THE HABSBURG EMPIRE:
FROM DYNASTICISM
TO MULTINATIONALISM

Paula Sutter Fichtner

Professor of History
Brooklyn College and the Graduate Center
City University of New York

AN ANVIL ORIGINAL
under the general editorship of
Hans L. Trefousse

KRIEGER PUBLISHING COMPANY
MALABAR, FLORIDA
1997

Original Edition 1997

Printed and Published by
KRIEGER PUBLISHING COMPANY
KRIEGER DRIVE
MALABAR, FLORIDA 32950

Library of Congress Cataloging-In-Publication Data

Fichtner, Paula S., 1935–
    The Habsburg Empire : from dynasticism to multinationalism / Paula
Sutter Fichtner.
        p.   cm.
    "An Anvil original."
    Includes bibliographical references and index.
    ISBN 0-89464-896-9 (alk. paper)
    1. Austria—Politics and government—1526–1848. 2. Austria—
Politics and government—1848–1918. 3. Nationalism—Austria.
4. Franz Joseph I, Emperor of Austria, 1830–1916. 5. Minorities—
Austria. 6. Austria—Ethnic relations.   I.Title.
DB80.F5 1997
943.6′04—dc21   96-36047
                                                       CIP

10 9 8 7 6 5 4 3 2

CONTENTS

PREFACE

Multinational states, both large and small, are rarely the outcome of deliberate design. They take shape as side effects of policies, or combinations of policies, which had quite other purposes. The Roman empire, which at its zenith encompassed most of the Mediterranean world along with a substantial part of Europe, was largely a by-product of military strategies created to meet defensive concerns. Similar problems drove the expansion of Muscovite and tsarist Russia. Though many now celebrate multiethnicity in the United States of America as an end in itself, the considerations which led to such a society were often far less visionary—the search for cheap labor, appeals to ethnic voting blocks, and the like.

And so it was with the Habsburg empire. When it collapsed in 1918, this sprawling structure included lands which now make up part or all of modern Austria, Hungary, Romania, Italy, Poland, Slovenia, Bosnia-Herzegovina, Croatia, Slovakia, Serbia, and the Czech Republic. It also numbered among approximately 51,000,000 inhabitants significant minorities, such as Jews whose historic statehood had roots outside of Europe altogether. The dynasty and the advisers who assembled this complex of territories and peoples were not morally and politically committed to heterogeneity. Some of these areas were conquered, a few purchased, some awarded in treaties or negotiations with local representative bodies which, as in the ancient kingdoms of Hungary and Bohemia, traditionally chose their monarch. A few lands, as the well-known aphorism "others wage war, you, fortunate Austria, marry" has it, came to the dynasty through marital alliances and subsequent inheritance.

For whatever reason they acquired these massive holdings, the German Habsburgs, like all of their princely contemporaries, thought of those whom they governed as subjects, whose allegiance was first and foremost to their ruler. Only in the nineteenth century did the dynasty's ethnic origins, so unlike the background of the majority of their population, become a topic for serious dispute. This was not because all of their lands passively yielded to the Habsburgs and the hereditary principles which their rule brought with it. Hungary was especially fractious. Yet, well through the eighteenth century, even those conflicts did not stem from ethnic differences between the politically dominant

Magyar nobility and their German-speaking sovereigns. What was at issue was how far the Habsburgs would respect the local understanding of the medieval Hungarian constitution which recognized elective kingship and the right to resist any monarch who overstepped his legal limits.

But, even as the Habsburg state reached its maximum territorial size in the eighteenth century, movements both within it and abroad were taking shape which would contest the house of Austria's government on national grounds. Habsburg rulers continued to view their empire as a kind of personal possession down to its bloody end. But they increasingly had to accommodate their dynastic sensibilities to an outlook which questioned whether any family, no matter how venerable, could legitimately rule peoples who differed from themselves in language, culture, religion, and historical origins. The values each side espoused may have been too polarized for them ever to have been reconciled. Legitimacy stood on the side of the monarchy, the democratic progressivism of nineteenth-century political and social thought reinforced the convictions of nationalists. The French Revolution translated notions of individual liberty into collective freedom of the nation, however that was defined. The spread of broad-based representative government and equality in all aspects of life created principled and permanent opposition to the elitism, traditionalism, and deference from which European monarchy, in all its forms, drew its sustenance.

The coming together of all these notions became even more dangerous for multiethnic states such as the Habsburg empire when foreign powers chose to sponsor the political aspirations of the Austrian dynasty's subject peoples. Governing what was called the Austro-Hungarian empire after 1867 was not only a question of mastering the national question on the domestic front; conduct of policy abroad was crucial as well. A state which centuries of negotiation had helped to create now maneuvered on the international scene for its survival. Throughout the last third of the nineteenth century, Emperor Franz Joseph (1830–1916) and his advisers worked to establish or to join alliances which they believed would defend the integrity of the empire. Increasingly, they saw tsarist Russia, as their chief threat. The Romanovs and their governments once made common cause with the Habsburgs against Napoleon. As the nineteenth century wore on, however, the regime in St.Petersburg grew ever more ready to intervene in eastern and southeastern Europe on behalf of peoples who shared the Eastern Orthodox faith and who were detaching themselves from the empire of the Moslem Turks. That both houses had much to lose should they clash over these matters ultimately made little difference. When war between the two great European multiethnic states came in 1914 it was clear that the international arrangements which had helped the Habsburgs to keep nationalist movements from unseating their rule were no longer functional. Nor were the peoples of their empire willing to sacrifice themselves indefinitely to what seemed to be the blatant self-interest of the dynasty and those close to it. The Habsburg empire did not survive the conflict. Nor, for that matter, did its Russian counterpart and enemy.

The
HABSBURG
MONARCHY
1815 – 1918

0   50   100   150
Miles

PRUSSIA

SAXONY

Elbe

Prague

BOHEMIA

MORA

Brno

BAVARIA

Danube

Inn

Linz

LOWER

Vienna

UPPER
AUSTRIA

AUSTRIA

Bratislava

Salzburg

SALZBURG

STYRIA

H

SWITZERLAND

VORARL-
BERG

Innsbruck

TYROL

CARINTHIA

Graz

ALPS

LOMBARDY

Milan

VENETIA

Venice

Klagenfurt

GORZ

CARNIOLA

Ljubljana

Drave

Zagreb

Save

CROATIA-S

Trieste

ISTRIA

Rijeka

Pulj

BO

ITALY

ADRIATIC

DALM

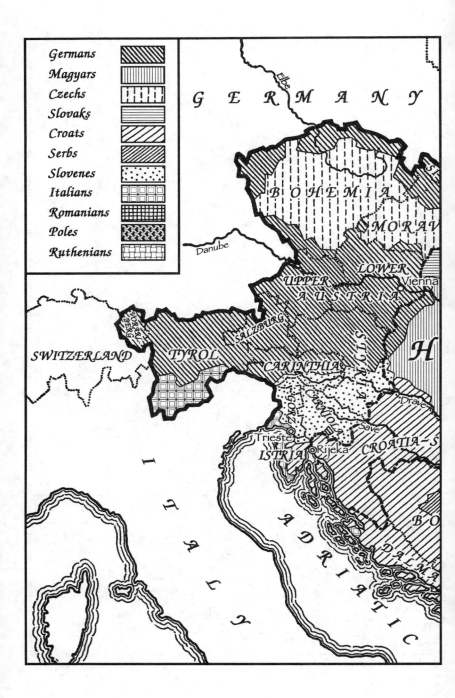

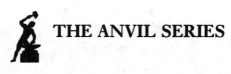 **THE ANVIL SERIES**

Anvil paperbacks give an original analysis of a major field of history or a problem area, drawing upon the most recent research. They present a concise treatment and can act as supplementary material for college history courses. Written by many of the outstanding historians in the United States, the format is one-half narrative text, one-half supporting documents, often from hard to find sources.

PART I

THE RISE AND FALL OF
THE HABSBURG EMPIRE

CHAPTER 1

TWO EMPIRES COLLIDE

The Origin of the Habsburgs. From medieval times to the beginning of the twentieth century, the Habsburg lands in central Europe lay across the paths of other powers eager to expand from the east. The dynasty, the house of Austria as it came to be called in the fifteenth century, had little choice but to defend its holdings. Sometimes its rulers justified their policies on religious grounds, but geopolitical considerations were usually uppermost in their thinking. That they fought a great deal was not because the Habsburgs preferred war to peace or were especially skilled in military affairs. Indeed, some of their most notable princes were poor commanders whom coalitions with foreigners often saved from humiliating defeats. But armed conflict was something they could not avoid if they wished to preserve the territorial and political position they came to occupy in central and east central Europe.

Originally from lands scattered throughout what is now Switzerland and southwestern Germany, the house of Habsburg launched its Europe-wide career in 1273. It was in that year that Count Rudolf of Habsburg (1218–1291) was chosen German king by the electors of the Holy Roman Empire, the loose union of ecclesiastical, secular, and municipal principalities, many of which are today part of Germany. The position was traditionally the stepping stone to coronation by the pope as Holy Roman Emperor; Rudolf, however, like several of his successors, was never able to get Rome to do this. Falling short of this honor did not weaken his ambition. He was eager to enlarge the territorial scope and influence of his house, and at least some of the German princes were willing to support him, provided that he could subdue the king of Bohemia, Otakar II (d. 1278), whose aggressive campaigns had recently brought him into lands that now lie in modern southeastern Austria. Not content with these conquests, he wanted the German crown as well, an ambition that troubled many. In 1278 Rudolf and his allies, some from the Bohemian nobility, crushed Otakar in battle; exercising his prerogative as German king, the Habsburg enfeoffed his family in 1283 with the Austrian lands which would become the core of their central European patrimony. To supervise his new acquisitions as closely as possible, Rudolf made Vienna the seat of his government.

Roughly corresponding to today's Upper and Lower Austria, they were important possessions, lying on the axes of the east-west and north-south trade routes of medieval Europe. The only city of any size was Vienna itself, but in the thirteenth century it was flourishing. However, Rudolf I's successors did not sustain his impressive start. From the beginning of the fourteenth to almost the middle of the fifteenth centuries, the Habsburgs lost control of the German emperorship. Though they added considerably to their family's holdings—today's Styria, Carinthia, the Tyrol, and principalities along the Adriatic coast from modern Slovenia west to Trieste—they fell to quarreling among themselves over dynastic territorial divisions, a common practice among German princes. Diminished resources diminished their standing in Europe as well. A serious menace from the southeast appeared in the Balkans at the end of the fourteenth century—the Moslem Ottoman Turks. However it was the kingdom of Hungary, not the archdukes of Austria, either in that role or as German emperors, which led Christendom in mounting whatever serious defense it offered.

Marital Diplomacy and Ottoman Expansion. The reversal of the Habsburg decline began with Archduke Frederick V (1415–1493) whose motto "the greatest happiness is being able to forget those things which are irrecoverably lost" would seem to have miscast him for this role. Often under serious attack from his own subjects as well as foreign rulers, most notably the king of Hungary, Matthias Corvinus (1440–1490), he was not an exciting intellect or personality. Contemporaries derided him as "the arch-sleepyhead" for his phlegmatic ways. Yet, he had an unwavering commitment to his dynasty's interests and the patience to work at realizing them. Nature was kind to him—at his birth the Habsburg Austrian holdings were divided among three branches of the house, one of which died out. Therefore at his death Frederick controlled all of the Habsburg Austrian holdings except the Tyrol and Vorarlberg. He also was elected German king in 1440, an office that, barring one short interlude, never slipped from the control of his family until Napoleon abolished the Holy Roman Empire in 1804. In 1452 Frederick received the imperial crown in Rome itself, the last of his line to do so.

All of these developments gave him enough credibility to negotiate succession agreements and marriage alliances which, if the contingencies specified in these arrangements fell properly into place, would dramatically increase the territorial power of the dynasty. His scheming came to naught in Bohemia and Hungary, elective kingships to which the Habsburgs long had unenforceable claims should local ruling lines become extinct. Very different were the results of the marriage in 1477 which he negotiated for his son, Maximilian (1459–1519). This union was with Mary of Burgundy (1457–1482), heiress to a wealthy complex of lands which were centered in the Belgium and Holland of today. Upon the duchess's death in 1482, her husband claimed the territories and managed to defend their integrity, with relatively few losses to the king of France who reasserted his feudal rights to the area.

By the end of the fifteenth century then, the Habsburgs were geopolitically well positioned to play a major role in central and west European affairs. The dynasty's international position improved even further in 1495 when Maximilian, who had followed his father in both the empire and in the Austrian lands, married his only male heir, Archduke Philip (1478–1506) to a Spanish princess, Juana (1479–1555), the daughter of Ferdinand of Aragon and Isabella of Castile. This was the relationship that paved the way for the couple's oldest son, Archduke Charles (1500–1558) to become king of Spain in 1516 and emperor in 1519. But Maximilian did not stop there. Like his ancestors, he was eager to have the closest ties possible with the Hungarian and Bohemian crowns. In 1515, he successfully promoted a double marriage for one of his granddaughters, Archduchess Mary (1505–1558), and either Charles or his brother Archduke Ferdinand (1503–1564). The young princess was betrothed to Prince Louis (1506–1526), the son of King Wenceslaus who ruled both Bohemia and Hungary. One of the emperor's grandsons—no one was quite sure which one—would be the husband of Wenceslaus's daughter, Princess Anna (1503–1547). Should Prince Louis die without legitimate sons, his sister would inherit the crowns of both kingdoms.

An energetic and extraordinarily imaginative man, Maximilian did more than plot advantageous marriages for his family. He tried to put the government of the Habsburg lands on a more rational footing. As emperor, he worked hard to modernize the administration, training, and outfitting of the imperial military forces which were notoriously unreliable. High on his list of priorities was persuading Germany's territorial rulers to allow the levy of a so-called Common Penny which would fund something like a standing army. These monies would lessen his dependence upon the extraordinary taxes which the estates traditionally voted on a campaign-by-campaign basis to finance military undertakings. The proposal was important; as emperor, Maximilian played a central role in keeping peace throughout the German lands and defending ancient imperial claims which reached far beyond Germany itself, most notably into Italy. Indeed, in theory, he was responsible for the welfare of all Christendom. It was this duty that made him keenly sensitive to the threat that the Turks posed for Europe generally, not to mention his Austrian patrimony. Though the Ottoman westward drive was occasionally set back or slowed, it had never been decisively halted. Constantinople had fallen to the sultan's forces in 1453. Despite often valiant opposition from Venice and the Hungarians, the invaders were, by the end of the century effective masters of the Balkans and appeared well on the way to dominating the Mediterranean world as a whole.

Much of Christian Europe was singularly uninterested in these events, in part because they took place far away, in part because local concerns loomed larger. The German estates were no exception; they were decidedly unenthusiastic about increasing the financial resources and independence of their emperor; they voted in principle for the Common Penny, but the tax was impossible to enforce. Maximilian toyed with the idea of undertaking a crusade and even founded a knightly order, the Order of St. George, to serve as its spearhead. Like many of his schemes, nothing came of it. The Turks continued to move episodically up the Danube valley, and both the Hungarians and the Habsburgs were directly in their path.

A Multinational State Begins. It was Maximilian's grandson, Archduke Ferdinand I (1503–1564), who was the first Habsburg to confront this last of the Islamic invasions of Europe which stretched back to the eighth century. In defending his patrimony, as he was called upon to do several times during the course of his reign, he enlarged it beyond its primarily German-speaking Austrian base to the multiethnic lands that were to the east and southeast. It was he, not his brother, since 1519 Emperor Charles V, who married Princess Anna of Hungary and Bohemia in 1521 as required in the Double Marriage Agreement of 1515. He did not claim the two kingdoms immediately—he still had a brother-in-law, Louis, the lawful heir to the lands who had actually been ruling them since 1516 when he was only ten years old. But age did not season this monarch's childish and self-indulgent character. The Turks took Belgrade in 1521, and Ferdinand had good reason to think that with such leadership Hungary would not be able to turn them back.

Without being too offensive to the influential Hungarian estates, he worked to manipulate Louis into reforming his ways.

None of these efforts were to great avail. Late in August of 1526, Louis met the Turks in a disastrous battle at Mohacs, in the southwestern corner of the kingdom. His strategy was impromptu at best, and the results, all but predictable. His forces were crushed; the king himself met his end when he slid from his horse into a swamp and drowned. The sultan, Suleiman the Magnificent, did not intend to stop there. He planned to go on to Vienna itself, and only logistical difficulties as well as the first chill of autumn persuaded him to postpone the attack.

Ferdinand had worked frantically to drive up additional aid for the late king from the empire and from his brother in Spain. But now that both the Hungarian and Bohemian thrones had become vacant, he wanted them for himself. As a younger brother to the emperor and king of Spain, he was eager to enhance his status among princes with a royal title. However, more considerations than raw ambition drove him to seek these crowns. He feared that the Hungarian and Bohemian thrones would fall to rulers who, themselves bothered by growing Habsburg power, might willingly strike deals with the Turks. This was a distinct possibility; succession agreements to the contrary notwithstanding, both kingdoms had long traditions of elective monarchy should their legitimate lines die out. Active candidates, who bore the house of Habsburg no great love, quickly surfaced. The king of Poland, Sigismund I, actually an uncle of the unfortunate Louis, was interested in Bohemia. So were the Wittelsbach dukes of Bavaria, long time rivals of the Habsburgs in the quest for preeminence in central Europe. A fraction of the Hungarian diet had already elected a native king, John Zapolya, one of the great landed magnates of Transylvania, an eastern Hungarian crownland today part of Romania. Indeed, he soon became a vassal of the sultan in order to keep the principality at least nominally independent of Constantinople. Ferdinand disliked submitting himself to the vote of each of the two kingdoms' estates and maneuvered tirelessly in future years to end such procedures. Nevertheless, he had little choice in 1526 and 1527 but to yield, if he wanted either title. By 1527, he had been chosen as king in Bohemia by its estates; in Hungary, a fraction of the diet not directly allied with Zapolya, accepted a Habsburg ruler.

Ferdinand I then, born in Spain, raised both there and in the Netherlands, was the true founder of the "multinational empire" which was a key feature of the European political landscape from the sixteenth to the twentieth centuries. The kingdom of Bohemia was made up of several so-called crownlands, chief among which was Bohemia itself. Corresponding roughly to the modern Czech Republic, it was among the wealthiest regions of Europe. Prague, the capital, was a major trading and manufacturing center. Productive silver mines were to be found in Jachymov to the north and west and Kutna Hora southeast of the capital. The other components of the kingdom were the margravate of Moravia, the duchies of Upper and Lower Silesia, and the counties of Upper and Lower Lusatia. To all of these, Ferdinand acquired the local ruling title as well. Thus, he was not only king of Bohemia, but margrave of Moravia, duke of Silesia, and so on.

Jealous as these principalities were of their local privileges, they were comparatively homogeneous demographically. Significant German settlements were to be found in all of them, especially in the cities. However, they were majoritarianly Slavic, and would grow more so. The presence of the Germans was unremarkable; medieval kings throughout east central and eastern Europe had welcomed them during the Middle Ages because of the farming and manufacturing skills the settlers brought to their realms. Ferdinand also had the advantage of actually ruling the entire kingdom, unlike his position in Hungary. Here Habsburg control was effective only over the western and northwestern part of the kingdom. The administrative center of the region was Pressburg (Hung.: Pozsony) today Bratislava, the capital of Slovakia. In 1542, Suleiman occupied Buda on the Danube, thus making the Turks masters of central Hungary, while Transylvania, to the east, protected the autonomy which Zapolya had sought for it.

With its associated kingdoms and principalities, Hungary was more ethnically and linguistically diverse than Bohemia as well. Though it preferred to administer and legislate for the realm in Latin, the kingdom's nobility spoke Magyar, a Finno-Ugric language quite unlike German, the Slavic tongues, or the Romance-based Romanian used by many in Transylvania. Substantial numbers of Slavic-speaking Slovaks lived in the northern reaches of the kingdom; to its south and west lay the equally Slavic kingdom of Croatia-Dalmatia-Slavonia which had been associated with the Hungarian lands since the twelfth century. The nature of that relationship was cloudy—the Hungarians argued that the realm had been incorporated into Hungary itself, the Croatians that they were simply part of a federation. Transylvania, where a wide variety of peoples had settled since the Middle Ages, also belonged to the crown of St. Stephen, the symbol of Hungarian territorial unity. Should Hungary ever be fully reunited, Ferdinand and his dynasty would come to rule this rich assortment of subjects as well.

Ottoman Decline and Habsburg Expansion. First the Turks had to be driven out, and neither Ferdinand nor his immediate successors could do this. While they were able to limit the Ottoman occupation to Hungary, the Austrian Habsburgs suffered one humiliating defeat after another in attempting to recapture the Hungarian lands which, as kings, they claimed. The Turkish forces were massive and frightening, but size by itself was not crucial. Ferdinand and his son, Maximilian II (1527–1576) often raised large armies against them, but neither man could organize and discipline them. To pay these forces and their captains, the sixteenth-century Habsburgs relied heavily upon the special contributions granted them by the estates of their own lands and the principalities represented in the imperial diet they called upon many times as German kings. Ferdinand received this title in 1531 because even though Charles V was alive, he needed his younger brother to supervise central European affairs. The emperor appeared in Germany very infrequently, as Spanish and Mediterranean matters took up great parts of his time. Both the German territories and the Habsburg provincial representatives usually voted the dynasty's requests; however, getting them to pay on time was another matter. Army morale disintegrated accordingly, and combat effectiveness even more. Disagreements among troops of different national origins and standards of training did not help matters either. The imperial standing force which Maximilian I once sought was very much needed, since one of the sultan's most effective tactical ploys was to soften up his Christian enemy with preliminary skirmishing. Though neither Ferdinand nor Maximilian II was able to win the Germans over to that proposal, the former was able to get support for the establishment of a permanent armed guard on the border of today's Croatia. These were the so-called *Grenzer*, at first Serbian refugees and their families who had fled their Ottoman-occupied lands further to the south and east. (*See Document No. 1.*) It did not trouble Ferdinand that they constituted yet another people with their own language and history in his increasingly heterogeneous lands. What was crucial for him—so much so that he granted them exceptional freedoms from taxation—was their willingness to fight for the Habsburg, and ultimately Christian, cause against the Turks. The system was later extended along borders farther east.

A kind of territorial stalemate developed between the two archenemies throughout the first half of the seventeenth century. Both were occupied with serious military enterprises elsewhere, the Habsburgs with the Thirty Years War in Central Europe, the Turks with the Persians in the Middle East. The quality of the Ottoman sultans degenerated after the death of Suleiman the Magnificent in 1566, as his successors neglected martial endeavors for private pleasure. The government in Constantinople fell increasingly into the hands of so-called viziers, or chancellors, chosen because they were personal favorites of the ruler, not necessarily because they were qualified for the office. Army discipline slipped as well. Nevertheless, these conditions did not rule out the possibility that ambitious viziers might appear who could rekindle lust for conquest. In 1656, the office fell into the hands of a veritable dynasty, the Kiuprili. Of Albanian origins, they used their power to restructure the army and overhaul Ottoman finance to the point where the Turks were militarily ready to challenge the house of Austria once again. This they did with indifferent results—the Habsburg forces defeated them in a major battle in 1664—but they continued warfare against Venice, Russia, and Poland. By 1682, they were again proceeding up the Danube valley. On July 17, 1683, they set siege to Vienna once more.

The emperor, Leopold I (1640–1705), was a cautious, indeed, somewhat timorous man. He and the court fled to Passau, about 175 miles by river from his capital. There he worked to organize Polish and German aid for the local defenders left behind in Vienna who mounted a heroic resistance in the face of increasingly desperate circumstances. For almost two months, the Turks did everything that continual assault and mining operations could do to destroy the elaborate fortifications that surrounded the center of the city. The long-awaited aid from Poland and the Empire arrived on the twelfth of September; by the end of the day the Ottoman forces were scattered into flight.

The lifting of the siege and the campaigns that followed began the reconquest of Hungary. For well over one hundred years, the Habsburgs had promised themselves and others to do this. This time, they fulfilled that vow, though like so many of their victories to come, they did not do it alone. Rather the house of Austria worked within a grand alliance made up of its own forces, along with Poles, Venice, and even the Russians, all of whom had territorial designs on the wide-flung lands of the sultan. For once the Austrian dynasty fielded genuinely capable military leadership. It was not, however, home-grown. A career officer, Prince Eugene of Savoy (1663–1736), who had been unable to find appropriate service with Louis XIV of France, had attached himself to the court in Vienna and commanded the Habsburg forces through a succession of major victories in eastern and southeastern Europe. In 1699 Leopold was able to conclude the treaty of Karlowitz (Serbo-Croat.: Karlovac) with the sultan which brought Hungary fully under Austrian control. This meant that he now had all of the land which comprises the Magyar-speaking Hungary of today, along with Transylvania and the parts of Croatia and Slavonia under Turkish rule. Eugene pressed on. In 1717 he captured Belgrade; the treaty of Passarowitz (Serbo-Croat.: Pozarevac) of 1718 added northern Serbia and the Banat of Temesvar, now Timisoar in Romania, to the house of Austria's possessions.

But here the Habsburg advance sputtered and died. In 1739 Emperor Charles VI (1685–1740) was forced to return the Serbian acquisitions to the sultan, though he did hold on to the Banat, like Transylvania a complex ethnic mix of Hungarian, Slavic, Romanian, and German-speaking peoples. The Habsburg possessions now stretched as far east as they ever would with one notable exception. This was Poland, a venerable Christian kingdom, not part of a Moslem empire, but one so politically hapless by the latter third of the eighteenth century that other powers, especially Prussia and Russia, found it convenient to absorb parts of it. The Habsburg court regarded such ambitions as serious threat to its territorial position. Though initially reluctant to dismember a traditional participant in the European state system and a one-time ally, the government in Vienna was nevertheless anxious about the westward expansion of Russia. It therefore joined in a three-way division of the kingdom. In the First Partition of 1772, the Austrian dynasty carried off Galicia and some other land in western Poland along with some of the area around the ancient Polish capital of Cracow. In the Third Partition of 1795—the Habsburgs had not joined in the second division which took place in 1793—they received the rest of the territory attached to the city. These additions incorporated not only large numbers of Polish-speaking Slavs into the empire, but also a substantial Jewish population which would continue to grow.

War and the diplomacy that attended it brought yet one other ethnic group into the orbit of the Austrian Habsburgs in the eighteenth century. While numerically small, compared to the over three million inhabitants in the new Polish territories, it would be responsible for the most serious challenge to dynastic rule that the house of Austria faced in the nineteenth century. These were Italians in whose lands the Habsburgs had a strong interest, indeed, one that antedated all of their expansion to the east. The last male heir to the Spanish line of the house, King Charles II, died in 1700. As grotesquely ugly as he was frail, he had lived longer than most had ever thought he would. Even before his death, potential claimants to the Spanish inheritance had made themselves known. Aside from his Austrian cousins themselves, there was Louis XIV of France. Married to Charles's half-sister, the Bourbon ruler also believed he had rights to Spanish-held lands in both Italy and what is today Belgium. His wife's dowry had never been fully paid, an insult that gave added force to his argument. The so-called War of the Spanish Succession (1701–1714) was the result. It did not bring the Austrian Habsburgs to the Spanish throne—that went to Louis's nephew who became Philip V of Spain. They did, however, receive significant pieces of the Spanish heritage outside of the Iberian Peninsula, most notably Milan and the Spanish Netherlands. Subsequent conflicts in the eighteenth century, along with inheritances, brought even more regions in Italy—Parma, Modena, Piacenza and Tuscany—under Austrian Habsburg control or influence.

Thus, dynastic interests and the policies employed to realize them created the multinational Habsburg empire. What contemporaries found noteworthy about all of this, at least until the middle of the eighteenth century, was not the variety of peoples that the dynasty controlled, but the size of the territory under its sway. What the house of Austria had accomplished, most European ruling houses would have done, had they had the same money, good fortune and opportunity. Peoples were subjects, politically and socially defined by their relationship to the ruler, not by the tongues they spoke or cultural norms peculiar to their group. While the Habsburgs, particularly during the sixteenth century, made unusual efforts to learn the languages of their various lands, their reasons were purely utilitarian. The Bohemian nobility functioned most comfortably in Czech, and Italian was both intellectually and diplomatically useful. No great philosophical or ideological significance was attributed to any one of the local idioms found in their lands, or, for that matter, in the household of the dynasty itself. From the middle of the seventeenth century to the a few years before the beginning of the French Revolution in 1789, Italian, then French crowded out German as the preeminent tongue at the court itself. Indeed, business and social exchange took place most easily in an artless blend of all three, with some Spanish and Latin thrown in for good measure. No one seemed to mind, especially the rulers themselves.

Such attitudes should not be read as signs that the Habsburg subjects were a uniformly docile lot, without all sense of local distinction and interest and ready to accept any order that came from Vienna. Quite the opposite was the case, as we are about to see. Nor were the Habsburgs blind to the difficulties that governing such a heterogenous group of peoples would bring with it. The serious problems that arose, however, came primarily from their constitutional relations with the traditional political orders of their lands, chiefly the nobilities. However, such conflicts were familiar to all of Europe's ruling houses. As long as their internal political problems followed this conventional pattern, the Habsburgs were on generally manageable ground.

CHAPTER 2

MAKING ONE OF MANY

Institutional Structures. From the very beginning of the Habsburg Empire in central and east central Europe, its most energetic rulers pursued one goal relentlessly. This was to preserve and strengthen the position of the house both in its traditional Austrian patrimony and the new lands which it had acquired after 1526. The more centralized the government of these far-flung and diverse territories was, the stronger the grip of the dynasty on them would be. Most of the Habsburgs understood this relationship clearly; what was difficult was getting their subjects, above all nobles who dominated regional estates and administrations, to accept the dictates of a regime based in Vienna.

Language barriers somewhat complicated this process. The Austrian estates themselves had reservations about Ferdinand I because he spoke practically no German upon his arrival there in 1521. The Bohemians grumbled when he brought German-speaking officials into the kingdom; indeed, they persuaded their new ruler to use them as sparingly as possible. Insofar as German was associated with the territorial pretensions and history of the Holy Roman Empire, both the Bohemians and the Hungarians had reason to be uneasy about Ferdinand's close associations to that polity. The Empire had long-standing feudal claims to Bohemia and its associated crownlands. Although these had not been seriously enforced for centuries, the king of Bohemia was still one of the seven imperial electors. The Hungarians, whose westward expansion had been checked by the Germans many centuries ago, were equally anxious to retain a separate identity. They did not care for the German-speaking entourage which Ferdinand's sister, Mary of Hungary, had cultivated at her court. But language issues, insofar as there were any, never became crises in the sixteenth century. Habsburg administrations in Bohemia loyally dispatched reports to Vienna in German. The Hungarian estates deliberated in Latin as they would continue to do down to the first half of the nineteenth century.

The Habsburgs also worked hard to ingratiate themselves linguistically with their new realms. Ferdinand I insisted that his sons know at least some Czech as well as other major continental tongues. Toward this end, he brought to his court the sons of nobles from his new lands, especially Bohemia, who chattered in their own idiom with the archdukes on whom at least some of this haphazard tutelage brushed off. Such practices also advanced the larger purposes of the dynasty by tying these aristocratic families to the Habsburg court more closely. Local interests and national distinctions colored their outlook less and less. Slowly but inexorably, they found themselves becoming an international class. The process accelerated in the seventeenth century when the monarchy once and for all made Vienna its permanent headquarters. Great nobles of Hungary, Bohemia, and from other areas of Europe who had entered Habsburg service—Eugene of Savoy was a conspicuous example—built magnificent palaces both in the cramped and winding streets of the Inner City and the area just outside of its fortified walls. The size and splendor of some of these edifices often rivaled the imperial residence, the *Hofburg*. In reality, however, the well-born men who established themselves so conspicuously in the imperial capital did so because, for all the diversity of their origins, the Habsburg monarchy had become central to their interests.

Nevertheless, the estates of the Habsburg lands were unwilling to allow major alterations in the balance of power with their rulers, precisely what the Habsburgs needed for them to make a coherent political whole of these lands. Ferdinand I experimented with joint meetings of the Bohemian and Austrian estates, but apparently dropped the idea. In the late 1520s, as part of a general administrative reform of his entire government, he tried to run the internal affairs of Hungary and Bohemia from Vienna. These, however, were soon returned to local control. In Prague royal officials managed such business as day-by-day supervision of the kingdom's treasury with a considerable degree of independence. In the last analysis, political and economic pressures, the need for experienced and respected officials, as well as their own belief in the hierarchical ordering of society, kept the Habsburgs of early modern Europe from challenging the constitutional balance of power in Bohemia and Hungary too aggressively. When they did so, it was either because they had no choice or because their chances for success were high.

The likeliest way to curb the influence and power of the estates was to turn both Bohemia and Hungary into hereditary, rather than elective monarchies where prospective rulers were often forced to trade financial, military and political favors for the votes of the estates. When he died in 1564, Ferdinand I had won the assent of the Bohemian and Hungarian estates to having his successor, in this case Maximilian II, chosen in his lifetime, and the Bohemians had indeed come very close to recognizing hereditary Habsburg rule. But they had hardly given up their rights altogether, and other issues continued to keep their relationship with the house of Austria on an uneasy footing.

Religious Problems and Confessional Uniformity. Preeminent control of their lands therefore eluded the house of Austria in early modern Europe, as local nobilities stubbornly refused to rearrange their constitutions to suit the ambitions of their new sovereigns. Diversity did reinforce their intransigence, but in a way not directly related to language or ethnicity. The Protestant Reformation of the sixteenth century gave rise to confessional divisions which were a major impediment to the unification of the Habsburg territories. As devout Catholics personally and Holy Roman Emperors publicly, the dynasty was obliged to defend the faith of Rome even as its subjects, especially in the Austrian patrimony and Bohemia were increasingly drawn to the various strands of the religious movement founded by Martin Luther (1483–1546). By the latter third of the sixteenth century, the Austrian lands, with the exception of the Tyrol, were either majoritarianly Protestant, or close to being so. The Bohemians had even taken the lead in the fragmentation of western Christendom. Confessional pluralism had existed in the kingdom since the fifteenth century in the form of Utraquism, so-called because its partisans took both the bread and wine at communion. (Lat.: utraque = both) The charismatic Bohemian preacher Jan Hus (1369–1415) was martyred at the stake for his cause, but the papacy had never succeeded in eradicating the church that grew out of it. The Habsburgs, like all of the kings of Bohemia from Hus's time onward, had been forced to recognize its existence as the part of the price for their election. Sixteenth-century Lutheranism, which spread quickly to the kingdom, only further complicated the religious picture there.

Christian faiths of all varieties found staunch defenders among the nobility in the estates throughout the Habsburg lands. In isolation from other factors, this situation would probably not have deterred the Habsburgs from doing their best to crush confessional heterodoxy. But these same Protestant sympathizers were often influential elements in the estates upon whom Ferdinand I and his successors depended for much of their help in the effort against the Turks. Quick to see how vulnerable the Habsburg position was, the estates demanded, and got, religious concessions as the price of military aid. For their part, Ferdinand I and Maximilian II avoided alienating these regional representative bodies permanently.

Their successors had greater opportunity to create a more favorable constitutional balance for themselves and their heirs. Among the most significant was Emperor Ferdinand II (1578–1637). A man of unyielding Catholic conviction, he had already done much, even before becoming emperor, to eradicate Protestantism in his native province of Styria. He would continue to pursue this policy throughout the entire Habsburg Austrian patrimony. His uncompromising outlook frightened the Bohemian estates into refusing to recognize him as their king in 1619. They turned to the Protestant Elector Frederick V of the Palatine, the son-in-law of James I of England, as their new ruler. Ferdinand responded by raising an army which shattered the Bohemian rebellion at the Battle of the White Mountain in 1620. With the Revised Land Ordinances of 1627, he established once and for all the hereditary right of his dynasty to the Bohemian crown. Whatever Protestantism survived in the kingdom went underground, and Protestant nobles had to flee abroad if they wished to remain in their faith. However, Ferdinand had no desire to destroy the nobility as a class; he merely reconfigured it confessionally. The Catholic aristocrats in Bohemia who had remained faithful to the Habsburgs were encouraged to stay on; others were imported from all parts of Europe, as far away as Ireland, for example. Those who came with no titles received them from the king. Their common denominator was loyalty to Ferdinand's dynasty and to Roman Catholic orthodoxy. Bohemia, then, had fallen under control from Vienna, a matter of great significance since the realm would be central to the monarchy's economic development in the next two centuries. Yet, the local legal and economic role of the landed aristocracy remained unbroken, leading to a political structure in this and other Habsburg lands that modern scholars call functional dualism. Even the right of the estates to approve taxes was never altogether eliminated, a power that would be crucial to the renewal of Czech national identity in the nineteenth century. Bohemian noble influence at the court actually grew, as the Habsburgs incorporated some of these men into their inner circle of advisers, one of the most powerful positions of the time.

Resistance in Hungary. As much as the Habsburgs would have liked to extend this policy to Hungary, they were unable to do so. From the sixteenth to the twentieth centuries, this kingdom managed to maintain itself as a special case among the Habsburg lands. The experience of Ottoman invasion and occupation had persuaded at least a sizeable group within the Hungarian estates to acknowledge Ferdinand I as their ruler. This was not because the youthful archduke personally had a great deal to offer them at the outset of his career. Rather they saw him as a useful conduit to his elder brother Charles, who as Holy Roman Emperor and king of Spain had formidable reserves of wealth. This, Hungarian supporters of Habsburg rule believed, could be tapped to defend east central Europe and, not incidentally, to help them regain personal properties lost in the Turkish conquest.

None of this worked out as planned. While Germany and Spain did contribute goodly amounts of men and money to the defense and re-unification of Hungary from the sixteenth to the eighteenth centuries, they did not do it regularly or always in the quantity needed. This situation put Ferdinand and several of his successors in a very dangerous position. Should they fail, as indeed they did for many years, to drive the Turks from Hungary, the estates there would call upon others to perform this task. The threat was virtual reality as far as the Habsburgs were concerned, and they acted accordingly. Unable to put an end to the Ottoman occupation, the house of Austria used financial and political concessions to keep its Hungarian supporters in line. The money for these and more substantive efforts to recover lost territory had to come from somewhere, but it was not from Hungary because only a third of it was in Habsburg hands.

Ferdinand and his successors therefore made liberal use of private credit to fund their campaigns. They also turned to the estates of their other holdings who grew increasingly resentful over being treated as little more than dutiful suppliers of troops and money. The Austrian lands themselves, particularly those in the east and southeast, were generally reliable. Their wealth was limited, however, and the Habsburgs eagerly sought deeper treasuries to draw upon. It was for this reason, among others, that Ferdinand I pursued the Bohemian crown so aggressively. The kingdom was rich, and he hoped that its taxes, especially a highly lucrative one on beer, would cover some of his military expenses in Hungary.

The Bohemian estates did not play this new part happily. Though both kingdoms were elective monarchies, the two had little in common. Aside from the deep linguistic gulf between Slav and Magyar, the realms had often been at war with one another in territorial disputes since the Middle Ages. With this history behind them, along with their normal resistance to taxation for whatever reason, the Bohemians dragged their feet when asked to fund the defense of Hungary. The margravate of Moravia, however, was a good deal more cooperative with its Habsburg prince, at least in the sixteenth century, but largely because its borders were far more exposed to invasion from the south and east.

Therefore well into the seventeenth century, the house of Austria struggled in Hungary not so much to curb its estates, but to control the entire kingdom physically and to get the rest of its lands to pay for the effort. What was left of the estates in the third of the kingdom under Habsburg sway continued to keep its options open. Its financial support of its own defence was erratic, and some members were quick to abandon the house of Austria for private negotiations with the Turks, should Habsburg policy in their realm displease them. The unwillingness of the dynasty to mount all-out offensives against the Ottoman occupiers and failure to take advantage of promising initiatives disappointed many Magyar nobles. Habsburg refusal to exploit a smashing victory over the sultan's forces in 1664 led to a conspiracy among several high-placed magnates to depose and kidnap Leopold I three years later. When the intrigue collapsed the emperor-king and his advisers used it to justify a broad-based attack on Hungarian privilege and on Protestant communities in the kingdom which had cooperated with the plotters. From 1671 to 1681, Leopold simply ignored the realm's historic liberties, not even calling a diet. The nobility lost its traditional exemption from general taxation, and a ruthless, much-hated, military occupation ensured that it would pay.

But renewed aggression from Constantinople and war with Louis XIV over Germany put Leopold in a position where he needed the Hungarian estates' good will and support. He convened the diet once again and returned the kingdom's treasury from Vienna, where he had relocated it, to Pressburg. In 1687, in conjunction with a joint meeting of the Hungarian and Croatian estates, Leopold restored the right of future diets to vote taxes and noble control over local legal and religious matters. He did carry away some important Hungarian concessions, however. The diet accepted the house of Austria as its hereditary rulers and effectively renounced the *jus resistendi*, the right to resist unconstitutional acts of the king without being tried for treason. As in Bohemia, a kind of court party began to develop among some of the Hungarian grandees, with Catholicism and the opportunities for great wealth serving to link them more closely to Vienna.

For all of these gains, Habsburg political control of Hungary remained less complete than in the dynasty's other lands. Many noblemen resisted co-option, especially in the eastern reaches of the kingdom and in Transylvania. Here, many of these people, along with more common folk, were Calvinists, who had further reason to differentiate themselves from the Catholic orthodoxy that the regime in Vienna was promoting throughout the empire. Nor did the government always behave with much political wisdom where the nobility was concerned. Habsburg resettlement policy in devastated sections of the kingdom, especially the central Hungarian Plain, still distressed many. Rather than allowing Hungarian landowners to purchase land in the area, Leopold and his advisers used it to place refugees from the Ottoman-occupied Balkans, among them numbers of Serbs. Many Germans were brought in as well. All these peoples, it was hoped, would restore the fertility of the area. By way of further insult, the diet was not called after 1687, antagonizing nobles who kept fast to their country estates.

High-handed ways such as these goaded a magnate from eastern Hungary, Francis II Rakoczi (1676–1735) into putting himself at the head of yet another rebellion against the central government in 1703. Ancestors on both sides of his family had fought against Habsburg rule, so that he was no stranger to sedition. Interested in becoming the local ruler of Transylvania, where his family had roots, he also demanded restoration of the *jus resistendi* and the abolition of hereditary succession. To attract support from Protestant Europe, he also asked for Hungarian religious freedom. By 1711, however, the revolt had collapsed. The new emperor and king, Joseph I (1678–1711), was able to make a peace acceptable to both sides. Joseph acknowledged most of the 1687 agreement, and the belligerents once again recognized royal authority. But it was clear that historical custom and right, especially in the Hungarian case, were tenacious growths. While the estates accepted hereditary dynastic monarchy as part of their constitution, they did so only on terms peculiar to Hungary itself.

Maria Theresa and the Reform of the Monarchy. Indeed, the unity of the Habsburg lands was still very much an issue, particularly in the mind of Emperor Charles VI (1685–1740) in 1713. With his late brother Joseph's two daughters as the nearest claimants to the central European lands of their house, Charles wanted to make sure that the Habsburg holdings would pass undivided to his own yet-to-be-born children without setting off a succession crisis. The outcome of his concern was the Pragmatic Sanction, a compact among members of the house, which restated the legitimacy of both male and female claims to the Habsburg lands. This, in itself, was nothing new. What Charles did in the document that was decidedly radical was to disinherit his nieces, a move that would cause no end of future grief for the dynasty. Both of these ladies married foreign princes who were eager to use their wives' connection with the house of Austria to justify rights in the Habsburg lands. The Pragmatic Sanction also strongly emphasized that the empire was "one and indivisible," a provision which Charles later came to feel required recognition from the various estates of his realms. (*See Document No. 2.*) This he eventually obtained. Once again, however, the Hungarians took the opportunity to extract promises that he and his heirs would call their diet regularly and preserve the integrity of the kingdom. The latter stipulation meant that the Habsburgs were not to incorporate the kingdom into any other of his realms. He then turned to persuading rulers throughout Europe to respect the arrangement.

Even though he lavished vast amounts of energy on this enterprise—some historians say to the neglect of more important political and economic matters—his ultimate goal eluded him. Contemporary states did acknowledge the territorial integrity of the Habsburg lands, but Charles had only to die in 1740 before the ambitious King Frederick II of Prussia, Frederick "the Great" to posterity, invaded Silesia. The area was a major center of textile production; to lose it would be a major blow to the Habsburg economy.

Charles's successor, Archduchess Maria Theresa (1717–1780), looked like an easy mark. Young and inexperienced, she had received little, if any training for the offices she assumed. Like some of her most notable predecessors, however, she possessed boundless reserves of determination. What she lacked in formal education she made up for with great common sense, shrewd political instincts, and skill in judging and handling—some would say manipulating—people. Married to Duke Francis Stephen of Lorraine (1708–1765) in 1736, she was pregnant with the future Emperor Joseph II (1741–1790) at the moment Frederick launched his offensive. None of this kept her and her ministers from rallying her lands and cobbling together alliances to defend the

Habsburg holdings. A particularly dramatic scene took place in 1741, when with the now infant Joseph II clutched in her arms, she appealed to the Hungarian estates for extraordinary aid in the emergency. The diet voted credits for a huge force, only a fraction of which ever materialized. Nevertheless, the gesture inspired other lands to contribute generously to the cause. While the Habsburg forces were unable to dislodge Frederick from much of Silesia, they were able to check further Prussian advances.

With the immediate threat at bay, Maria Theresa and her advisers began working to regain the lost territory. To do this the queen, whose husband actually held the title of Holy Roman Emperor, realized that she needed far more effective armies. Her Hungarian performance in 1741 had been undoubtedly compelling theater. She might have blunted Frederick's attack sooner, however, had she been able to mobilize men and money without having to go through the cumbersome ritual of coaxing such aid from regional estates. Radical restructuring of the entire Habsburg government, particularly its fiscal affairs, was called for. Guided by a new chief minister, the Silesian Count Frederick William von Haugwitz (1702–1765) she set about persuading these bodies to grant their contributions, some for as long as ten years, to the central government in Vienna rather than regional treasuries. Such changes allowed for a degree of planning and central control over finance that the Habsburg government had never had.

She also united the administrations of the Austrian and Bohemian lands. In Hungary, however, the diet resisted this move and the queen, ever careful not to weaken her position by overreaching herself, granted the kingdom a separate chancellory. Nevertheless, the Hungarians paid something for the concession. To improve the revenue flow and strengthen the economy after the loss of Silesia, Maria Theresa made the empire a customs union for the first time in its history. The only exception was Hungary which she treated essentially as a foreign country within the monarchy. Heavy duties were levied on its exports; wares sent into the kingdom from other parts of the monarchy discouraged domestic manufacture. The government hoped in this way to offset Hungarian reluctance to pay a greater share of the contribution assessed upon the kingdom and to protect agricultural enterprises in other Habsburg lands, particularly wine production in Lower Austria. However, this policy only reinforced the notion of Hungarian exceptionality, something the Habsburgs would come to regret.

Maria Theresa won back only a fraction of Silesia after the Seven Years War ended in 1763. Nevertheless, her administrative reforms significantly shifted the balance in the relationship between monarch and estates in favor of the crown. The nobility throughout the Habsburg lands had much to lose. It often administered its properties as feudal lords, with judiciary powers over the local peasants and rights to labor dues from them as well, but it did not put up great resistance to many of the Theresan reforms. Disadvantageous though some of these changes may have been, Prussian expansionism appealed to the Habsburg aristocracy even less. This feeling was especially strong in Bohemia. Complain though she did about the local particularism that made it very difficult for her government to focus on the larger interests of the monarchy, Maria Theresa avoided challenging this condition systematically. (*See Document No. 3.*) In Hungary she went out of her way to appease the nobles, even founding a special honorary guard in which they could serve her.

Enlightened Despotism and Revolt. However shakily Maria Theresa's reign began, it ended with the Habsburgs enjoying considerable good will among all the social classes of their empire. Nevertheless these feelings evaporated quickly during the ten-year reign of her son, Emperor Joseph II (1741–1790). Among all the rulers produced by the house of Habsburg, or Habsburg-Lorraine since Maria Theresa's marriage to Duke Francis, Joseph's career was perhaps the saddest. Opinionated and impatient beyond what was normal even in an era of restless and ambitious monarchs, Joseph was imaginative, intelligent, and often courageous. Inspired with the Enlightenment passion for reason and order in government and society, he worked tirelessly at putting it into practice. The Habsburg Empire was to be centralized administratively, and its social order and economy reconfigured to further the well-being and prosperity of its citizenry and the dynasty which ruled them. Traditional arrangements of all kinds, including the functional dualism which had defined relations between the Habsburg rulers and local political powers since the sixteenth century, had little place in his schemes.

Maria Theresa had pursued many of these objectives as well, but always with a firm sense of what was politically possible. Her cautious tactics often left her eldest son torn between fury and despair. He swung into high gear as soon as he came to power in 1780. Much of his program continued the Theresan reforms, but he reached far more deeply into some of the most venerable institutions of his realms. Serfdom was largely abolished throughout the Habsburg lands; the secularization of education and society was moved forward precipitately with the dissolution of large numbers of monasteries and nunneries. This last measure stemmed from the emperor's conviction that many monks and nuns spent all too little time in useful labor. Joseph granted confessional toleration to the major Protestant sects, Lutherans and Calvinists, as well as to Jews.

Like so many visionaries, the emperor paid little heed to the practical impact on people affected by these changes, even when these measures brought more pain than relief. Impoverished serfs did not have the capital to turn themselves into self-supporting free farmers overnight; their noble masters throughout the Habsburg territories lost a crucial supply of agrarian labor. Many in cloistered vocations, especially women, had left secular life as girls; the world to which they returned utterly bewildered them. To these injuries Joseph added radical administrative reforms that had particularly heavy repercussions in Hungary, the Austrian Netherlands, and northern Italy where the Theresan innovations had been more limited. In 1784, he declared that German would be the official language of government and education throughout his lands, an especially provocative step in Hungary where Latin was still used in the diet. The latter was a dead language, reasoned the emperor, and the kingdom was better ruled in a tongue the modern world understood. All state employees and provincial administrators had three years to master enough German to perform their duties. His next step was to get rid of the historic counties into which the kingdom was divided. These he replaced them with ten administrative districts of roughly equal size supervised by a commissar of his own choice. He refused to convoke the Hungarian diet; indeed, he refused even to submit to the separate ceremonial crowning of the Hungarian ruler on Hungarian soil. Similar policies appeared in the Habsburg Italian territories as well as in Belgium.

These measures quickly led to armed uprisings in several parts of the Habsburg lands. Joseph combatted these both militarily and with the vigorous censorship and police activity that as a child of the Enlightenment he had once scorned. When he died in 1790, exhausted and embittered and with his realms still in an uproar, even though he had revoked many of his measures. It fell to his brother, Leopold II (1747–1792), to remedy the situation. Like Joseph, Leopold was deeply

committed to political, economic, and administrative reform; as Grand
Duke of Tuscany he had turned his lands into a showcase for enlightened government and its promise to advance the welfare of the entire
principality. But having inherited a good measure of his mother's political common sense, he knew that he had to restore order to his lands,
and not only for domestic reasons. A massive revolution had begun in
France the year before which threatened aristocracies and crowned
heads throughout Europe. His sister, Marie Antoinette, was married to
Louis XVI of France, and there was a distinct possibility that he might
have to go to war to defend her position and that of her husband.

Leopold pacified the Hungarians by agreeing to call the diet. (*See
Document No. 4.*) Nobles from all parts of the Habsburg lands felt more
easy when he modified the terms under which serfs could be released
from compulsory labor. Landlords could negotiate these arrangements
without government interference; nor were they obligated to grant their
servile populations their freedom if satisfactory contracts could not be
arranged. The Belgian uprising fell apart under military pressure and
because of local disagreements between the aristocratic and more democratic elements among the dissidents.

Thus at his death, Leopold had contained the worst of the troubles
that his brother's policies had created. And in many ways, the monarchy
was far stronger administratively than it had been at the outset of the
Theresan era. While Maria Theresa and her sons never fully realized
some of the more far-reaching reforms they had in mind, Habsburg government was structurally and financially sounder than it had been in
1740. A functional bureaucracy was now in place—perhaps Joseph's
most lasting achievement—imbued with Josephinian commitment to
the general welfare and impartial execution of policy and law that would
carry over into the next century. Fostered by generous tariff protection,
domestic industry had expanded considerably, and agriculture had
grown more productive as well. Both conditions markedly improved the
revenue flow to the government in Vienna. Finally, aside from the loss
of Silesia to Prussia, the monarchy had indeed hung together, something not altogether predictable in 1740.

But the upheavals which many of Joseph's measures provoked showed
that the Habsburg monarchy was still very much a conglomerate of
lands, ready to defend their local identities and socioeconomic arrangements against the interests of a central government should the latter
overstep the general understanding of its limits. This attitude had

proven how dangerous it could be in a largely domestic crisis. How the peoples of the Habsburg lands would react to pressures from abroad, especially when these celebrated the virtues of national particularism, although not for traditional reasons, had yet to be tested. That challenge would not be long in coming.

CHAPTER 3

BETWEEN THUNDER AND LIGHTNING

The Habsburg Empire and Napoleon I. "Liberty, equality, fraternity," the motto of France's revolutionaries, had a deep and lasting impact on the multiethnic dynastic empires of central and eastern Europe. Radical intellectuals and others dissatisfied with their political situation quickly grasped both the logical and moral relationship between the rights of individuals and the collective rights of nations.

The revolutionary armies of Emperor Napoleon I (1769–1821) reinforced these notions among those attracted to them, and Bonaparte himself showed how to create political and administrative structures that would realize these goals. By consolidating some of the smaller principalities of the Holy Roman Empire and Italy into larger entities, he alerted many people, particularly of the middle classes, to the legal and commercial benefits of more centralized government. He had a scheme for the reunification of Poland. Moreover, in battle after battle, he had defeated the major ruling houses of Europe, the Habsburgs among them. Occupying Vienna in 1809, Napoleon humbled the house of Austria through marital diplomacy as well. The following year, Emperor Francis I (1768–1835) betrothed his daughter to his French rival as the price for temporary respite from military conflict. The union of the Corsican commoner-emperor and Archduchess Maria Louise may be said to have recognized the victory of talent over lineage, one of the more constant elements in French revolutionary thought. Napoleon, of course, had not destroyed dynastic monarchy in Europe. He intended to establish an imperial house of his own and was as anxious to sire a legitimate heir of impeccable family background as any conventional prince. Nevertheless, his successes, temporary though some of them were, made it clear that Europe's venerable ruling families could not survive upon tradition and deference alone.

The idea of the nation as the individual writ large had populist implications that threatened all dynastic monarchs. The failure of the first revolutionary government in France to reconstitute Louis XVI as a national, rather than proprietary, King of France bode ill for the future of such efforts elsewhere in Europe, especially in the Habsburg Empire.

If such a transformation could not take root in the comparatively homogeneous linguistic and ethnic setting of France, it was even less likely
to prosper in a state made up of many different peoples and cultures.

Metternich and Nationalism. Napoleon's imperial ambitions
eventually turned not only his formal enemies, but even many of his
early supporters against him. By 1815, a great coalition of Austria, Russia, Prussia, and Great Britain had decisively beaten him. The victori-
ous powers gathered at a congress in Vienna (1814–1815) to restore
Europe along lines more to their liking. Both Prince Clemens von Metternich (1773–1859), the Habsburg chancellor and the driving force at
the meeting, and Francis I were eager to quiet the national passions
which Napoleon and his armies had aroused. Like so many German territorial officials of his time, well-born in territories too small or poor to
employ them appropriately, Metternich had made his career abroad. A
Rhinelander, he had served the Habsburgs in several ambassadorial
posts during the first decade of the nineteenth century, including a stint
in Paris between 1806 and 1809. Few people could have been less given
to patriotic enthusiasms. His tastes and view of the world were those of
an unregenerate cosmopolitan; local sensibilities, ethnic or otherwise,
were significant only should they threaten a social and political system
in which he and his kind could flourish. (*See Document No. 5.*) On these
grounds, he was occasionally willing to continue supporting the study
of indigenous cultures which had begun under Maria Theresa. As late
as 1846, upon the founding of the Imperial Academy of Arts and Sciences, he ordered that the languages spoken within the confines of the
empire receive special attention; the first members of the organization
were to come from all the areas of the Habsburg state.

Generally Metternich discouraged national sentiments, and the idea
that nationality should be central to the structure of government and
official policy was altogether abhorrent to him. This was true even when
such notions could possibly work in the Habsburg interests. In the effort
to whip up public opposition to Napoleon, some publicists and political
leaders, including members of the dynasty, had tried to develop a kind
of "Austrian" patriotism. Among these was one of the Emperor's
younger brothers, Archduke Johann (1782–1859)—" . . . to the affairs
of state, the affair of the nation . . . " was the way he put it. Part of his
inspiration came from anti-French guerilla warfare then going on in
Spain which had accomplished enough to convince him that broad

popular mobilization was the key to military success. Local militias had to be created; these would bring "the masses" to bear in the struggle. The term "fatherland" cropped up frequently in military orders as well as in propaganda broadsides.

These ideas fired the imaginations of intellectuals as well as many among the common folk. Some German Romantics such as Frederick Schlegel (1772–1829) came to view the independence of the German territories as a whole and the independence of the Austrian monarchy as one and the same thing. Indeed, Schlegel and like-minded contemporaries in Austria dreamed of reestablishing the Holy Roman Empire with the Habsburgs at its head. Even as the war with the French emperor was going on, they converged upon Vienna to promote this scheme. Though both they and some Habsburg bureaucrats who supported them knew well that non-Germans were part of the Habsburg state, they believed that their vision of Austrian patriotism was comprehensive enough to speak to all the empire's peoples. Metternich feared that such notions were likely to reignite the controversies Joseph II had provoked not so many years before when he tried to Germanize his administration. While he did not openly forbid the activities of Schlegel and his cohorts, he saw that they never received the highest official support. Spurned by the very government which was supposed to advance its program, the movement gradually fell apart.

Thus both Metternich and Francis I had good reason to approach the negotiations in their capital city with one goal in mind—the reconstitution and preservation of the Habsburg state. They began that process even before the congress started. Francis had resigned himself to Napoleon's abolition of the Holy Roman Empire in 1804 and his recreation two years later as Francis I, emperor of the new Austrian Empire. The Treaty of Paris, signed on 30 May 1814, returned to the Habsburgs lands they had lost in various treaties with Napoleon from 1797 through 1809 (Campoformio 1797; Luneville 1801; Pressburg (Bratislava) 1805; Vienna, 1809). These included those Italian possessions ruled either from Vienna or by close relatives of the house, the Tyrol, and parts of Croatian Hungary as well as other areas. Though he had claim to further restorations, Francis was willing to sacrifice these to the greater advantage of territorial contiguity. He therefore gave up lands in southwestern Germany, which the Habsburgs had held for centuries but lost to Napoleon in 1805, as well as the area which was to become modern Belgium. As compensation, he received Lombardy-Venetia, now fused together as a kingdom, and the archbishopric of Salzburg, both better fits with the general outline of the Habsburg empire.

The German Confederation. The settlement Metternich did much to arrange at the Congress of Vienna was designed to thwart national movements as much as possible. Metternich believed that the Habsburg government was incapable of enforcing such a policy alone; the Napoleonic wars were, among other things, a financial catastrophe in Vienna and other parts of the empire. Alliances and agreements with like-minded states to stabilize European politics domestically and internationally were his answer to the problem. He came closest to realizing his designs with the creation in 1815 of the German Confederation. This was a loose organization of those German states still sovereign after Napoleon's reworking of the political geography of central Europe. Theoretically all of the rulers represented by envoys in its diet were equal, but Habsburg Austria held the permanent presidency over its gatherings.

The purposes of the Confederation sounded routine—securing German independence, territorial integrity, and domestic tranquillity. But the second and the third easily lent themselves to curbing national revolution, and Metternich was quick to activate them in his cause. Middle class intellectuals, students and university professors among them, had continued to call for a united Germany after 1815. They argued that if all Germans were to enjoy the rights to which the French Revolution had awakened them, they would have to live under one government rather than many. A stirring assembly of nationally minded university students took place in 1818 at the Wartburg Castle in what today is Thuringia, where Martin Luther had once hidden himself from a hostile pope and Habsburg emperor. The gathering was followed by the assassination of a conservative journalist and writer August von Kotzebue (1761–1819) at the hands of someone who was thought to be a liberal nationalist. Metternich persuaded the German Confederation to adopt the Karlsbad Decrees which obligated each of the members to promote good order in their institutions of higher learning and in the press, a euphemism for severe restrictions on freedom of speech and learning. A further, and especially important, series of agreements were signed among Austria, Prussia, and Russia in 1833 committing the three powers to aid one another against both domestic and foreign enemies.

Political and Financial Affairs. Francis I shared Metternich's traditional view of social and political relations along with the conviction that stability, not reform, was essential to the preservation of his monarchy. Indeed, so committed was the emperor to established ways of doing things that he sometimes rejected Metternich's own administrative proposals. The chancellor very much wanted to serve as a prime minister within an organized cabinet, but Francis stubbornly held to dealing one-on-one with his chief officials in time-honored Habsburg fashion. This practice made the emperor work very hard, but he also had full control of the decision-making process within his government. The court remained the center of events in the Habsburg realms, and frustrated though he may have been, even Metternich complied.

Consistent with his general purpose of bringing calm to his lands after the upheavals of the Napoleonic interlude, Francis changed the structure of the Habsburg regime only where doing so engendered little trouble. The need to reconstitute local government in areas the French or their allies had controlled did allow him to curtail the powers of provincial estates further. Officials appointed by the emperor's government, rather than traditional local authorities, took over more functions in regional administrations. When a new civil code for the empire was introduced in 1811 along with changes in the system of taxation, Vienna did not consult with the estates.

These were tactics which would have provoked vehement protests, especially from the aristocracy, in an earlier age. But new times had arrived, and nobles worried as much about the constitutional liberal currents running through Europe as did their Habsburg sovereign. They were on the whole willing to let Francis have his way at home, so long as he continued to draw upon them, along with his dynasty, for his chief ministers and advisers. Even the Hungarians had supported the anti-Bonaparte cause, though such cooperativeness was short-lived. In 1811, the general diet of the kingdom rejected a general devaluation of paper currency issued during the war; Metternich retaliated by not calling that body for thirteen years. Instead, he turned to the estates in individual Hungarian counties when driving up subsidies and recruits for the war effort. However, these local gatherings refused to go along with this charade indefinitely; in 1825 the chancellor had to return to the practice of calling the national assembly every three years as had been agreed earlier. Furthermore, a serious Hungarian reform party had begun to take shape, which the government in Vienna would find ever harder to control.

The greatest immediate problem that the Habsburg government had to solve if it hoped to preserve itself was financial. Inflation had devalued the currency so badly by 1810 that when a rumor circulated that the regime was allowing this to go on as a way of lightening its own fiscal troubles, bondholders demanded immediate redemption of their credit. The empire had never been a center of commercial capitalism, for all that seventeenth- and eighteenth-century mercantilists in Habsburg service stressed its importance. Western Europe had expanded overseas, generating a good part of the wealth that would underwrite the industrial revolution of the nineteenth century. The Habsburgs, on the other hand, had poured three centuries of resources, either their own or borrowed, into rescuing Catholicism and themselves from Protestants, Turks, Louis XIV, Prussians, and Napoleon. The overwhelming majority of their subjects in 1815 were impoverished peasants who, despite Joseph II's declaration, were still largely serfs or virtually so. While a commercial bourgeoisie existed, it was small and concentrated in the western territories of the monarchy. Its opportunities for growth were still limited by archaic guild restrictions and by its own aspirations to acquire noble titles and privilege as soon as possible, rather than to exploit its wealth in further entrepreneurial investment. Such ambitions were shared by their counterparts in England and France, but the depth of prosperity among the middle classes in the latter was far greater.

The Habsburg lands had some mineral resources—iron, gold, lead, copper, and silver. However, many mines had long since run out or become too costly to exploit for what remained in them. Furthermore, in proportion to the territorial mass of the empire, its fertile land was limited. Mountains to the west ruled out large-scale agriculture. As one moved toward the Hungarian plain, the terrain became far more suitable for extensive cultivation of grain and grazing animals, but returning the area to an arable condition after the Turkish withdrawal took some time. The textile manufacture in Silesia lost to Prussia in the Seven Years War had been restored elsewhere, both creatively and profitably. In Bohemia and Lower Austria some enterprising nobles had begun producing these goods on their estates. But these pockets of economic dynamism were few and far between, and Metternich was well aware of how vulnerable this condition left the state which he served.

Therefore, while political liberalism was wholly uncongenial to the opportunistic chancellor, its economic counterpart was not. Habsburg influence abroad and economic growth became, in his eyes, two sides of the same coin. He was even more inclined to believe this as he watched the *Zollverein*, a Prussian-led tariff union, draw the northern and central principalities of Germany together. The rapidly industrializing German lands might, he thought, lure away skilled workers from Bohemian textile and glass factories which were right on the border of Saxony. Austria was not a member of the *Zollverein*; export of its goods to member German lands would decline since a stiff duty had been placed on them.

The answer to this problem was to make the Habsburg lands more productive. Only if the empire's currency were stabilized would this take place, and here the regime in Vienna was genuinely successful. The huge supply of paper currency in circulation was absorbed through a variety of schemes offered to creditors. The interest-bearing debt of the empire declined substantially as a central bank with officers both from the government and the public was given sole authority to issue new tender and grant credit to the state. The government failed, however, to revise the tax system in ways that encouraged major economic growth. By 1830, income was in excess of expenditure, but only because Habsburg authorities were reaching deeply into the pockets of the empire's peoples. The policy was stirring considerable resentment among the estates in Hungary and Bohemia, which had retained some say in fiscal matters. Some signs of major industrial development were visible; the first steam-driven railway opened for service between Vienna and Galicia in 1836. However, the scale of industry was still comparatively small. The center of textile manufacturing was in Lower Austria where 40 factories employed 7,493 workers. Bohemia was far more efficient— there 81 establishments had 7,524 laborers. Styria and Carinthia, including Carniola, had only one textile mill apiece!

An Age of Culture in an Age of Repression. The Habsburg government therefore discouraged political innovation at the same time it fostered a more dynamic economy. Each program had the same goal— to enhance the power of a dynasty badly shaken by the humiliation of the Napoleonic years. Of the two, however, it was the repressive thrust that had the greater immediate impact, settling upon the empire a tone of quietism which never disappeared, especially in Vienna itself. The dynasty and its advisers had, of course, long experience with such poli-

cies. Indeed, a mechanism was already in place to minimize public opposition to the regime. Joseph II had used censorship and police surveillance to combat sedition; reinforced by the Karlsbad decrees, Metternich and Francis availed themselves frequently of both strategies,
along with arbitrary imprisonment of those believed dangerous to their
vision of the state.

The impact of such measures stretched far beyond politics and administration. Intellectual life suffered heavily, particularly at its highest
levels. Speculative philosophers, Kant and Hegel among them, were
proscribed reading. Classics of the eighteenth-century German theater
were crudely rewritten to please both state and Catholic orthodoxy.
Gottfried Ephraim Lessing's great eighteenth-century brief for religious toleration, *Nathan the Wise*, was a prominent victim. The play's
chief protagonist, a Jew, is asked which of the three major religions,
Christianity, Judaism, or Islam, taught him the most. Before the arch-
bishop would allow a public performance to go forward, the names of
the faiths were dropped, to be replaced with "truth," "doctrine," and
"opinion".

Higher education lagged far behind its counterpart in the better
German universities to the north, notably Göttingen and the new establishment in Berlin. The latter, following the reform program of
Wilhelm von Humboldt, treated teaching and research as two sides of
the same intellectual coin. Francis I's approach to these endeavors was
altogether different; he announced in 1821 that the two activities should
remain separate in order to create good citizens and pliant subjects.
Writers and scholars often had no choice but to go into exile or to publish their work abroad. Among the most notable of these emigres was
Karl Anton Postl (1793–1864) who went to America in 1823 and took
the pen name of Charles Sealsfield. (*See Document No. 6.*) Though he
returned to Europe in 1831 to live in Switzerland, he traveled to the
New World many times after that. His novels about the struggle of the
North American Indians and the rebellious uprisings against Spanish
government in Mexico and in Texas were thinly masked protests against
the conditions he had fled in the Habsburg lands.

Yet, the general cultural environment of the years 1815–1848,
soporific and stifling as it may have been to some, had its distinct
charms and satisfactions. Increased economic activity and stability gave
the urban middle classes the discretionary income to cultivate the aesthetic side of their private lives. The German term applied to the period,

"Biedermeier," comes from a style of interior decoration which featured solid, yet classically graceful furniture and accessories. To this day, it betokens a world of cozy domesticity and bourgeois self-confidence. And, for all of its official constraints, the Austrian Empire was far from a spiritual wasteland between the years 1815 and 1848. Music, of all the arts, the most immune to censorship, flourished. Though not a native of Vienna, Ludwig van Beethoven (1770–1827), the preeminent composer of his age, lived there permanently after 1792 when he began a two-year period of study with Joseph Haydn (1732–1809) to whom he dedicated his second piano sonata. There he wrote all of his most important work which enjoyed immense popularity and support among the city's elite. His funeral from the Church of the Holy Trinity, was worthy of a major state figure. One of his greatest contemporary admirers was Franz Schubert (1797–1828). While his output found its audience in somewhat more modest social circles, he raised the German art-song to a heretofore unsurpassed level of inner expressiveness.

Literature, of course, was scrutinized far more systematically by the authorities. Yet, some of Austria's most important authors emerged during this period. Those very same obstacles that government oversight imposed gave their writing a unique tone and outlook which it retains to this day. The nineteenth-century novelist and painter Adalbert Stifter (1805–1868) created an aesthetic that gave both artistic freedom and the requirements of state their due. In the introduction to a collection of his stories, *Many-colored Stones* (1853) he claimed to be guided by what he called "the gentle law"—taking the things of this world for what they are rather than looking behind or into them for deeper meaning. Though later Austrian authors and intellectuals would explore material which Francis I and Metternich's censors would have rejected out of hand, they would never abandon this principle altogether.

Viennese theater actually thrived. Public enthusiasm in the capital for the stage antedated the post-Napoleonic era by a century or more. However, both comedy and drama rose to classical status between the years 1815–1848. It was during this time that Austria's three greatest playwrights, the dramatist Franz Grillparzer (1791–1872) and the popular comic writers Ferdinand Raimund (1790–1836) and Johann Nestroy (1801–1862) did all, or in Nestroy's case, a good part, of their most important work. Raimund, a complex and hypersensitive man, who ended his life in suicide, was intellectually the least controversial of the three. The sweet-tempered moralizing of his plots lay in his char-

acteristic balance of traditional virtues which stressed both the absurd-
ity of trying to rise above one's station in life and the lessons which the
ordinary folk of this world had to teach their betters. Especially good
examples of the genre are *The Peasant as a Millionaire* and *The Spend-
thrift*. At a yet deeper level, Raimund's characters are engaged in a quest
for their true selves, a theme especially well-realized in his *The King of
the Alps and the Misanthropist*. Indeed, the subject permeates Austrian
literature as a whole. Grillparzer is among the most important dramatic
poets to have ever written in the German language. His plays on historical themes, *King Ottakar's Fortune and End*, *A Quarrel among Brothers in the House of Habsburg*, as well as classical subjects such as *Medea*,
are both linguistically accomplished and psychologically compelling,
even for modern tastes. Grillparzer's frustration at the hands of censors
as well as disappointment over public reaction to some of his plays did
lead him to abandon writing for the state service long before he died.
His output before that decision, however, was more than enough to give
him major status in the German literary canon. Nestroy was equally
active before and after the revolution of 1848; while his roots in the venerable Viennese popular comedy were as strong as those of Raimund, his
work grew more sharply critical of social arrangements once the Metternich regime collapsed. (*Freedom in Krähwinkel*, *The Unimportant
Man*). Nestroy's earlier plays were less bitter, though their comic impact
remains fresh. One of them *On the Town* (*Einen Jux Will Er Sich
Machen*) has worked its way into the English-speaking theater in several
versions, among them as the original source of the book for the American musical *Hello Dolly*. Part of the effect of his memorable characters
comes from their dazzling verbal endowments expressed in improvisa-
tions, bizarre juxtapositions of images, and puns, all of which distinguished Nestroy himself who often performed in his plays. It was one
of his comic figures who gave some of the earliest, and perhaps wisest
advice on the Habsburg national question, even as it was becoming an
earnest matter in the empire: "the best nation is resignation."

National Stirrings. Nor was Vienna the only literary center of the
empire. Nineteenth-century Romanticism did not have official support
in the Habsburg capital, if, for no other reason than the stress which the
movement placed upon the uniqueness of national endowments. For this
reason alone, however, it made great inroads among the non-German
peoples of the Habsburg lands, even when the general thrust behind it

was not in the dynasty's interests. Heavily influenced by Lord Byron, the English Romantic, and the German dramatist Frederick Schiller, the Czech lyric poet Karel Hynek Macha (1810–1836) finished the stunningly beautiful epic *Maj* (*May*) in 1836. Popular folklore served as the basis for many poems of the Hungarian Alexander Petofi (1823–1849) whose "Arise Hungarians" would become the anthem of contemporary and future revolutionaries. Silvio Pellico's (1789–1854) tragedy *Francesca da Rimini* was translated into English by Byron and is the source of the libretto for the opera of the same name by Ricardo Zandonai. Imprisoned by the Habsburgs for his nationalist activities, he wrote *My Prisons* a graphic and moving description of his unhappy fate which, when circulated abroad, did much to foster the reputation of the Habsburg state as a "prisoner of nations."

Thus, behind these impressive upsurges of cultural consciousness lay that larger awareness of national identification which Metternich had been so anxious to keep at low ebb. The Habsburg Italian lands were especially volatile. In 1816, only a year after the close of the Congress of Vienna, reports from that area showed clearly that the stuff of revolution, inspired by the contact with republican and Napoleonic France, was still very much there. The thoughts of independence which Bonaparte's armies had brought with them would not go away. In Lombardy, which the Habsburgs had tried to turn into a showcase for enlightened monarchy, the largest part of the educated among the population supported the idea. Postwar economic hardships weighed on this group heavily; former officers who had been cut in rank, merchants ruined by the giddy fluctuations of the empire's currency, lawyers, a few scholars—all had little to lose, as one observer noted, and therefore had little to fear from change. Even within the Apostolic Congregation in Rome, there were groups—the "Sanfedists" in particular—who were calling for a break with Vienna.

These sentiments as yet lacked someone to turn them into coherent and active policy, but they were nonetheless dangerous to the dynasty's position. Though the Habsburg holdings remained outwardly tranquil during revolutionary upheavals on the peninsula, Habsburg armies participated in efforts to put them down—in Naples in 1823 and in Parma, Modena, and the Papal States during the 1830s. Their campaigns were on the whole successful, but one thing was abundantly clear to anyone who wanted to see. Metternich's grand scheme of European stabilization had achieved only a limited hold on the continent.

CHAPTER 4

REVOLUTION FROM WITHIN

The Seeds of Upheaval. Emperor Francis I died in 1835. Although a convinced autocrat, he was personally unpretentious, and he had been genuinely popular, at least among his Viennese subjects. His domestic lifestyle was that of the well-to-do Austrian bourgeoisie. In conversation he preferred their *patois* as well. Called *Wienerisch*, it is an urban variant of the south German dialect to which have been grafted bits of the many tongues spoken in the Habsburg capital. His successor had many of these qualities, but was a sorry replacement. Ferdinand I (1793–1875), known colloquially as Ferdinand the Benevolent (*Gütig*) or, less kindly, Ferdinand the Cretin (*Trottel*) had been epileptic since childhood. He was not altogether mentally dysfunctional—he played musical instruments and was a serious scientific amateur. Nevertheless, his ailments had made his education and behavior erratic. To compensate for his eldest son's present and future deficiencies his father had left the day-to-day government of the empire in the hands of a State Conference headed by the new emperor's uncle, Archduke Ludwig (1784–1864), a man of considerable intellectual vigor and imagination. Other members were a second, and far less consequential, archduke, Franz Karl (1802–1878), Metternich, and Count Franz Anton Kolowrat (1778–1861), a Bohemian nobleman whose nominal position was that of minister of the treasury but whose word counted for much in the general conduct of domestic affairs.

In historical retrospect, the calm of the Biedermeier era seems altogether deceptive. In fact, it was a time when structural changes were underway in the societies and economies of Europe which led to widespread revolution in 1848. For scholars of the Habsburg monarchy, 1840–1848 is called the "Vormärz" or "pre-March," a way of saying that the antecedents of these outbursts in Austria, Hungary, Bohemia, and elsewhere were taking shape during this period. Metternich's diplomacy had contained the liberal and national aspirations of the Napoleonic era. He had not, however, eradicated them. Furthermore, a new element had been added to these now familiar political and cultural discontents. This was the call for greater social and economic justice for rural and industrial workers. The Habsburg monarchy was vulnerable

38

to this unrest as well. The impoverished and servile status of their peasantry had troubled Maria Theresa and Joseph II both for moral and
utilitarian reasons. Although each ruler had made serious efforts to remedy these conditions, their successful promotion of manufacturing in
their lands had aggravated economic inequalities in both town and
countryside. These grew worse as the war economy of the Napoleonic
era spurred industrial output even beyond the level it had reached under
the shelter of high protective tariffs during the late eighteenth century.
Increasing quantities of textiles and iron were being turned out in the
eastern Austrian lands and Bohemia. Vienna and Prague had become
growing industrial centers as were smaller cities such as Brno (Brünn)
where the opportunity for work in wool mills led the population to double. The living conditions and often the wages of these people were ap-
palling, however, and demands for serious improvements began to cir-
culate. The middle classes in the Austrian lands, especially in Vienna,
were the chief beneficiaries of these changes. Yet, they felt that their
government had not done enough for them. If anything, their greater
well-being only increased their appetites for more of the same. Durable
artifacts of a much older regime—the privileged position of artisan and
trade guilds and the restrictions they placed upon production and commerce, the forced labor still required from peasants in many parts of the
empire which discouraged cultivation of cheap food needed for urban
workers—all stood in the way of their ambitions. Merchants and factory
owners were joined by many in the professional classes and an assortment of bureaucrat-intellectuals still true to the Josephinian belief that
a more centralized government would further the economic development of the entire empire. While such people did not seek to abolish
the monarchy, they wanted a constitution that assigned real power to
some form of popular representative body. Specifically they wished significant control over taxation, expenditure and state policy as a whole.
They also asked for exercise of such basic civil rights as freedom of the
press, speech and the right to assemble.

The push for far-reaching reform did not stop in Vienna. Enthusiasm
for serious change was developing throughout the empire, though unlike the liberals of the capital, their counterparts in Bohemia, Hungary,
and elsewhere thought primarily in terms of national interests. Habsburg governments from Maria Theresa on had hoped that their various
peoples could fulfill their need for greater national identification
through cultivation of their linguistic and literary heritage without un-

dermining their loyalty to the dynasty. Among the Slavic peoples of the empire, at least the first part of that policy had yielded impressive results. This was especially true among the Czechs, whose language, under the relentless inroads of German, had fallen to the status of little more than a popular idiom. Ironically, it was under the influence of the German philosopher Johann Gottfried Herder (1744–1803), that this state of affairs began to turn. Herder stressed the uniqueness of national cultures in his writings, thereby furnishing justification for both scholarly studies of Czech language and literature as well as new creative writing in Czech, often on national themes, which appeared at the beginning of the nineteenth century. The linguist Joseph Dobrovsky's (1753–1829) grammar of the Czech language, which came out in 1809, is regarded as the formal beginning of modern Slavic philology. The founding of the Czech National Museum in 1818 further accelerated these developments.

Such interests led inexorably to larger questions about the history of the Czechs as a whole and their relationships to the peoples around them, especially the Germans. Generally acknowledged as the father of modern Czech historical scholarship, Francis Palacky (1798–1876) argued in the first volume of his *History of Bohemia* (1838), written in German, that Czechs and Germans had been one another's long-term enemies and that the Czech nation should have an autonomous position within the Habsburg state. Fearful that his people could never remain independent in the face of stronger states such as Russia, he was nevertheless careful not to overstate his political program. He therefore would be the spokesman for the moderate side of that issue for many years to come. (*See Document No. 7.*) After 1830, the Czech national movement grew increasingly divided over its relationship to fellow Slavs, particularly those in imperial Russia. It also acquired a democratic wing that aroused apprehension within the Bohemian nobility, who otherwise generally supported the idea of greater local freedom, especially in financial matters. But intellectuals and aristocrats in the Bohemian diet alike, could agree on the importance of fostering Czech literature and science. As early as 1816, Czech was declared the language of instruction in the secondary schools, though the measure was repealed following the mandate of the Karlsbad Decrees (see p. 30).

More profiled national identities were also taking shape among the South Slavic subjects of the monarchy. However, these people were less hostile to the Habsburgs and German culture than to the Magyar assertiveness which the resistance to Joseph II's measures had intensified. During the brief Napoleonic occupation of the Dalmatian coast, the Croatian Louis Gaj (1809–1871), educated in Graz and Vienna, founded the so-called Illyrian movement which advocated joining the Serbs, Bosnians, and Croatians to defend their interests, primarily against the Magyar ethnic hegemony now emanating from Budapest. A cornerstone to Gaj's program was the creation of a South Slavic literature in a common language. For this he chose Stokavian, one of the three dialects of the Dalmatian region; he then promoted its use through a reading society and library which he founded in Zagreb, the Croatian capital.

Though it had been affiliated with Hungary for centuries, Croatia had, at one point in its history, been an independent kingdom. But national sentiments in the pre-1848 Habsburg empire were not exclusively found among people who could claim statehood, however long ago that may have been. Slovaks, settled heavily in the mountainous regions of Hungary, also began to take a scholarly interest in their linguistic history, and to celebrate the achievements of Slavic peoples generally. The same concerns were stirring among the Romanians of Transylvania.

Indeed, from the standpoint of the Habsburg empire, the most complex amalgam of nineteenth-century liberalism and nationalism arose in Hungary. Haunted by Herder's prediction that the Magyars would inevitably disappear as a nation amidst the more numerous Germans, Slavs, and Romanians who surrounded them, Count Stephen Szechenyi (1791–1860) had emerged as the chief spokesman for a many-sided program of reform to rescue his native kingdom. Unlike many continental liberals, he was more influenced by English models than by French ones; both England and Hungary, he believed, had strong parliamentary traditions. Admiration of the economic progressives among the British landed classes led him to think that forward-looking magnates like himself should take the lead in modernizing Hungary. By bettering the lot of the nation as a whole, they would be enhancing their own fiscal position as well. Above all, he wished to improve Hungarian agricultural production and transportation. He had other important goals as well. Hungarians' interest in cultivating their tongue had already quickened in the latter years of the eighteenth century; Szechenyi was convinced that political and economic advances could not take place without an informed public. He therefore worked to continue raising the quality of the press and fostering Hungarian vernacular and national culture in general. In 1844, the kingdom finally dropped Latin as the official administrative and legislative language of the realm in favor of Magyar.

Szechenyi's activities ran generally along the lines of policies being followed in Vienna between 1815 and 1848. But there were Hungarian nationalists who had quite different ideas. These often were intellectuals, who supported the count's reforms but who had few ties to the landed aristocrats whose circles Szechenyi frequented. As these radicals saw it, Hungarian interests would be served better by ridding the kingdom of control from Vienna altogether. Among such men, informed by the egalitarian ideals of the French Revolution, Louis Kossuth (1802–1894) had an increasingly prominent voice. With some experience in Hungarian local government, he was making himself a national figure as a political journalist. In this role, he had begun editorializing for the complete political separation of Hungary from the rest of the Habsburg empire. He took scant account of the national aspirations among the Slavic and Romanian minorities in his kingdom, thereby laying the groundwork of trouble for future Hungarian politicians who supported his program.

A Year of Revolution. There was a more moderate faction among the Hungarian reformers whose demands centered around questions of civil liberties and modernization of the social structure of the kingdom. Count Francis Deak (1803–1876) had emerged as the spokesman for the generally liberal group. The Hungarian diet was actually discussing his proposals with the regime in Vienna on March 3 of 1848 when news of a revolutionary outbreak in Paris brought the talks to a halt. Kossuth demanded a government for Hungary alone, and revolution was on. Indeed, all of the national discontents smoldering throughout the Habsburg empire suddenly ignited. Budapest was, of course, far away, but the dynasty really knew that its troubles were serious when on March 13, large demonstrations took place in Vienna itself. Led by students, more radical members of the middle classes, and increasingly, industrial workers, crowds called for a constitution that established popular representation. While they did not challenge the unique privilege of the house of Austria to furnish a sovereign for its lands, they wished to be ruled in more egalitarian ways. The Habsburgs were asked to rid themselves of advisers who were unsympathetic to revolutionary views. Above all, the insurgents meant Metternich. The house of Austria had sacrificed men who served it well many times before if circumstances required it to do so; the chancellor was no exception. He fled to England.

Ferdinand the Benevolent's regime then made even larger concessions. Censorship was ended, and on April 25, 1848 a constitution was issued. It provided for a bicameral legislature, but allowed only a restricted franchise. When the mobs in the street rejected this arrangement, the government promised a unicameral legislature which would be chosen popularly throughout every place in the empire, save Italy and Hungary. Having yielded so much, the dynasty withdrew from its capital city to Innsbruck. There was some reason to fear for its safety. The bulk of the Habsburg army was by this time deployed in putting down rebellions in Bohemia, Hungary, and Italy, and therefore not available for duty in Vienna. Elections took place for the assembly in June and July, and the new legislature actually began its work. Its great accomplishment would be the general abolition of serfdom, though it took many years to work out the terms on which this was done.

The Dynasty Reasserts Itself. But it was not long before the Habsburg forces began to reverse most of the revolutionary tide. Under Palacky's aegis, an international Slavic Congress with representatives both from the empire and abroad had come together in Prague during June of 1848. It asked for a constitution guaranteeing a form of representative government for Bohemia. It also proposed federalizing the Habsburg state to give the Czechs equal status with the Germans and Magyars. The gathering was dissolved with relatively minor resistance by Habsburg forces under Prince Albert Windischgrätz (1787–1862). The truly venerable Field Marshall Joseph Radetzky (1766–1858), who had begun his military service as a boy under Joseph II, successfully put down the revolutionary outbreaks in Lombardy-Venetia in July. These had been led by King Charles Albert of Sardinia-Piedmont who then abdicated in favor of his son Victor Emmanuel. The dynasty returned to Vienna in August, though agitation had not yet stopped. Indeed, it became more radical as workers stepped up their calls for greater economic justice. This alarmed many middle-class property owners who had once supported the uprising. Peasants grew less sympathetic as well, now that they had the right to own land. Once again in October the dynasty withdrew, this time to Olomouc in Moravia. The revolutionary legislature was prorogued to Kromeriz (Germ.: Kremsier) where it was to write an administrative constitution for the empire.

By the end of 1848, however, the Habsburgs were firmly in control of almost all their lands. The police and the army had silenced the unrest in Vienna, often mercilessly. Some of the most radical spokesmen for change such as the socialist Robert Blum were executed. Equally significant for the future of the house of Austria, its members had agreed upon a new emperor to rule its lands. In December, Ferdinand the Benevolent yielded to the entreaties of his relatives and advisers and abdicated in favor of his eighteen-year old nephew, Franz Joseph (1830–1916). The slender and straight-backed young man, while not brilliant, was at least mentally normal and adequately trained. He was also, even as a youth, very circumspect, a quality which would serve him well throughout his lengthy career as would his natural dignity, courtesy and sense of duty.

Subduing Hungary. The lone area which had yet to be pacified was Hungary. Here, under Kossuth's leadership, the revolutionary program posed ever more serious threats to the integrity of the monarchy. In the face of great pressure, the Habsburg government had quickly met the demands for autonomy coming from Budapest. The Hungarian March Laws of 1848 created what was, in important respects, a genuinely liberal constitution for the kingdom. Heavily indebted to the thinking of Francis Deak, the new instrument provided for a popularly elected assembly, guaranteed civil liberties, abolished serfdom, and made all subject to taxation. Transylvania, Croatia, and the Serbian Vojvodina to the southeast were incorporated fully into the revolutionary state, to the bitter resentment of the nationally minded in those areas. The Habsburgs remained as kings of Hungary, but only by virtue of a personal union. This meant that laws applicable to the rest of the Habsburg territories did not have force in lands which belonged to the Crown of St. Stephen. In December, spurred on by Kossuth's fiery oratory, the Hungarian parliament refused to recognize Franz Joseph as its king in any kind of relationship. He had not been crowned and there was little likelihood that he would be, since Habsburg efforts to bring the Magyars to heel militarily had so far failed.

By the beginning of 1849, however, the dynasty's fortunes took a turn for the better. Budapest was retaken, forcing the new parliament and Kossuth to transfer themselves to Debreczen in the eastern part of the kingdom. There on April 14, 1849, they declared the dynasty deposed and proclaimed Hungary to be a republic. (*See Document No. 8.*) But at this point, the government in Vienna received unexpected assistance from abroad. Tsar Nicholas I of Russia had no sympathy for revolution of any sort. Following his obligations made to Austria in 1833, he offered to intervene in expectation that the Habsburgs would one day reciprocate the favor. Franz Joseph took him up thankfully, though as the Russians would discover in the near future, that gratitude was short-lived. By August the Hungarian forces surrendered. Kossuth fled the kingdom, first to Turkey, then to the United States, which celebrated him as a hero of democratic republicanism, and finally to Italy where he developed far more generous views toward the non-Magyar peoples of his native land. However, he lived long enough to gain iconic status among generations of Hungarian nationalists to come. His popularity remained especially strong among the peasantry. He left a brutal Austrian occupation behind him. Nine Hungarian high officers were hanged, four others shot. The relatively moderate Count Louis Batthyany (1806–1849), the first prime minister of the new Hungarian parliament, was executed as well.

Neo-Absolutism. For those who supported national causes in the Habsburg lands, this chaotic year seemingly did little to advance their goals. Indeed, the revolutions on many fronts fell apart as much because of dissension among their supporters as they did because of Habsburg repression. Furthermore, the regime that Vienna imposed on all the Habsburg territories was about the last thing that any of them had wanted. Not yet nineteen when the Hungarians finally surrendered, Franz Joseph followed the advice of two counselors very closely. One was Prince Felix von Schwarzenberg (1800–1852), who, along with the young emperor's mother, had been instrumental in persuading Ferdinand I to abdicate. The other was Alexander Bach (1813–1893), a onetime radical liberal for whom absolutism became the key to reform during the upheavals of 1848. Both men believed only tightly centralized authority in Vienna could restore the monarchy to viable statehood.

Some of the changes brought about in 1848, particularly in the socioeconomic area, were compatible with the goals of both men and therefore endured. Legal serfdom would never return, though much of the agricultural population remained mired in the status of a rural proletariat. Such commercial anachronisms as trade guilds and their crippling restrictions on manufacture and trade were put on notice that their privileges would come to an end, as they largely did. Municipal franchises were considerably broadened. But in imperial political and administrative affairs, Schwarzenberg moved swiftly and illiberally. He dissolved the 1848 parliament still meeting in Kromerziz where it was polishing the so-called Kromerziz constitution, perhaps the most serious effort to work out the relationship between central government and local administrative and popular interests that the monarchy would ever see. Its provisions were never adopted. In its place would eventually come the Sylvester or New Year's Eve Patent of 1851 which gave short shrift to representative government and national sentiment. It clearly affirmed the supremacy of the emperor and his regime; there was no room for popular input of any kind. More than anything else, the arrangement seemed designed to curb Hungarian separatism. That kingdom, like almost every other area of the monarchy save Lombardy-Venetia and Polish Galicia, was divided into administrative districts directly controlled from Vienna. Transylvania and the Serbian Vojvodina were excised from the Crown of St. Stephen altogether and governed directly from the Habsburg capital, as was Croatia. The policy led some in that kingdom, who had supported the Habsburgs during 1849 in the hope of gaining greater freedom from the revolutionary government in Budapest, to remark that what the Magyars received as punishment from their sovereign they had received as a reward.

New Developments in Nationalism. Once again, a superficial calm returned to the empire, but it was the result of crushed idealism and close police surveillance, not broad and genuine consensus. The themes and goals of the revolutionaries, while defeated, had not been eradicated. Political and social unrest during 1848 and after throughout Europe put ideas into circulation which would have a heavy impact on a multinational state at the center of the continent. Several uprisings had taken place in the lands of the German Confederation which had led to the calling of the so-called Frankfurt Parliament in 1848. Many Germans supported forming a unified state of their own to the north of the Austrian empire. Should such a creation arise, it would drastically alter the geopolitical structure of the region. Dominated by liberal intellectuals, a large number of academics among them, this gathering forged ahead with writing a constitution for a single Germany. To the question of what role the Habsburg empire would play in the new order, the answer of the delegates had finally been "none." Having completed its work in 1849, the gathering offered the crown of the nation not to the house of Austria, which had traditionally held primacy of place in German affairs, but turned to the Hohenzollern Frederick William IV, the king of Prussia. Recognizing that the democratic implications of the invitation could gravely compromise his own position within such a polity, he turned it down. Indeed, the Prussian army finally dispersed the entire conclave. But a vocal constituency had made clear its position on the role of the Habsburgs in Germany. This, even though one of Franz Joseph's uncles, Archduke Johann (1782–1859), who was something of a German patriot, had actually presided over the conclave for a time. Such a view raised the serious possibility that should ethnic particularism ever burgeon among the numerous Germans within the Habsburg lands, whose loyalty to the house of Austria had never been in question, they would find that the political center of their linguistic identity lay beyond the borders of the dynasty's holdings.

But more immediately significant were the changes which revolution in the name of national liberation had begun to work in the political organization of eastern and southeastern Europe. Some had occurred even before the upheavals of 1848. Greece had won its independence from the sultan in 1831; while there was no significant Greek minority within the Habsburg empire, its struggle for statehood had inspired many of Europe's subject peoples. More troubling for the regime in Vienna was yet another rebellion in Serbia which had been under Ottoman control since the end of the fourteenth century. An uprising had taken place against a Turkish garrison in Belgrade during the Napoleonic Wars. Encouraged by indigenous writers and by nationalist partisans in the Serbian settlements of southern Hungary, the insurgency had assumed international dimensions. The Habsburg Serbs had turned for support to their fellow-Orthodox Christians, the Russians; the government in St. Petersburg obliged. In 1817, the sultan recognized Milos Obrenovic, the head of one of the two influential local families who would rule Serbia into the twentieth century, as hereditary prince in the territory. The treaty of Adrianople in 1829 raised Serbia to an autonomous province within the Ottoman empire. By the 1840s, national leaders had already begun to speak of a greater Serbia. Initially they understood this term to mean a land cleared of Ottoman rule, not as a challenge to the right of the Habsburgs to rule the Serbs within the dynasty's territories.

Complete independence for Serbia would not come until 1878, but the very ambition had worrisome implications for the Habsburgs. The

Serbs in Hungary had already indicated that they would resist Magyar efforts to control their domestic financial and military affairs. And, as the Illyrian movement during 1848 had shown, there was some sentiment throughout the South Slavic areas to join more closely together should Magyar hegemony advance.

Finally, there was the role of Russia in all of this. Even before the French Revolution, the government in Vienna had grown increasingly wary of tsarist designs in Ottoman territory where the sultan's control appeared to be less and less effective. The need for Vienna and St. Petersburg to cooperate during the Napoleonic era had temporarily quieted these concerns; with the French threat now gone, this rivalry could grow to even larger proportions, should the opportunity present itself. Nicholas I's aid to Franz Joseph in quelling rebellion in Hungary in 1849 demonstrated that the two great multiethnic empires of Europe could still work together. But that, of course, depended upon a perception of mutual interest. Circumstances where those interests diverged sharply could destroy such harmony very easily. It was clear that the future integrity of the Habsburg empire depended both on the skillful conduct of foreign relations and on minimizing the role of liberal republicanism and ethnic particularism at home.

CHAPTER 5

SURVIVAL ABROAD,
EXPERIMENTS AT HOME
1848–1867

Foreign Powers and the Habsburg Monarchy. The Turkish sultan had already found that the cultural, ethnic, and religious particularisms of his subjects, singly or combined, easily converted themselves into demands for autonomy or outright independence. Moreover, these movements quickly won support and sympathy abroad, making them more difficult to control by raw force. One reason that the rebellions in Greece and Serbia had succeeded was that foreign powers were happy to exploit the discontents in the Ottoman empire to improve their own positions in the eastern Mediterranean. Russia had long sought naval access to the Dardanelles and westward; it had also conferred upon itself the role of protecting Eastern Orthodoxy and Slavic peoples generally. Both policies made the tsarist empire a major factor in the struggle for political nationhood among the Balkan peoples in the nineteenth century. England was keen to reinforce its commercial preeminence in the Levant and farther to the east. The Habsburg empire had a central role in the region as well, but it was a very complex one. With Russia's ambitions in the region growing, the government in Vienna looked ever more favorably on the "hereditary enemy" of former times as an ally. Should their interests require it, however, Franz Joseph and his ministers were ready to convert Ottoman land into Habsburg territory, regardless of how exposed they themselves were to the same kind of treatment.

Concessions at Home. Like Metternich, Bach and Schwarzenberg hoped to quiet internal political unrest which might open the Austrian empire to adventurism from abroad. They thus put much effort into bettering the lives of the young emperor's subjects, and managed to do so in several important respects. Heavily bureaucratized and intrusive though it was, their regime substantially advanced the economic and social welfare of the monarchy's peoples. Indeed, some of their most effective measures had genuinely liberal features. The vastly enlarged official apparatus was more honest, conscientious, and industrious than what had preceded it. The New Year's Eve Patent of 1851 guaranteed equality before the law. The removal of customs barriers between Hungary and the rest of the empire created more favorable conditions for trade and commerce, and the expanded police force, while oppressive to some, increased personal security throughout the Habsburg lands.

Franz Joseph's reign had also begun with ringing declarations of the right of all his peoples to cultivate their own language and culture. This principle had especially far-reaching consequences for the educational system of the empire. Classes in primary schools were conducted in the tongue of the majority of the people in the area. The language of instruction for a high school or *Gymnasium* remained the subject of dispute in areas of mixed population, but was practically circumvented through a locally conditioned bilingualism in which German and the tongue predominant in the school district were used, depending upon the nature of the work a student was doing. Both German and the regional idiom were taught.

Elementary schools, both secular and religious, remained heavily under the control of the Catholic clergy; the position of the latter was even enhanced in the Concordat which Franz Joseph signed with the papacy in 1855. However, standards of secondary and post-secondary education improved markedly, despite an undersupply of faculty qualified to give advanced training in certain disciplines. Religious instruction was obligatory, though it now was organized according to the confessional affinities of students. Secular teachers were used in history and the natural sciences as well as in both classical and modern languages, still the heart of the curriculum. (*See Document No. 9.*) To graduate from a *Gymnasium*, or high school, students had now to attend for eight years rather than six. Universities adopted a more modern outlook as well. The study of arts and sciences, which until the middle of the nineteenth century acted as a kind of preparatory division for the vocational divisions of law, medicine, and theology, became equally professionalized. Achievement in these disciplines was measured more and more in terms of specialized research, a change already in place throughout leading German universities to the north. Institutions of higher education were also given wider autonomy in managing academic affairs.

But if they were to survive the challenge of European nationalism, particularly where it was supported by foreign powers, the Habsburgs needed a loyal and well-schooled army. Thus, the commitment of the regime to more equitable treatment of its subjects extended to required military service as well. This burden was spread to include men from social and economic classes heretofore lightly touched. Beyond this, the actual call to duty—eight years, liberally broken with furloughs, and two more in the reserves—was done by lot. Such measures were supposed to improve morale and commitment, qualities Franz Joseph found very quickly that he had to test in defense of his holdings. For the nationalism of the Habsburg lands, like similar movements in the Ottoman empire, was indeed prone to foreign exploitation, a card Kossuth tried to play as soon as he fled Hungary in 1849. (*See Document No. 10.*) However, it was not in that rambunctious kingdom but in Italy where the trouble began.

The Unification of Italy. Italian nationalism had been suppressed in 1848, but it had not been eradicated. Instead, the movement acquired a coherence and a steadfastness of leadership during the 1850s it had heretofore lacked. The driving force behind this development came from the northwestern kingdom of Sardinia-Piedmont with a new ruler, Victor Emmanuel II (1820–1878) and his prime minister, Camillo Count Benso di Cavour (1810–1861). A man of rare political and diplomatic talents, Cavour had a grand vision of a single Italy whose mission and influence stretched beyond its borders. None of this, however, could take place without the tolerance, not to mention active backing of other European countries. Throughout the 1850s he pounced upon every opening that came his way to ingratiate himself and his kingdom among those powers which could help advance his schemes. He was particularly successful in Paris. Here there once more was an emperor, Napoleon III (1808–1873), the nephew of Napoleon I. Elected president of the short-lived Second Republic in France in 1848, he transformed this into an empire toward the end of 1852 with himself at its head. He and the Sardinian minister had something to offer one another; Nice and Savoy, on the French-Italian border had gone back and forth several times between France and Piedmont over the centuries, and the emperor wanted them to become French once and for all. Something of a populist, Napoleon was also anxious to be known as a friend of national struggles. He was especially partial to Italian aspirations, given the Corsican origins of his family.

Clumsy diplomacy from Vienna and Cavour's manipulative tactics led Franz Joseph's government in 1859 to go to war in Italy. French support contributed significantly to bloody battlefield stand-offs between

Austria and Sardinia-Piedmont at Solferino and Magenta in that year. Though the Habsburg army had not been decisively defeated, Italian principalities under the dynasty's influence or outright control—Parma, Modena, and Tuscany, most notably—voted in 1860 for annexation to Victor Emmanuel's realm. The failure of the Habsburg government to roll back these initiatives led to the Treaty of Villafranca (1862). Franz Joseph turned over Lombardy to Napoleon who in turn presented it to Victor Emmanuel. Only the Italian alpine regions and Venetia remained under Austrian control.

The Italian debacle—Franz Joseph had led his forces into combat himself only to prove that, while he was brave, he was a bad strategist— quickly reverberated throughout the now smaller empire. None of the changes of the Bach regime, beneficial though some may have been, had sufficed to rescue Lombardy-Venetia for Franz Joseph during 1859. Though its spirit had been good, the army was, in fact, not adequate to its task, largely because the Habsburg high command followed tactical doctrines which had long since outlived their usefulness. For these men cavalry rather than infantry was still the core of offensive maneuvers. Setbacks in combat moved political leaders at home to question the soundness and legitimacy of a regime which many found unsatisfactory on other grounds. Financial upheavals that came after the defeat undermined its credibility even more. The integrity of the monarchy had been successfully challenged on national grounds for the first time; others would be quick to press claims of their own.

Constitutional Experiments. Like many of his Habsburg forebears, the emperor had a strong pragmatic streak. In his case, this trait was probably more a sign of weak imagination rather than innate flexibility, but it was an advantage to him in the political climate he now faced. While temperamentally he was more at home in a relatively authoritarian state, he was willing to explore different constitutional arrangements if he thought they might save his throne. Opponents of the reigning neo-absolutism from all quarters of society wished a greater role for their own voices in their government. Landed aristocracies throughout the monarchy urged that local diets once again have the authority they had lost after 1848, especially in fiscal matters. Middle class liberals, the initial revolutionaries in Vienna in 1848, still endorsed the idea of a more centralized monarchy but were anxious to have constitutionally explicit guarantees of civil liberties. Germans throughout the monarchy dominated both groups, though they had yet to identify their cause with their language and ethnicity. Others were not so hesitant to resurrect national causes. The Hungarians, for example wished to reinstitute the March Laws of 1848 that had granted them virtual autonomy. Liberal thinkers among them such as Baron Joseph Eotvos (1813–1871) argued that the very integrity of the Habsburg empire depended upon the monarch's willingness to act as the protector of the historical rights of all the nations under his government. While not totally incompatible with the principle of equality among the Habsburg nationalities which the Bach regime had espoused, this idea nevertheless had its problematic side, especially when it came from Hungary, where treatment of non-Magyars had been a divisive issue in 1848–49.

Franz Joseph's response was the October Diploma of 1860, the first among a series of efforts to strike some compromise between centralized and decentralized authority. Issued ". . . in the interest of our house and our subjects . . ." the Diploma conferred legislative power upon legally assembled provincial diets, or, in Hungary's case, the parliament in Budapest, in a wide range of regional affairs. Hungary was once again divided into its historic counties and was to be ruled by its historic constitution. An Imperial Council (*Reichsrat*) consisting of one hundred members appointed by the crown and drawn heavily from the propertied classes of the entire monarchy could participate in the development of the state budget and inspect it when finished. This body also had the right to approve the taxes needed to support the projected expenditures. The conduct of foreign relations, however, along with administrative control of the military, remained the exclusive province of the emperor.

Not all the peoples of the Habsburg empire applauded this adaptation of limited monarchy. It enraged many German liberals who saw provincial nobles reacquiring feudal powers which had been supposedly eradicated after 1848. Even the Hungarians in Budapest, some of whom were great landowners and had cause to cheer the restoration of their political status, were not altogether pleased. The more nationally minded among them still balked at participating in any central institutions outside of the kingdom such as the *Reichsrat*. Franz Joseph's own advisers, Ignaz von Plener (1841–1923), his minister of finance, and Anton von Schmerling (1805–1893), the minister of state, were much against the idea. They believed that even experiments with decentralization might end in the wholesale financial ruin of the monarchy.

The October Diploma never went into effect. It was replaced in 1861 by the February Patent, which was less driven by conservative and aristocratic interests. The *Reichsrat* was recast into a genuine parliamentary organ, empowered to initiate legislation and to pass an annual budget. Yet, though it moved the Habsburg empire further along the path of constitutional monarchy, the Patent was hardly a radical departure from past practice. The Imperial Council consisted of two houses, a senate composed of the Habsburg archdukes, high ecclesiastical figures and men nominated by the monarch, and a 300-member house of representatives. Members of the latter branch were chosen by local diets, which meant that the traditional monied classes still had much to say about the course of policy in Vienna. The emperor retained control of foreign affairs and the military; he could also call and dismiss the *Reichsrat* at will.

These arrangements brought forth their own set of heated objections. The more conservative aristocratic and urban elements of the empire feared that the expanded franchise promised in the document would lead to greater social democratization. The German liberals held the Habsburg army and its performance in Italy accountable for the breakdown of the Bach regime. This, for all its oppressiveness, had carried out many of their administrative ideals. They were therefore eager to do whatever they could to punish the military, but while they were able to block expenditures for the armed forces, they could not touch their general structure, since the Patent left this in the hands of the emperor. But it was the redirection of power toward Vienna that most bothered the politically minded among Franz Joseph's subjects. When the newly elected *Reichsrat* convened in May of 1861, it was boycotted by the Magyars, Croatians, and remaining Italians. Many Czechs, Poles, Serbs, and Slovenes who also did not like being forced to represent themselves in the Habsburg capital of the monarchy, were no less displeased, all for their own reasons.

From 1861 to 1865 when it was suspended, the Patent set the legal framework for Habsburg government. This did not mean that it was genuinely functional. Indeed, it served to make the domestic weaknesses of the monarchy more visible. The Hungarians had never been reconciled to the arrangement, which meant that half of the monarchy all but abstained from participation in its legal political structure. It was clear that some way had to be found to overcome this impasse. Otherwise, Franz Joseph could be faced with the same combination of problems that had led to his calamitous adventure in Italy. Internal national unrest might be turned to the use of ambitious foreign powers should it suit the interests of the latter to do so. All of this could force him once again to scale back his empire.

The Unification of Germany. The creation of a single Germany could open this problem among Franz Joseph's German subjects, that group which was the least likely to resist Austrian rule on ethnic grounds. Frederick the Great had already shown in the eighteenth century that the kingdom of Prussia was ready to rework territorial arrangements in the Holy Roman Empire at the expense of the Habsburgs, though he did not openly contest the house of Austria's long-standing hold on the imperial title itself. By 1848, German liberals were ready to reject these traditional relationships altogether. Though it had no legal standing, the revolutionary Frankfurt Parliament called for unification along the lines of the "small Germany" (*kleindeutsch*) principle, meaning that the Habsburg empire was excluded altogether. Economic policy in Berlin following the Napoleonic wars had encouraged this thinking. As we have already seen, Metternich himself had been deeply troubled by the political and economic implications of a Prussian-inspired German tariff union (*Zollverein*) in which Austria had no place.

Sitting both as a Prussian representative and as an observer for a conservative Berlin newspaper at the Frankfurt Parliament, Otto von Bismarck (1815–1898) began putting together some far-reaching thoughts about the future of German nationalism. He despised the progressive ideal of civil and economic freedoms for all Germans that many participants at the congress saw to be the chief goal of unification. He nevertheless sensed the historical dimensions of the movement and believed that its appeal would last. A unified Germany, he concluded, was inevitable, but when it came, it would best be on Prussia's terms. He did not have great sentimental attachment to the reigning house of Hohenzollern, though he did enjoy reasonably good relations with his king, William I. Rather he wished to preserve the political and economic position of landholding nobles like himself whose privileges were entrenched locally through such mechanisms as the Prussian three-class voting system which was weighted in favor of large property-holders. Following his return from Frankfurt, he spent a few years as Prussian ambassador to St. Petersburg and to Paris. Returning to Berlin, he took up the position of Prussian minister-president, or prime minister.

In this role he planned the political and military strategy that would create a single Germany, not by persuasion, as he said, but by "iron and blood." War, in his view, was necessary against the two foreign governments most likely to oppose the new state. One was France which over many centuries had consistently blocked German unification in any form. It also possessed rich coal and iron deposits in Lorraine, an area that the medieval Holy Roman Empire had once claimed. The other was the Habsburg regime in Vienna. The dynasty had been the titular, and in many instances, real leader of the German lands for over four hundred years. On historical grounds alone, Franz Joseph and his ministers had a vested interest in keeping Germany as a collection of small and medium-sized states. The house of Austria was in a position to make things uncomfortable for Bismarck on confessional grounds as well. The Hohenzollerns were Protestants and so were the majority of their subjects. The kings of Bavaria and Saxony, however, were Catholic and could be expected to look to Franz Joseph for support should Prussia challenge their sovereign status in any way.

Bismarck's first move was to draw Austria into a position where he would be able find a way to push both states into war. In the name of preserving the integrity of the German Confederation, the two powers mounted a grotesquely unequal offensive in 1864 against Denmark whose king was pressing dynastic territorial claims in Schleswig and Holstein on the Danish-German border. Though they cooperated in the venture, the government in Vienna believed that the Prussian minister-president was preparing to drive unification forward and strip the Habsburgs of active influence in Germany once and for all. To assure himself of Hungarian loyalty during the crisis to come, Franz Joseph reluctantly decided that he had to reach a political modus vivendi with the kingdom. Its politicians and peoples had waged a stubborn and often ingenious campaign of passive resistance to the February Patent which included tax evasion, among other things. In 1859, a kind of Hungarian government in exile had won at least temporary support of its quest for independence from Napoleon III. At the end of 1864, therefore, Franz Joseph delicately began exploring new political relationships with Francis Deak. The latter had been a persistent spokesman for the reactivation of the 1848 March Laws, but he was flexible enough to work productively with the government in Vienna. Unlike some of the more radical nationalists among his countrymen, he wished to continue some form of Hungarian membership in the Habsburg empire. A truly independent state, he feared, would be short-lived.

Their discussions were going on as Austria and Prussia fell to quarreling about the rights of each state in the administration of Holstein, occupied by Austria following the Danish conflict. Prussia launched its expected offensive into Habsburg territory in June of 1866. The Habsburg army and navy scored some successes against Italy, whose support Bismarck had cultivated with promises of the remaining bits and pieces of Venetia should Austria lose the war. However, combat with Prussia itself was yet another disaster for Franz Joseph's forces. In July they suffered a humiliating defeat at the hands of Prussian tactics and technology at Königgrätz (Hradec Kralove) in Bohemia. The need to accommodate the Hungarians was greater than ever. The Habsburg negotiators had tried to recycle an argument put forth years before by Schwarzenberg that the Hungarians had lost any claims to their constitution by rebelling against the house of Austria in 1848. With military defeat and even further disintegration of the empire staring them in the face, however, they abandoned legal niceties for hard bargaining with Deak and his party.

The Compromise of 1867. The result was the Dual Compromise (*Ausgleich*) of 1867 which created Austria-Hungary, the last form that the Habsburg monarchy would take until its collapse and dissolution in 1918. Formally the empire was divided in two with the boundary being the Leitha (Hung.: Latja), a river of no great distinction which runs south to north for a time in the eastern Austria of today, then crosses into Hungary where it flows south again toward Lake Balaton. What was generally north, northeast and northwest of this was called Cis-Leithenia, or the lands this side of the Leitha, all of which quickly, though unofficially, became known as Austria. Though less cumbersome, the term was very imprecise, since it included not only the former Austrian, and heavily German-speaking patrimony of the Habsburgs, but Bohemia, Galicia, and other lands as well. The other part was Trans-Leithenia, or Hungary for short. This encompassed not only the Hungary of today, but Croatia, Transylvania and what is now called Slovakia. Franz Joseph and his heirs carried the title emperor in Cis-Leithenia, but king in Hungary. Hence the abbreviations "k.-k." "imperial-royal" or "k.u.k" "imperial and royal" (Germ.: *kaiserlich-köni-*

glich or *kaiserlich-und königlich*) which are still affixed to many public buildings of the former empire in central and east central Europe.

The two political divisions of the Austro-Hungarian empire as it was first known—the term Austria-Hungary quickly supplanted it—shared the same monarch in a personal union, a common army—that Franz Joseph insisted upon—and a common foreign policy. This was the area where the Hungarians yielded ground, since, in the view of those who demanded the return of the March Laws to the letter, treating relations with other states as "common affairs" diminished the Hungarian right to self-government. A joint finance ministry existed as well, but its competence was limited since both halves of the new state paid only for the upkeep of the military and diplomatic establishments. The emperor-king had the power to appoint and dismiss the ministers to head these offices, but they were also accountable to their respective parliaments. A joint commission met every ten years to settle whatever fiscal affairs had to be worked out between them. The two parts would use the same postal system and currency; the customs union which dated from the Bach era would remain, though on terms to be renegotiated every ten years, along with related commercial and financial issues. Each parliament appointed delegations to discuss other matters of common concern. Though they met alternately in Vienna and Budapest, they were to communicate only in writing, unless they came to an impasse at which time they could deliberate together. Should they not resolve their differences, the decision rested with the monarch. (*See Document No. 11.*)

The management of domestic affairs in both divisions was left largely to their parliaments and local authorities. Both Hungary and "the kingdoms and lands represented in the *Reichsrat*," the tortuous legal designation of Cis-Leithenia or Austria, wrote constitutions or bundles of basic laws which established the legal and political ground rules in each division. Hungary moved briskly to turn itself into a centralized national state. Some real concessions were made to ethnic sensibilities, though as time went on the government concerned itself less and less about engratiating itself with its non-Magyar peoples. Croatia-Slavonia, for example, had a separate diet with autonomy in legal and educational affairs, but Budapest had control over the defense, fiscal, and commercial policies of the territory. There was a Croatian parliamentary delegation to the capital, but the far more numerous Magyar representatives could always outvote it. The Hungarian prime minister nominated the governor of Croatia who was then appointed by the king.

The constitutional environment in the "Austrian" half of the monarchy developed somewhat differently. As we have seen, the Habsburgs themselves had declared even in 1848 that they would recognize and defend the national and linguistic particularity of their subjects. The goal of the dynasty was to preserve their empire as a whole and to find some political structure in which they could do this comfortably. Issued in 1867, the December Laws, the constitution of Cis-Leithenia, openly proclaimed that part of the Habsburg lands to be a state of many peoples. (*See Document No. 12.*) However, after much wrangling, the negotiators left unspecified whether government officials were required to master a local tongue in order to hold a position in a given district. This was a distinct concession to the Germans who felt themselves much put upon by repeated demands in Bohemia that they know Czech, the language of what had become the majority of the population in many areas. The Germans throughout the western and northern half of the monarchy were advantaged by another provision as well. This was the decision to continue the weighted system of voting used in the February Patent of 1861. Since large landholders and the well-to-do urban middle classes were heavily German, except in the Polish lands, they in effect enjoyed the same privileged position in their half of Austria-Hungary that the Magyars did in theirs.

Indeed, the upper classes of Hungarian society believed that they had a vital stake in preserving a society in Cis-Leithenian Austria which was symmetrical to their own. A parliamentary Hungary was far from a democratic Hungary, the propertied and noble having retained the upper hand there once again. (*See Document No. 13.*) And since, legally speaking, the Hungarians could correctly argue that the December Laws were part of the entire constitutional package which they had accepted in 1867, they in effect retained a veto power over the conditions under which they would remain party to the agreement as a whole.

Basic political reform in the Cis-Leithenian half of the monarchy was henceforth awkward, although the December Laws in themselves significantly advanced the liberalization of government and society there. The devolution of power to Hungary had distressed the German liberals to the point where Franz Joseph and his ministers needed to make substantial concessions to them to win their support for the arrangement as a whole. Full civil rights finally came to the Austrian division of the state. Censorship was largely abolished, freedom of public assembly, confession, and the right to form political parties granted, and the freedom to own and acquire property, and to choose one's employment and profession recognized.

Thus the Compromise of 1867 was far more than yet another way of patching together the monarchy of many peoples which had been so distressingly vulnerable to the military challenges of Italy and Germany. From the standpoint of civil rights alone, within at least part of the Habsburg realms, it brought some positive and widely longed-for reforms. And the promise in the December Laws to respect the national and linguistic rights of minorities was no empty one. Complaints did indeed arise; these went through prescribed juridical processes in the imperial court which often found in favor of the aggrieved. But, very dangerously, there was a basic unfairness to the *Ausgleich* as well, which, the nonprivileged nationalities, especially the Czechs were very quick to recognize. Having called, at least since 1848, for something like the status now granted to the Magyars, they protested vociferously against the arrangement. Others would be quick to follow, especially as the government in Budapest became increasingly chauvinistic. Predictable difficulties were therefore on the way. The distinction that was drawn between the terms "k.k." and "k.u.k." in the two halves of what might still best be called the Habsburg empire, was a sign that the Compromise of 1867 had left hanging some crucial issues between the Hungarians and the rest of the dynasty's realms. "K.k." was preferred among the Hungarians since this implied that the monarch, in this case Franz Joseph, was simply emperor in one half of his lands and king in another. The expression "imperial *and* royal" meant to politicians and nationalists in Budapest that there was yet a collective authority which on the highest level spoke only once for together the two parts of the monarchy, something which the Hungarians had historically denied.

Clearly the purpose of the Dual Monarchy was not to make government easy, but, like all of Franz Joseph's constitutional experiments since 1848, to buy time for Habsburg rule. From that standpoint, the *Ausgleich* could be called a qualified success. It lasted longer than any of his previous attempts to erect a workable structure of government for his lands, and, as we shall see, allowed them the room to develop economically and make important cultural contributions to Europe as a whole. However, its most widely acknowledged flaw—its unequal political weighting of the nationalities—could not be reformed without bringing the entire apparatus down, and this did not bode well for future stability. But for the time being, it more or less worked, and the Habsburgs rarely thought in long-range terms.

CHAPTER 6

KEEPING THINGS TOGETHER: THE ECONOMY

Historical and Material Background. By accepting the Compromise of 1867 Franz Joseph tacitly admitted that his empire could not withstand the challenges of nineteenth-century nationalism from abroad unless the he took serious steps to meet them at home. Bismarck had at least thought about using the ethnic *ressentiments* of some in the Habsburg empire to promote German unification. The problem was likely to become truly chronic and therefore even more complex, as new national kingdoms appeared in the Balkans during the second half of the nineteenth century, most notably Serbia and Romania. These were generally more than eager to represent the interests not only of their own peoples, but those of their ethnic, linguistic, and confessional brethren within the borders of the new Austria-Hungary.

As we have already seen, the *Ausgleich* resolved some, but not all of the national grievances in the Dual Monarchy. The outlook for its continued existence was thus precarious at best. Yet, endure it did, for another fifty years, and, in some ways, brilliantly. Modern historians normally approach the Habsburg empire as a study in great-state collapse. However, history concerns itself with continuity as well as change; in view of Austria-Hungary's tenacity, even as the corrosive power of ethnic particularism strengthened throughout Europe during the latter third of the nineteenth century, one can instructively ask how it managed to last at all. The economy in all likelihood offers part of the answer.

Down to the beginning of the nineteenth century, the sole common feature of the monarchy's economic life was its generally agrarian base. The farther east in the empire one looked, the more this was true, but the rule prevailed throughout the entirety of the Habsburg realms. Economic coherence had always taken second place to political considerations, the long treatment of Hungary as essentially a foreign country in matters of import and export tariffs as the most conspicuous example. During the eighteenth century, the government actually founded an overseas trading company, but the emperor's dynastic concerns about ensuring a female succession displaced fiscal innovation very quickly. In some ways the empire would always be a field of broken dreams for the clever and enterprising. Rural societies and traditional handicrafts always produce certian poeple who see ways of improving the tools and machines of their trades. Even today, museums thoughout the lands that took the place of the Habsburg monarchy display local prototypes of mechanical inventions which were, however, developed to their full commercial potential in parts of the world which had the capital resources to exploit them privately. It would be fair to say that the Habsburg empire suffered from all of the drawbacks of mercantilism, while enjoying few, if any, of its advantages.

Industrialization in the Habsburg Empire. As we have already seen in the Metternich era, the rulers and peoples of the Habsburg lands were more receptive to economic liberalism than its political counterpart. The latter, as a modern Austrian scholar, Gerald Stourzh, has observed, legitimized the civil and human rights of individuals. Its application to collectivities, while defensible, only led to dangerous strife, both among the ethnic communities in the empire, or between them and their sovereign. The material variant of these principles has, theoretically, no ethnic or linguistic application. The marketplace works impersonally; those operating in it are driven by financial and psychological considerations, not cultural and historic ones. Prosperity is the result of individual, not group, initiative. Only very gradually would large numbers of people in the empire associate economic status with national membership. Even then, such thinking did not always divide along the crude lines of rich and poor but the more subtle one of comparative advantage.

The dynasty's needs for economic growth, regardless of the ideological auspices under which it took place, were immediate and clear-cut. For military reasons alone, the Habsburgs were drawn to modern transportation technology, especially the railroads. Though developing these ate up vast amounts of speculative capital, the government pushed ahead on the project with unusual purposiveness. In 1841 it promised a certain level of return to investors in rail track construction. Europe's first mountain locomotive facility over the Semmering Pass between Lower Austria and Styria was begun in 1852; by 1870 Vienna, Budapest, Prague, and Trieste, the Adriatic seaport of the Austrian half of the monarchy, were all linked by the steam engine. This activity placed great productive demands on iron and coal mines as well as on heavy metal industries and led to a major economic boom in the years 1867–1873, especially in eastern and southeastern Austria and in Bohemia. During 1869 alone the government of the Austrian half of the monarchy chartered over 1,000 new companies. Textile manufacture expanded rapidly in these regions as did sugar refineries, taking local advantage of a craving that seized the entire continent during the nineteenth century.

Between 1848 and 1859, the empire took other decisive steps toward reaching the economic standards already present in many parts of western Europe. The final lifting of serfdom in 1848 made it easier for agricultural workers to migrate to manufacturing and commercial centers. In 1859, guilds were at last abolished, an act which fostered a far more positive climate for new industrial and commercial undertakings. The tax system was unified and standardized as well. General income and property taxes and a residential impost on rental earnings in cities were introduced. All of these measures took a certain amount of capital out of the hands of private investors, but made the financial behavior of the state more predictable. Vienna grew from 842,951 inhabitants in 1869 to 2,031,498 by 1910. Prague and Budapest developed similarly. Money once exclusively concentrated in agricultural undertakings now flowed into business and industry. With the encouragement of the government, banks to mobilize investment capital sprang up. The most famous of these was the Austrian Credit Bank for Trade and Manufacture (*Österreichische Credit-Anstalt für Handel und Gewerbe*) owned by the Rothschild banking house, originally of Frankfurt, more recently of London and Paris, and from 1855 on, a major force in the financial world of Austria-Hungary. The *Credit-Anstalt*, as well as the numerous other private banks, did not normally make direct loans to enterprises, particularly those looking for start-up funds. Their preferred clients were the government and the nobility, who then, as the consistently richest segment of the population, put money into commercial and manufacturing enterprise. In general, the bank whose policies did the most for the economic development of the empire was the Austro-Hungarian National Bank. Though it too, extended credit only to the most wealthy and reliable, it held official interest rates steady, a condition business ordinarily finds attractive.

Prague also became a major financial center; indeed its Bank for Trade (*Zivnostenska Banka*) became the first investment bank in the

Habsburg lands to draw its capital solely from within the empire itself. Budapest, while less important financially, burgeoned industrially. Grain was the chief crop of the kingdom's agricultural hinterland; its premier city became a hub for the transportation and processing of flour which had a large market not only within the empire but in the newly united Germany. Under pressure from both agricultural and industrial interests elsewhere in the Habsburg lands, the imperial government imposed a substantial import tariff in 1879. Thereafter, Hungarian flour sales slowed somewhat, but continued to be a profitable sector in the Hungarian half of the empire's economy.

The industrialization of the Dual Monarchy had its troubled moments. The boom between 1867 and 1873 encouraged banks, railroads, and industries to declare huge dividends and joint stock companies to water shares already oversubscribed. The predictable crash came in 1873, bringing with it multiple business failures, unemployment, and sagging wages. A recovery, though considerably less frenetic than the activity which took place between 1867 and 1873, was underway by the late 1870s. Prosperity returned, but more in spurts than steady growth. Nor would the empire ever be a major force in world commerce. During the 1850s and 1860s the government in Vienna generally subscribed to the free trade models current in Europe. This policy was not always to its advantage, but it did help the empire preserve its trading connections with the German states gradually coming together in the *Zollverein*. The Habsburg empire was late to follow other European powers after 1873 in converting to the gold standard, including the new Germany. Silver remained the basis of the currency until 1892, much to the disadvantage of Austria-Hungary, since the value of the metal fluctuated wildly in the latter third of the nineteenth century. Such unpredictable conditions complicated the mechanics of international commerce and finance and made doing business in the Habsburg empire trickier than elsewhere.

Spreading Prosperity. Yet, episodic though economic development within the Habsburg lands might have been, it helped raise the living standards for large numbers of people from many walks of society. Construction work for the unskilled was readily available in all the major cities of the empire, thus blotting up agrarian labor made redundant by shifts in the world commodity markets. The Vienna *Ringstrasse*, the circumferential boulevard which separates three sides of the central district of the city from all of the outlying ones, had major ramifications for real estate and housing development throughout the city. An inspiration of the post-1848 era, it is lined with massively proportioned government and cultural buildings that took countless numbers of hands to erect. Moreover, in order to realize the elegant thoroughfare, medieval fortifications which had once discouraged both entering and leaving inner core of the city, had to be razed. Once this had been completed in 1860, tract housing sprang up throughout the Habsburg capital, providing not only jobs but cheaper quarters for those who came to Vienna to better their lives. Even the more ordinary among the empire's bourgeoisie found their domestic circumstances improved. Moderately well-to-do families, and not only in Vienna and Prague, could afford at least one "serving girl for everything" as countless advertisements in the newspapers of the time put it.

A sizeable and often sophisticated class of wealthy businessmen, bankers, and industrialists emerged. Among them were some who were affluent enough to become major patrons of the arts, once the exclusive function of the ruling dynasty and the great nobles associated with it. The career of Karl Wittgenstein (1847–1913), the father of the philosopher Ludwig Wittgenstein (1889–1951), shows what a man of brains, energy, and no little luck could accomplish in what was a heady period for many. He was born in Germany to Jewish parents who had become Protestants. The family emigrated to Vienna in 1851; the son became an engineer despite a spotty educational background. As a young man he traveled to the United States, supporting himself by playing the viola in American orchestras. The drive and imagination of American businessmen deeply impressed him. A lifelong admirer of Andrew Carnegie with whom he exchanged hospitality, Wittgenstein heartily endorsed American political and economic freedoms which he believed allowed such people to flourish. Though he chafed at the restrictions on business and manufacture that the political needs of the Habsburg empire forced upon him and his kind, his was one of the great success stories of the 1870s. Beginning with some rather murky financial speculation, he acquired substantial interests in iron, steel, mining, and railroad undertakings. In 1877 he founded the first railroad cartel in the empire and was the owner of the two leading complexes for iron and steel production, one outside of Prague, the other, the Alpine Mining Company, in the southeastern province of Styria. He was a great supporter of the arts as well. Musicians such as Brahms and the young cellist Pablo Casals played at his home; and he collected significant painting and sculpture.

It was always possible for national strife within the empire to interrupt industrial and commercial growth. Indeed, a temporary slowdown at the turn of the twentieth century was due in part to Czech–German conflicts over the Badeni language ordinances (see p. 77), which would have forced German-speaking officials in Bohemia to learn Czech. There were always those who were quick to attribute any economic difference between groups, regions or both to national bias on the part of some official agency or another. Interest rates in the more highly capitalized areas of the monarchy were always somewhat lower than in the less developed ones, something the Hungarians often pointed to as evidence of economic discrimination against them. The same suspicions existed in Bosnia about Budapest when the control of local banks and credit institutions was at stake. (*See Document No. 14.*) Then too, there were people such as Wittgenstein for whom the economy could always do better. He and those who shared his outlook were very critical of any political concessions to ethnic sensibilities, however useful, if they thwarted the entrepreneurship which was for them the engine of material progress. (*See Document No. 15.*) These views were often based upon subjective perception and personal self-interest rather than informed analysis. Yet, whether empirically verifiable or not, they had a way of becoming the concrete issues of political life. They posed very real, and therefore potentially very divisive problems for any government that had to confront them if it hoped to survive.

Economic Development and Habsburg Survival. Did the economy of the empire between 1867 and 1914 tie its various peoples together more than it divided them? The scholarly jury has yet to render a final decision on the case. Some regions of the Habsburg monarchy undeniably prospered more than others such as the regions of Lower Austria and Bohemia which were close to the rapidly industrializing new German empire. The farther east one went in both Austria and Hungary, the more impoverished was the overwhelmingly rural population. Bukovina and Galicia, in Cis-Leithenia and Transylvania in Hungary were, in general, the most economically backward of all. Emigration from the empire to the New World as well as to other countries in the Old, remained high, especially from the kingdom of Hungary, a sign that whatever prosperity the empire was enjoying had not reached all who lived there.

Nor was the spread of industrial capitalism in the empire a positive experience for all. The growing efficiency of agriculture, so necessary to sustain the urban working classes, came at the expense of many small peasant farmers in both halves of the monarchy. Recently unfettered from the last vestiges of serfdom, they found themselves caught up in the boom-bust economic cycles of the late nineteenth century which often forced them to sell to large proprietors. Free farmers for only a short period of time, they became tenants once again on lands they had struggled to own outright. Worse yet, they might be dispossessed altogether, turned into agrarian farm and estate hands who lived at subsistence levels. This was especially true in Hungary where there were large landed properties which required many workers to cultivate them.

The cities, particularly those that developed large industrial infrastructures, became centers of assimilation, but also the locus of new tensions. By the beginning of the twentieth century, Vienna was a carnival of tongues. Around half of its inhabitants were immigrants from all parts of the empire—the Czechs were especially numerous—who quickly set up their own newspapers and cultural centers. However, intermarriage among all these groups, as well as into the more established German element, began fairly soon. The practice cut across religious lines as well, including Jews and Christians. Such population redistributions swelled the legions of cheap labor, but not to everyone's advantage. Factories and their employees became the direct competitors of traditional small artisans. No longer protected by guild regulations, the latter were often unable to run their shops and small enterprises profitably. Their wares were often the shoddy handiwork of sullen apprentices whose dismal living conditions antagonized them toward everything, their jobs included. Such shops were not in any case oriented toward mass consumption.

Entrepreneurial manufacturers had quite different goals. To capture the widest possible market for their machine-made and, in many instances superior, products, they sold them not only in stores but through peddlars. The latter were often recent Jewish emigres from the easternmost parts of the empire, whose presence alone was enough to intensify the anti-Semitism that had long existed in this area of Europe. Acting, however remotely, as agents of an economy which was stripping both livelihood and status from a traditional class of urban society, Jews became even more exposed to hostilities that could be mobilized against them at any time. But it should be remembered that industrialization stirred up similar problems even among Christians. Once a majoritarianly German city, Prague became a Czech and Slavic one in the nineteenth century, the result of immigration and a much higher birth rate among the Czechs than the Germans. The latter greatly resented being crowded out of their dominant position in the capital. Perhaps of greater future significance was the reaction of some Germans to the increase of Czech workers in the industrialized northern regions of the kingdom. It was here the first German National Workers' Party was created in 1904. Though its concern for the laboring man had Marxist roots, the movement had little use for the ideal of proletarian solidarity. Rather it, and its organ, *The German Workers' Voice* (*Deutsche Arbeiter-Stimme*) went out of its way to report cases of boorishness and criminality among the Czech working classes. (*See Document No. 16.*)

Thus it is clear that the industrial revolution and the social and economic changes it promoted often drove the nations of the Habsburg empire to dislike one another vehemently. Yet, there is enough serious data to support a more positive view of the impact these developments had on ethnic relations in the monarchy. While industrial capitalism might not have reconciled its peoples to one another, Austria-Hungary's regional economies did become sufficiently interdependent to make Franz Joseph's subjects think twice before casting off Habsburg rule altogether. Patterns of domestic migration coupled with production figures indicate that many expected and found opportunity somewhere in the empire. Eastern Austria, with Vienna at the center, and Prague were particular targets for those who believed that a better life awaited them if only they moved to take it. Of course, hope did not correspond to reality in every instance. Nevertheless, as long as people had reason to think that Austria-Hungary's economy had something to offer them, they were not prepared to sacrifice this prospect to the urgings of national agitators.

Recent research suggests that the regional economic inequalities of the Habsburg empire evened themselves out over the course of the nineteenth century. While during much of the period interest rates were lower in the more advanced German lands, the general tendency was for them to equalize throughout the Dual Monarchy rather than to spread apart even more. Vienna and Prague supplied credit to the hinterlands as a whole; as the resources of these centers increased, the empire began to look more and more like an integrated capital market, even though foreign investment, especially from Germany continued to play an important role in the development of the area. From about 1895 on sustained growth was taking place even in such peripheral territories as Galicia, Bukovina, and Transylvania; and incomes throughout the empire as a whole were converging. The Compromise of 1867 freed Hungary to foster industrialization on its own terms which it did through direct subsidy of industry. Agricultural production in that kingdom grew too, as great landowners incorporated inefficient small plots into their own estates. These men, though among Europe's least enlightened in matters of labor and social policy, were quick to raise their productivity with these new lands. Thus, one of the basic prerequisites for the development of an industrial economy—a reliable agrarian sector to feed an urban manufacturing population—was now in place. Though not especially well-endowed with mineral resources, Hungary produced important staple crops—grain and increasingly sugar beets—which were easily refined into basic foods for which there was a large and steady consumer appetite.

The principal beneficiaries of these developments were those entitled to handsome returns from their investments—the financially sophisticated among the nobility, those members of the middle-class who had laid the groundwork of their fortunes in the first half of the nineteenth century. There were many failures—the number of bankruptcies in the crash of 1873 was staggering. Yet, there were many people—Karl Wittgenstein being only an unusually brilliant example—who had much to thank the monarchy for in terms of personal betterment. In the case of the Jews, this was true for a substantial number of a very specific ethnic group. Through the centuries the Habsburgs, like other European rulers, had treated these people both as favorites and outcasts. Leopold I had settled the Jews of Vienna in their modern ghetto, the *Leopoldstadt*, which became the second district of the city. As we have seen, Joseph II had taken the first move to bring them into the mainstream of civic and economic life, allowing them access to public places and to engage in most trades. Until 1848, however, the community was liable to a special tax (*Judensteuer* = Jew Tax), paid every two weeks, and forbidden to acquire land and to enter the civil service or legal profession. By that time, however, they had already begun to cluster heavily in finance, handicrafts, medicine and private teaching. Around 1850, they represented only 1.3 percent of Vienna's inhabitants. By 1890, they made up about 12 percent of the population of Vienna, and though that figure sank back to about 8.6 percent by 1910, this was due to heavier immigration to the capital, largely from Bohemia, than to a reduction in their absolute numbers.

The reason for the sharp increase is not hard to find. The Dual Compromise of 1867 gave full civil rights to all Jews in the Habsburg monarchy. They quickly became some of the empire's leading economic immigrants, coming especially from Austrian Galicia, to Vienna and secondarily Prague for the financial and educational opportunities which both cities offered. Sigmund Freud's father, for example, a Galician wool merchant, brought his family to Vienna in 1859 from Pribor (Germ.: Freiberg), a town in northeast Moravia because the weaving trade there was declining. With no formal restrictions on their choice of career after 1870, they went into the learned professions, law, and journalism in large numbers. By 1890, Jews made up 33.6 percent of all those enrolled at the University of Vienna. As early as 1880, they comprised almost 39 percent of students in the medical school and 24 percent of those studying law. Their ability to gain access to this and the other major universities of the empire—Prague, Budapest, Zagreb, Cracow, and Graz—in turn depended upon the newly secularized system of secondary education now ready to teach them as well as Catholics and other Christians. Sigmund Freud (1856–1939) was a star student at one such institution. Jews also began to enter the lower ranks of the civil service, though the diplomatic service, traditionally staffed by men from social circles closest to the imperial house, remained forever barred to them. All of the major private banks in Vienna were in Jewish hands with the exception of one which was owned by a Greek. Not all Jews were, of course, in a position to profit so handsomely from the business and educational opportunities which the late nineteenth century Austro-Hungarian economy had to offer. There were also the aforementioned house peddlars among them, hawking their wares in one inner courtyard after another of the vast stretches of apartment complexes lining the streets which radiated from the center of the city outward. But Jews prospered in Budapest as well, where the environment had long been far more tolerant toward them than in Vienna.

Thus for them and many others, the Habsburg empire had become an arena of opportunity, not with the rich possibilities of the New World, or even perhaps of industrializing Germany, but one where the hope of substantial material improvement existed for many and not only in the realm of private fantasy. This was especially true on a mass basis after 1867. Frictions there were, and serious ones at that. But these were problems for the political system to work out, and few were willing to say that this could not be done. Major restructuring of the multinational empire for the past one hundred years had come, by and large, as the result of foreign, not domestic catastrophe. If all was at peace abroad, there were sound material reasons to think that things could work out at home.

CHAPTER 7

POLITICS IN A MULTINATIONAL SETTING

National Relations in Austria-Hungary. In creating a species of parliamentary government in each half of the Habsburg empire, the authors of the Dual Compromise took a major step forward in bringing the political life of the monarchy into line with the other leading powers of western and central Europe. Though the electoral base in both halves of the empire was very narrow at the outset, pressure for democratization was relentless, especially in the Austrian lands. It was now legal to organize political parties, and almost all of them had a crucial interest in enlarging their constituencies. This could come only by expanding the numbers of those eligible to vote. The emperor himself was not beyond supporting a widened franchise if he saw that he could gain something by playing off one group of voters against another. By 1914, universal manhood suffrage had been all but realized in the Austrian half of the empire, though not in Hungary. Public political life was very lively, to say the least. When the First World War broke out in 1914 there were around fifty factions sitting formally in the imperial *Reichsrat*. Some of these were tightly organized and spoke for large memberships; some had no more than two or three delegates. But regardless of their practical effectiveness, many of these people came away from their experience as legislators knowing more than they once did about the mechanics of representative government, its possibilities, and, as soon became apparent, its limitations.

Predictably enough, national causes shaped the agendas of several parties in both halves of the monarchy. In Hungary, where in 1905, only 5 percent of population throughout the entire kingdom had the franchise, constitutional provisions for ethnic representation virtually invited such thinking. The quotas of non-Magyar representatives were actually fixed in such documents as the Hungarian-Croatian Compromise, the *Nagodba* of 1868, which governed relations between the two kingdoms. However, electoral districts were drawn so as to ensure the dominance of the Magyars. Budapest exercised a great deal of central administrative authority as well. Therefore, national resistance to these and other policies came more in local demonstrations, sometimes informal, sometimes in regional representative bodies. Episodes of anti-Magyar rioting took place throughout the 1890s in villages with Croatian, Romanian, and, in the east, Ruthenian inhabitants. Though widely scattered, they could not be taken lightly since all the ethnic groups of the realm seemed prone to them. In 1895, a congress of non-Magyar nationalities actually took place in Budapest. Yet, as stormy and sometimes violent as some of these protests were, they did not bring government in the kingdom to a halt. Antagonisms which Hungary's peoples held toward one another—the Serbs and the Croats being an especially conspicuous example—enabled the politicians in Budapest to survive through the age-old tactics of divide and conquer.

In the Austrian half of the monarchy, where the franchise was considerably broadened by 1914, national hostilities occasionally paralyzed parliamentary life altogether. The environment did little to reinforce anyone's faith in the effectiveness of representative government. Ministries were named in the hope of creating greater harmony among the delegates of the empire's peoples, only to fall over the most parochial of disputes. This happened in 1895 when the question of whether to build a Slovenian-language high school in Cilli (Slov.: Celje), a German-speaking town in rural Slovenia, came to Vienna for administrative resolution.

All of the empire's nationalities begrudged Habsburg concessions to Hungarian statehood in the Dual Compromise, and all had to be pacified in some way. The Poles were probably the easiest to deal with. Indeed, from the standpoint of Franz Joseph and his ministers, the bargain which they struck in the Galician lands was genuinely productive. In effect, the emperor handed over a domestically autonomous Galicia, along with adjacent Ruthenia, to the management of the local Polish aristocracy. Polish became the language of administration, the courts and legal structure, and secondary schools. In return, the Galician nobility supported whatever government the emperor named to deal with the Vienna parliament. More than a few Poles became prominent imperial ministers. Though some among them dreamed of a reunited Poland, they realized that the climate of European state relations in the last third of the nineteenth century ruled this out. Only extraordinary circumstances would persuade Germany and Russia to yield their share of the fragmented kingdom, and Franz Joseph himself was the last man to dismember his state voluntarily.

Czechs and Germans. The Czechs were far more intractable. The transformation of the Magyars into a governing nationality in the 1867 Compromise deeply offended the so-called Old Czechs. These were what remained of the aristocrats, intellectuals and the more well-to-do elements of the middle class who were the core of the revolutionary uprising in Bohemia during 1848 and who still led the national movement there. They quickly undertook a series of negotiations with Franz Joseph and his ministers to win something like equivalent status for the kingdom. In particular, they wished to have Czech recognized as the language of instruction and administration in the realm. This could best be realized, they argued, if a certain measure of autonomy were granted the kingdom. Some among them had even more radical ideas. They called for establishing a Trial, rather than Dual, Monarchy. The third element was to be made up of the Slavs, by far the most numerous among Franz Joseph's peoples.

This scheme gave rise to every Hungarian politician's darkest fears—if ever there was a linguistic minority in the empire it was the Magyars. Many Germans did not like the prospect either. Greater autonomy was less drastic however, and for a time it appeared that the Czechs might achieve it. In 1871, the emperor's government put forth a program to the local Bohemian diet. It proposed to establish a unified assembly of delegates from Bohemia, Moravia, and Silesia. This body would have wide internal administrative powers and could even have a voice in the monarchy's foreign relations. The Czechs themselves had supported it on the plausible assumption that since they were the majority nationality in the kingdom, they would be able to dominate political life on the local level. There they could inaugurate the reforms they wished to make. The two ruling nationalities were not to be persuaded, however; in fact, neither of the provincial diets of Moravia and Silesia was ready to take the step either. By 1871 the emperor yielded to the Hungarian argument, legally correct, that these measures broke the terms of the Dual Compromise.

Not unexpectedly, however, the Czech issue did not go away, either regionally or in the parliament in Vienna. Communities made up of both Czech and German populations experimented with separate school boards for both language groups after 1873. This did not always work out happily. Speakers of either tongue often had good economic reasons to master the other. Contested ethnic identifications in school board elections sometimes went to the High Administrative Court in Vienna which ruled opaquely in 1879 that one's ethnic identity was a matter of personal declaration. In this and other decisions, the court was moving away from the concept of a civic polity based upon membership in a state to one based on membership in a national group. As Gerald Stourzh has observed, such thinking was fraught with sinister implications for central European political life following the First World War.

But first and foremost, none of these schemes softened the demands of Czech nationalists. What did change was the leadership of their cause, passing from the aging Old Czechs, who were still fundamentally loyal to the dynasty and socially quite conservative, to another faction, the Young Czechs. Spearheaded by two brothers, Edward and Julius Gregr, the newer movement grew even more stridently nationalistic. It acquired a broader popular base as well, since large numbers of its members were Czech peasants, small tradespeople, and artisans. This fresh political tone and the people who espoused it significantly altered the civic life of the kingdom. As the nineteenth century came to a close, more and more Czech-speaking peasants were drawn into the cities of the Bohemian crown, lured by the hope of employment in thriving textile and heavy metal factories. There they confronted an older, German-speaking urban population, who resented both the demographic shift which threatened their long-established domination of commerce and manufacturing, and the ideology which legitimated it. (*See Document No. 17.*)

The Czech-German issue therefore became the central national problem in the empire during the latter third of the nineteenth century, especially in the Austrian half. This was not because Franz Joseph favored German interests in his ministerial appointments. Indeed, he had no great love for the Liberal party which traditionally represented the German point of view and only worked with them until the faction began angling in the parliament for more control over military funding and foreign affairs. After 1879 his governments were drawn from men who came from all regions of the monarchy, Bohemia included, or were part of the dynasty's court circle.

But the polyglot backgrounds of these minsters were alone not enough to end the Czech language question, either administratively or in parliament itself. The Czechs' demands for the use of their tongue in both legal and administrative affairs grew louder, even in regions of Bohemia where they were still a minority. Almost all educated Czechs could function with some degree of comfort in German, but the reverse was not true of the ethnic Germans in the kingdom, since Czech was not commonly offered in their schools. After becoming minister-president in 1879, Count Edward Taaffe (1833–1895), a long-time friend of the emperor, organized a parliamentary coalition in ways which he thought would move the Czechs to cooperate more closely with the government in Vienna. Known as the "Iron Ring" it did include Czechs as well as Poles, Catholic clericals, and German conservatives. Their common interest was opposition to the liberals and their centralizing and secularizing policies. But the Czechs were not to be appeased, at least over the long run. Elections to the regional Bohemian diet in 1883 brought a landslide of Czech-speaking representatives. This in turn prompted local German demands for partition of the kingdom along ethnic lines, something the Young Czechs would not even consider.

The issue of franchise reform brought down Taaffe's government in 1893. The emperor and some of his advisers had come to the dubious conclusion that expanding the right to vote beyond the nationalistic middle classes might take some of the edge off of ethnic tensions. In 1895, under the ministry of the Polish Count Casimir Badeni (1846–1909) near-universal manhood suffrage was indeed introduced. Contrary to the government's hopes however, national discord in the parliament worsened. Elections in 1897 only strengthened the Young Czech faction. The bloc was outnumbered by the Germans, but the latter were splintered into several hostile wings. Needing the support of the Czechs for other initiatives, Badeni sanctioned two decrees, the so-called Badeni language laws in that same year. These ordered that all government employees in Bohemia and Moravia, regardless of rank, speak and write both Czech and German by 1901.

The Hungarian government in Budapest deplored any concessions to Slavic nationalism. However, its objections were relatively temperate compared to the fierce German protests which brought parliamentary debate in Vienna to a standstill. Nationally minded German students demonstrated in the Habsburg capital and Graz, the chief city of Styria to the southeast. Badeni resigned, and his program was withdrawn. This led, however, to even angrier disturbances in Prague in December of 1897. Spurred on by Czech national radicals, crowds ransacked shops, homes and schools of their alleged German oppressors, along with those of Jews, whom the mobs often took for German as they often spoke that language by preference. The diet of the kingdom could not function as a deliberative body as deputies encouraged raucous protests and outright brawling. Similar outbreaks took place in 1904–1905 and 1908 upon the defeat or frustration of some aspect of the Czech nationalist agenda. The appearance of a single German university student on the streets of Prague in protest against the Czech national program sometimes triggered these outbursts.

The depth of antagonism between two groups that had lived in the kingdom for centuries shocked many throughout the empire. Relations grew ever more bitter as the Germans developed their own protective strategies. After 1897, demands among them for splitting the realm along ethnic lines grew louder and more frequent. "Los von Prag" ("away from Prague") became a favorite slogan of the Germans in the northern border areas of Bohemia where they were concentrated, even though it meant that they would abandon the ever-shrinking number of their ethnic cohorts in the capital city. Not all the Prague Germans, however, had responded that enthusiastically to the call at any time. Many in the capital were middle-class and often very prosperous, compared to the northerners who lived in more modest circumstances. While they did not like the Slavicization of their environment, they had much to lose by leaving it altogether. An element of economic conflict thereby crept into the national question, complicating even more the task of holding the monarchy together.

In the Vienna *Reichsrat* these conflicts only marginalized parliamentary life in a political culture where it had not been at home for very long. Faced with legislative deadlocks that kept any business from getting done, the Habsburg government fell back on emergency procedures provided under article 14 of the 1867 Compromise. This enabled the emperor to rule through decree when the *Reichsrat* was not sitting. Down to the outbreak of World War I, the number of political parties continued to grow. What did not develop was either a mechanism or outlook which encouraged them to work together for any length of time toward the interests of the monarchy as a whole. (*See Document No. 18.*) Therefore, the newly representative parliamentary life of the empire, for all of its positive features, further unsettled the relationships of its peoples, both among themselves and to their government.

The Christian Social Movement. Nor was nationalism the only cause of political turmoil in the monarchy between 1867 and 1914. Large numbers of Franz Joseph's subjects had far more urgent concerns than being able to conduct a lawsuit in their native idiom rather than German. Indeed, the overwhelming majority of them did not have the money either to prosecute anyone or to defend themselves for any length of time. It was to such people, among the ordinary middle and lower middles classes concentrated in the increasingly urbanized empire, that the Christian Social party and its leader Karl Lueger (1844–1910) spoke.

This movement took shape in the latter third of the nineteenth century, though its ideological roots lay in the Catholic conservatism of the Metternich era. Its advocates, often among the urban parish clergy, hoped to push the Church of Rome into responding vigorously and creatively to what they saw as mounting spiritual despair of the empire's city dwellers. Industrialization, big capital, and bureaucratic indifference both in the state as well as religious institutions, were undermining the social and economic position of artisans and small tradesmen long accustomed to supporting themselves independently. Marxism, to be discussed below, required them to proletarianize themselves voluntarily in order to benefit from the answers offered by socialism. Christian Social policy made it possible for them to avoid this, for central to its program was a promise to better the daily quality of life for people of limited means.

Vienna, in the second half of the nineteenth century, continued to be a hard environment for most of its inhabitants. Rents were high, quarters scandalously cramped, and municipal services were both poor and costly. The city was acknowledged to be the worst-lit major capital in Europe. A British concern with little incentive to improve either its product or delivery of same had held the concession to supply gas for decades. The local government, though aware of the shortcomings in this arrangement, could not raise the money to build its own utility. Once he became mayor in 1897, Lueger launched an extensive a program of public works that made him one of the great municipal officials of his century, and arguably in all of European history. A variant of today's "junk bond" financed many of these undertakings. Creditors lent the required funds on the promise that their investment would eventually pay handsome returns. Such policies saddled the municipal government with a heavy burden of debt, the full impact of which hit the city only after the end of the First World War when the capital resources of an empire were gone. But the more immediate, and therefore politically significant, outcome of Lueger's efforts was to give the Habsburg me-

tropolis a first-rate public transportation system, its own gas works, and
a drinking water supply that was the envy of Europe. The funeral of the
enormously popular mayor in 1910 was a memorable public spectacle,
even for a city steeped in Baroque theatricality.

In general, the Christian Social movement shunned the factionalism
of national politics, in part because of its ideological link to Roman
Catholic universalism, in part because its constituency had no steady
interest in such matters. Opportunist that he was, Lueger often used
ethnic and national invective to tactical advantage both in the Vienna
city council and in the imperial *Reichsrat* where he also had a seat. His
opponents charged him with unprincipled behavior, but his larger constituency never seemed to mind. (*See Document # 19.*) In any case, the
chief targets of his rhetoric were Hungarians and Jews, both of whom
were conventional scapegoats for the afflictions, real and imagined, of
many Habsburg subjects in the Austrian half of the monarchy. The
Czechs and the German lower middle classes of Vienna, the dominant
ethnic groups of the city, could only applaud his sentiments, since both
Jews and Hungarians, particularly those in Budapest, were beginning
to challenge German Vienna's commercial preeminence in the empire.
This support of the so-called *Mittelstand*, shopkeepers, petty officials,
artisans and the like tightened behind the Christian Social party even
more as Lueger emerged as their advocate in the imperial parliament.

Social Democracy. The other mass political organization which
took shape even more self-consciously as an alternative to national ide-
ologies was Marxist Social Democracy. For industrial labor throughout
the empire, this would become the party of choice. Karl Marx had spent
a few days in Vienna during the turmoil of 1848, only to come away
persuaded that conditions there were unpromising for an eventual revolution. Nevertheless, discussion of his ideas went on in the city. Encouraged by the right of free assembly now in the Austrian constitution of
1867, workers' associations sprang up. The year 1868 brought forth the
first of their manifestos, asking for free and universal suffrage, freedom
of the press, and—something Franz Joseph would never countenance—
abolition of the standing army, among other things. At first the movement was split between two major factions—a radical one heavily
influenced by the violent wing of nineteenth-century anarchism and a
more moderate side which believed that socialism could achieve many
of its goals through cooperation with the crown and sympathetic mem-

bers of the enlightened middle classes. The two positions were drawn together to a point which made political cooperation possible through the work of Victor Adler (1852–1918) and Karl Renner (1870–1950). The former was born in Bohemia, the latter in Moravia, but both spent their active careers in the Austrian capital. For each of them compromise and consensus were avenues to social progress, a view that considerably moderated the revolutionary fervor of Austro-Marxism. The Bolshevik ideologue Leon Trotsky, who was in Vienna on and off in the early years of the twentieth century, eventually derided them as " . . . the guardian angels of the *Kreditanstalt* . . . " the great Rothschild bank of the empire discussed in the previous chapter.

Trotsky's contempt, while perhaps understandable in view of his political enthusiasms, showed little appreciation of the extraordinary difficulties any supranational movement faced in the Habsburg Empire, even one which proposed to better the lives of its dreadfully exploited working classes. The relentless pressure to fragment along national lines accounts in part for the failure of Social Democracy to develop any wider following than it did before World War I. Even in Vienna, the seat of its largest constituency, men and women who eked out their meager lives through wage labor distinguished themselves from one another in many ways, religion, language, and land of origin prominent among them. The periods 1891–1900 and 1906–1910 brought a great surge of domestic immigrants to the imperial capital. The most poverty-stricken of these were from Hungary and Italy, people who knew little or no German, and had no way of communicating with the German-speaking working classes of the city. Poorly skilled, they often worked seasonally, and thus lacked the fixed proletarian identity which Marx set as an axiom for his revolutionary working class. These deficits were less characteristic of the huge numbers of peoples to arrive from the lands of the Bohemian crown. Between 1856–1910, roughly one-half of the city's population consisted of first, second, and third generation residents of Czech-speaking families. Some among them, with long experience in the Bohemian textile industry, were accomplished tailors. They were already part of the middle class and intended to make Vienna their permanent residence. They opened shops in more well-to-do districts of the city, where they found a clientele with the discretionary income to employ them steadily.

Others among their fellow-migrants from the Bohemian lands, less well-trained and speaking German more poorly if at all, retreated into the protective anonymity of ethnic enclaves. Czechs particularly found their way to Favoriten, the tenth district of the city, which unofficially came to be known as the *Böhm*, "Czechdom," where, in 1900 45 percent of its residents had been born either in Bohemia or Moravia. Though they managed to find jobs in factories and the construction sites that abounded in the city at the turn of the twentieth century, they were not welcomed among the German-speaking working families who still lived in the district. Common membership in the working classes did not keep the latter from taunting the newcomers for their linguistic failings. The longer term German residents of Favoriten even ostracized some Czechs for where they lived. One of the major enterprises of the district was the Wienerberger Brick Works which housed its virtual army of employees in barracks-like quarters, squalid even by local standards. When the children from the buildings broke their isolation by attending school, they were mocked by those fortunate to have marginally better homes outside of the giant industrial complex and pleased to find a cohort of people more deprived than themselves.

Philosophically and tactically, the national question tormented the upper echelons of the social democratic movement as well. Marxist ideologues were coming to believe that nationalism reinforced late nineteenth-century imperialism. The Social Democrats of the Habsburg lands had enough to contend with in an old-fashioned dynastic empire let alone this newer and more crushing variant which only added to the miseries of industrial labor and the humbler classes of society generally. Beyond the ethnic tensions which demographic shifts created within the proletarian generality, nationalism absorbed the political energies found in other classes of Habsburgs subjects whose support Adler and other Social Democrats hoped to enlist for their cause. Peasants still made up the bulk of the empire's population; with the expansion of the franchise, every political movement in the Austrian half of the monarchy needed their help. Rural populations, however, were often vulnerable to nationalist appeals, particularly when they came from their employers—landlords whose views they dared not contradict. Even more prone to radical Pan-German and Pan-Slavic ideas were students and intellectuals whose revolutionary enthusiasms could do much to advance the socialist program.

However, both hard work from its leadership and good luck enabled the party to avoid disruptions over the national issue. Renner, on the theoretical front, and Adler in organizational affairs, did much to reduce these dangerous tensions. Along with bringing together the anarchist and moderate wings of the party in the Hainfeld Conference of 1888, Adler stitched together a modus vivendi between its Czech and German leadership. This relationship would remain somewhat fragile; the Czech trade unions continued to chafe at the heavy influence of the Vienna Germans in the party. At the very least, they wanted some sort of guaranteed representation in the policy-making councils of the Social Democrats; by 1896 they were calling for some sort of autonomous standing within the organization, a striking parallel to the way Czech-German relations were developing throughout Bohemia as a whole. Accommodations were nevertheless made to both Czech and German sensibilities in Prague itself. There German-speaking workers were not wholly comfortable with a Czech-dominated party which required linguistic assimilation as an informal, but real, condition of rising to high position in the organization. The Czechs agreed to allow a Society of German Workers and permitted the latter to use their facilities. For their part, the Germans did not support radically national groups among their linguistic cohorts. On the theoretical level, Karl Renner made important progress in harmonizing the imperatives of social justice, democracy, and nationalism. Arguing that the Habsburg empire should once and for all constitutionally fix the relationships of the various nations within its borders, he called for the creation of a state of nationalities (*Nationalitätenstaat*). This would be a democratic federal state which would serve as a paradigm for the socialist restructuring of the entire world.

More than intraparty compromise and futuristic visions helped keep the Social Democrats from falling apart over national grievances. There was good reason for workers to support the party. It promoted some notable reforms which opened the way for wage laborers of all ethnic origins to better their situation. The last major expansion of the franchise in the Austrian half of the monarchy in 1907 was in good part due to Social Democratic pressure. Pure circumstance helped as well. The generally growing economy was not due to Social Democrats. However, prosperity eased the lot of the working man, regardless of nationality, and inclined him to be at peace with his neighbors, no matter what language they spoke.

However, Socialists were not always so anxious to bridge political differences. The opposition which they aroused among the more conservative groupings in the empire, particularly those of clerical leanings, brought out the most intransigent elements on all sides. A good part of the solidarity within the Christian Social movement was negative—born not out of belief in a distinctive program but out of resistance to the atheism and rejection of private property which the Marxists of the day espoused. Each bloc demonized the other. Despite the general show of popular good will at the first May Day celebration in 1897, which many had predicted would mark the outbreak of proletarian revolution, Christian Socialists and Social Democrats began emotionally arming themselves against one another. They thereby laid the groundwork for the so-called armed-camp mentality (*Lagermentalität*) that defined their tragically hostile relationship in the interwar period.

How could a party based on radical egalitarianism live under the Habsburg regime? The Social Democratic program of 1899, written at a conference in Brno, the Moravian capital, proposed that the empire be turned into a democratic federation of nationalities. No one publicly suggested that the Habsburg dynasty remove itself from the political scene altogether. Indeed, from both the ideological and practical point of view, there was some advantage for the socialists in keeping the empire intact. It was still, as they saw it, a bulwark against the nationally divided proletariat which the collapse of the monarchy would promote.

And here, the socialists were at one with all of the other political factions of the Dual Monarchy. There were very few of Franz Joseph's subjects who did not have some reservations about ridding themselves of his government between 1867 and the outbreak of the First World War. All of them, with perhaps the exception of the Pan-Germanists and some agitators among the South Slavs, still had some interest in protecting the arrangements which even the disputed Compromise of 1867 had brought to them. Long-desired changes had actually occurred, particularly for the middle classes; even the situation of the working man seemed to promise future improvement. Yielding to Hungarian national interests had been a mistake, certainly in the eyes of the Slavs. However, yielding to others, perhaps even the preferences of one's own group, might have even more serious consequences.

CHAPTER 8

AN EMPIRE ON NOTICE

Europe and Austria-Hungary. The Ottoman Empire, the once-dreaded nemesis of the Habsburgs, broke apart along national lines during the nineteenth century in part because foreign powers supported the process. With chronic national discontent at home and an army that had twice been found sorely wanting on the battlefield, the Dual Monarchy seemed open to the same fate. The emergence of a new kingdom in Italy showed the world at large that the empire was fracture-prone along linguistic fault lines.

But most of Europe's states, great and small alike, did not exploit this weakness to its logical end. With the inconsistent exception of Napoleon III (1808–1873) in France, no one saw any great advantage in dismembering either Austria, or, after 1867, Austria-Hungary. England viewed the Habsburg empire as a strategic obstacle to Russian expansionism and overly assertive French foreign policy on the continent. For his part, Napoleon III quickly came to regard the unification of Germany as the chief threat to France and realized that he needed all the allies he could line up, Franz Joseph included. Loud irredentism remained, and even grew, among Italians scattered around the empire's Adriatic ports, Trieste and Fiume, and in the southern regions of the Tyrol. Nevertheless, the government in Rome was not all that eager to nibble further on the Habsburg lands. First and foremost, Italian relations with France cooled markedly in the latter third of the century. Napoleon III and the Second French Empire disappeared from the political scene in 1870. The Third Republic which replaced him embarked on an active program of expansion in North Africa at the same time Italy developed imperial ambitions in the region. Furthermore, Victor Emmanuel's successor, Umberto I (1844–1900) was under fire both from the Vatican, which had bitterly opposed Italian unification, and the republicans. He was therefore willing to cooperate more closely with his fellow continental monarchs, not only in Berlin but in Vienna too. In 1882 the three states signed a defensive treaty, the Triple Alliance, which obligated each member to aid any among them who was attacked from without. The pact was renewed four times, the last in 1912 when all the signatories promised to use their influence to counter any threat to each other's territorial integrity. Austria-Hungary and Italy specifically agreed to maintain the status quo of their respective boundaries in the east. Should some territorial adjustments in the Balkan kingdoms or in the Ottoman empire prove unavoidable, these should take place only with prior consent of both parties and with either state receiving just compensation for whatever gains the other might make.

Russia and Austria-Hungary in the Balkans.

The great state which had gradually come to displace the Turks as the prime rival to the Habsburg empire in the east was Russia. The tsarist government had long wished to expand westward and southwestward, a path that put it on a collision course both with the new Germany and the Dual Monarchy. During the 1870s, Franz Joseph had Count Julius Andrassy (1823–1890) as his foreign minister, an erstwhile Hungarian revolutionary of 1848, who had urged his sovereign to take a greater military and economic interest in the Balkans after the Prussian debacle of 1866. He was also convinced that Russia was the principal threat to the kingdom of Hungary. Ethnic Magyars were outnumbered in their own kingdom by both Slavs and non-Slavs of Eastern Orthodox faith such as the Romanians. Russia claimed to speak for both, and Andrassy wanted to contain these ambitions as much as possible.

Despite this tension, Habsburg-Romanov relations had not been altogether hostile. The Grand Alliance against Napoleon had brought the two multinational states together as allies. Helped along by a shared conservative outlook, they remained on relatively good terms, down to the middle of the nineteenth century. Aid from Tsar Nicholas I in 1849, as we have already seen, was crucial to Franz Joseph's subduing the Hungarian revolutionary forces. But the youthful emperor did not return the favor when Russia entered the Crimean War against England and France in 1853. Nicholas and his successors felt deeply betrayed, and Habsburg-Romanov relations were never quite the same after that.

Nevertheless, both circumstance and self-interest prevented a complete rupture between the two multiethnic empires. Even in moments of genuine crisis, they did not challenge one another militarily. In 1875 two Ottoman provinces—Bosnia-Herzegovina and Bulgaria—rebelled against the sultan. A year later, the autonomous provinces of Serbia and closely related Montenegro, sensed that territorial gains could be made in this fluid situation. Theoretically still under Turkish suzerainty, they declared war on their overlord. The sultan's armies, who characteristically pulled themselves together in times of peril, were able to beat off the Serbs. Indeed, they inflicted permanent humiliation on the ruling prince, Milan Obrenovic. Russia intervened in the next year. The announced purpose was to defend the Orthodox Christians, particularly in what was to become Bulgaria, where Moslem officials and armies were exacting grisly retribution from the subject population. War between Russia and Turkey broke out, with the former emerging the victor.

Before the tsar's government had entered the conflict, it promised Austria-Hungary the major part of Bosnia-Herzegovina, still under Ottoman control. However, the treaty of San Stefano signed by Russia and Turkey in 1878 violated that understanding. Russia was to become the guarantor of a huge new Bulgaria to be lopped off of Turkey. This arrangement, which alarmed much of Europe, did not cause any immediate discomfort in Vienna. However, the compact called for a joint Austrian-Russian administration of Bosnia-Herzegovina. The two provinces were on the border of Croatia, part of the kingdom of Hungary. The ever-vigilant Andrassy protested that this was not what he and the Russian foreign minister, Alexander Gorchakov, had once agreed upon for the region.

In 1878 a major diplomatic congress organized by Bismarck met in Berlin to resolve these disputes. Andrassy extracted a mandate from the gathering to administer Bosnia-Herzegovina, though technically the lands remained under Ottoman sovereignty. The arrangement had, at best, a mixed reception in the two provinces. Roman Catholic elements of the population welcomed the appearance of the Austro-Hungarian army and bureaucratic apparatus. The Moslems, however, would have preferred to stay directly under the control of Turkey. Eastern Orthodox Serbs were not happy with either alternative, and their Russian patrons deeply resented having to scale back their hold on the Balkans.

The tsarist regime could have tried to destabilize the Habsburg state from within by exploiting ethnic unrest. Among those embittered by the Dual Compromise, the Czechs seemed very likely to look eastward for support. The Pan-Slavic idealism of 1848 and after cast Russia as its chief advocate and protector. Yet, Czech politicians in 1867 and for some time after that, held back from identifying themselves with an ideology that could force them to break completely with their traditional Habsburg rulers. At first, they confined themselves to taking out their frustration on the Austrian parliament where they kept business from going forward again and again. By the end of the century, a new generation of Czech nationalists under the leadership of Dr. Karl Kramar (1860–1937) began to see Russia in more positive lights. However, even this new-found interest was more intellectual than practical.

Moreover, Pan-Slavism, while tactically convenient for the government in St. Petersburg, did not drive its larger international strategies. These had Middle Eastern and Asian, as well as European, dimensions. If such concerns overlapped with the protection of Slavic peoples, this was all to the good. However, the Russians were usually ready to sacrifice ethnic interests to geopolitical ones if necessary. Even as their Slavic cohorts in eastern and east central Europe looked increasingly to Russia for leadership at the end of the nineteenth century, the tsar's government was preoccupied in the Far East. Here Japan had become a vigorous competitor for influence in the Pacific. Destabilizing the Habsburg monarchy was therefore not high among anyone's diplomatic priorities in St. Petersburg.

For its part, Franz Joseph's government became more solicitous of Russian concerns. Andrassy's immediate successors as foreign ministers, Counts Gustav Kalnoky (1832–1898) a Moravian, and Agenor Goluchowski the Younger (1849–1921) a Pole, both cultivated good-will in St. Petersburg. The League of the Three Emperors (1881), made up of imperial Germany, Austria-Hungary, and Russia, reaffirmed the Balkan settlement of 1878 and explicitly acknowledged that all three had legitimate interests in the region. Should there be further changes in the political geography of European Turkey, these would only take place following discussions among the signatories. An additional protocol affirmed Habsburg Austria's right to incorporate Bosnia-Herzegovina into itself at an "opportune" time. This moment was to be determined by Vienna itself. In 1884 the agreement was renewed.

The Habsburg Empire in Bismarck's Alliance System.
Nor, though Austria was Prussia's chief rival for preeminence in central Europe, was Bismarck eager to crush the venerable monarchy altogether. Even during the Austro-Prussian War he had fended off pressure from both the Prussian High Command and King William himself to follow up their quick initial victory with a more devastating blow to the Habsburg state. The goal of the conflict, as Bismarck saw it, was as much to bring the other medium-size kingdoms of Germany into the new Hohenzollern empire as to cripple Austria. Bismarck did not want

to be put in a position where he might have to be overly punitive toward future members of his fledgling political creation, some of whom actively supported the Habsburg side. He did have plans to enlist Magyar and Czech nationalism to his cause if that were the price of success, though whether he could have done so is open to question. Fears of German influence from outside the Habsburg realms continued to make the Czech national movement wary of close contact with the Wilhelmine empire. But in any case, the new imperial German chancellor never made any serious moves along these lines. He was firmly convinced that Prussian victory at Königgrätz had excluded Austria from the all-German polity about to be born. A more cordial approach to the Habsburgs might persuade southern Germany's principalities, particularly Catholic ones such as Bavaria, to accommodate themselves to leadership from Berlin. Lastly, unlike Frederick II in the eighteenth century, the chancellor did not want any territory from the Habsburgs. Their heterogeneous peoples had no place in a Germany unified, by and large, on national principles. Bismarck saw little reason to complicate what was already a challenging task of domestic state-building. He therefore backed a treaty in which Austria was let off very lightly.

Had Bismarck wanted to undermine the Habsburgs at home after 1867, there were Germans there who would have welcomed his encouragement. He did at times use press campaigns to support the German liberals within the Dual Monarchy. His strategic motives, however, were political and diplomatic, not ethnic. With the more rabid pockets of German nationalism in the Austrian lands, he would have nothing to do. In the late 1870s, Georg von Schönerer (1842–1921), a petty Austrian nobleman and parliamentary delegate, began calling for the fusion of the Habsburg German regions to the Wilhelmine *Reich*. Voters returned only a tiny fraction of his movement's candidates to the Austrian legislature. Nevertheless, he had an enthusiastic following among pro-German students at the Austrian universities. He also became a self-styled spokesman for Austrian peasants and artisans of German stock, prominent among those suffering visibly from the effects of rapid social and economic change. Strident anti-Semitism was a staple of his rhetoric as well, though Jews, among whom there were many Germanophiles, sometimes sympathized with the general thrust of his thinking. Notable examples were Viktor Adler and Heinrich Friedjung (1851–1920), who would become a major historian. Indeed, some of his most important work dealt with the Habsburg-Hohenzollern rivalry in central Europe.

Both men helped to draw up the Linz Program of Schönerer's German National Party in 1882, which reached a level of ethnic particularism exceptional even for the Habsburg monarchy between 1848 and 1914. Its call for as tight a union as possible of the Habsburg German peoples, including those in Bohemia and Moravia, added up to the deconstruction of the monarchy. In their territorial enclaves, German culture was to flourish and German be the lone official tongue. The scheme did allow for some choice in the language of instruction in problematic school districts where pupils came from households where German was not spoken. By the time a boy or girl came to the so-called middle school, however, German was obligatory, and no student could be forced to learn any other vernacular. Hungary would absorb the Cis-Leithenian Adriatic territories, along with Bosnia-Herzegovina. Galicia and Bukovina were to be joined with Hungary as well or given some unspecified form of autonomy in Cis-Leithenia. Curiously, the manifesto called for a customs union of both the Austrian and Hungarian lands with the German empire, a proposal that the latter would resurrect during World War I.

None of this appealed to Bismarck. The document also talked of reviving the German Confederation, about the last thing the chancellor wanted to hear. Nor were Pan-German organizations within the new *Reich* to the north much attracted to their counterpart in Austria-Hungary. Schönerer's rather bizarre personality put them off, and he eventually alienated many of his Austrian supporters too. His point of no return came in 1888 when he was jailed for leading a violent attack on a newspaper editor. Schönerer and his student followers believed that the journal had cynically exploited the death agony of Emperor William I by publishing two contradictory reports—one announcing the ruler's passing, the other correcting this—simply to sell their paper.

The All-Germans to the north also thought that their new empire had done enough to protect the German-speaking peoples of the Habsburg empire. This notion was an outcome not of Bismarck's domestic worries, but of his military and diplomatic concerns. The unification of Germany landed a resentful France on his western boundary and an ambitious Russia on his eastern frontier. The chancellor had good reason, therefore, to foster cordial relations with Franz Joseph and his ministers. The possibility of a two-front war haunted him. The French began working to reverse their defeat in 1871 as soon as the war ended. While it was highly unlikely an Austro-French alliance would reopen hostilities with Prussia in the immediate future, Bismarck was not one to allow that future to take its own course. At the outset of the Franco-Prussian War the majority of Franz Joseph's closest advisers as well as the Habsburg military establishment had actively hoped that the French would win; Bismarck did not want Vienna ever to think that way again.

However, it was the Russian problem that brought the governments in Berlin and Vienna together, a relationship that endured even after the Prussian chancellor left office in 1890. As early as 1871, Bismarck opened negotiations with Austria-Hungary on an alliance. Later that year, the talks gathered real momentum with Franz Joseph's appointment of Andrassy as his foreign minister. Ideally the latter wanted an updated version of the Grand Alliance that had once defeated Napoleon I. This time, however, it was to be made up of Germany, Austria-Hungary, Great Britain, and Italy, and it was to check Russian, rather than French, expansionism.

The outcome of these exchanges was the Dual Alliance. Signed by Austria-Hungary and Germany in 1879, it was not made public until 1888. The antagonists of 1866 became the guarantors of each other's territorial integrity. As explained in its introduction, the compact was to help both states foster the security of their lands and the tranquillity of their peoples. The Berlin settlement of 1878 was to be maintained as well. The heart of the arrangement however, was a mutual defense treaty which applied to the eastern frontiers of both states. Germany and Austria-Hungary pledged to aid one another militarily should Russia attack either of them. Were a country other than Russia to open hostilities against either Germany or Austria-Hungary, the unaffected signatory would observe a "benevolent attitude" (*wohlwollende Haltung*) toward its partner and not help the aggressor. If, on the other hand, Russia supported the offending belligerent, then the provision calling for mutual defense was to be activated. After five years either party could request that the pact be renewed. If neither government asked to reevaluate the arrangement within the first month of that last year, it would run for another thirty-six months. In 1883 the Habsburgs signed a similar alliance with the new kingdom of Romania, thereby gaining some influence on the political and military calculations of yet another state.

Aside from specifying the behavior of each partner in the face of outright attack, all of these agreements were rather vague about the contingencies that would set them in motion. Nor did they specify the limits, if any, the contracting parties were prepared to set on their military commitments. Were there threats, for example, short of actual war that could be construed as dangerous to the territorial integrity of Germany, Austria-Hungary, or, after the creation of the Triple Alliance, Italy? And once such a condition was clearly evident, where did the dividing line between self-protection and offensive engagement fall? As the diplomatic historian René Albrecht-Carrié once pointed out, such distinctions were not always obvious. In defending one's own lands it was often tactically desirable to move armed forces beyond established borders. Such questions were barely raised, let alone answered in these documents. But by making the Habsburg empire an important partner to so many major international agreements, the states of Europe had affirmed that the continued existence of Austria-Hungary was important, regardless of the ethnic troubles that beset it at home.

The Emergence of the Serbian Problem. Thus, neither the Russian nor the German empires programmatically encouraged the Dual Monarchy's peoples to challenge or to cast off Habsburg rule altogether. It was a much smaller realm, at least as high officials in Vienna saw it, that was to play that role. Among other provisions in the 1878 treaty of Berlin was one that recognized the independence of Serbia, Montenegro, a mountainous principality to the southwest of Serbia with a basically Serbian population, and Romania. Now a kingdom, Serbia ruled only part of a people who lived as national minorities in several areas throughout eastern and southeastern Europe. Many of them were in the various lands of the Hungarian crown, as well as in Bosnia and Herzegovina. The Berlin accord contained several provisions to ease Austria-Hungary's worries about the future political influence this new state might have among the Habsburg Serbs. The government in Vienna was permitted to administer the Sanjak of Novi Pazar, a sliver of land which was actually closer to the heartland of historic Serbia than Belgrade, but now separated Serbia and Montenegro. Not only did this arrangement block the union of Serbia and Montenegro; but as long as some form of the Ottoman empire stood in the east and southeast, Serbia was surrounded by states anxious to keep it as small as possible.

Taking advantage of Russia's military exhaustion following the Turkish war of 1877, Andrassy's successors in the Habsburg foreign office were able to make Serbia something of a client state. The task was made considerably easier by the damage that the reputation of the new king,

Milan Obrenovic, had suffered in his failed strike against the sultan. In 1881, Austria-Hungary and Serbia secretly pledged their mutual friendship in a treaty which gave the Vienna regime some formal input into the conduct of the small kingdom's international affairs. In return, the Habsburg government guaranteed Milan's throne and indicated that it would not oppose any plans he might have to expand his borders in an eastern or southeastern direction. A year later, Milan actually discussed allowing an Austrian occupation of the kingdom should he abdicate. Hungarian fear of bringing any more Slavs into the Dual Monarchy squelched this idea. Nevertheless, it betokened the respect which the Habsburg government commanded in Belgrade. Indeed, its power to control events stretched even farther to the east. In 1887, Austria-Hungary made its diplomatic muscle felt in Bulgaria, till then, informally, but nonetheless clearly, a Russian client. Along with Great Britain, the foreign office in Vienna supported the installation of a new Bulgarian tsar, Duke Ferdinand of Coburg, whom the national parliament had voted into the office over the objections of the regime in St. Petersburg. But once again the Russians had concerns that forced them to cultivate good relations with Franz Joseph. In 1897, preparing to confront the Japanese challenge in the Far East, they concluded an agreement with the Dual Monarchy to respect the status quo in the Balkans.

From the diplomatic standpoint therefore, Austria-Hungary was well situated at the opening of the twentieth century to contain territorial irredentism in the Balkans. Yet, the empire's position had a serious weakness. It had little beyond diplomatic skill to maintain its claim to being a great or even regional power. Given its relatively low rate of capitalization, the Dual Monarchy could not exert serious economic pressure over the long term on the independent Balkan states—this role was falling to the Germans even before World War I. Having performed dismally in Italy and against Prussia, the effectiveness of the yet-untried common army was questionable at best. Should the talents of the foreign office in Vienna falter, or should Franz Joseph's military and naval forces be put to a test they could not handle, Austria-Hungary's place in southeast Europe would be precarious indeed.

More troubling yet, its foreign policy was tied very tightly to domestic concerns. England, France, and Germany were not completely free from such pressures either; but it was only in Austria-Hungary where the very integrity of the state depended so heavily upon keeping other countries from competing for the loyalties of its many peoples. Working in this context, political and military leaders could easily read domestic crises as foreign ones and the other way around. Mistakes in judgment could easily become a problem for the entire continent, given the elaborate alliance system of central Europe of which Austria-Hungary had become an integral part. Outwardly recovered from both its Italian and German humiliations, Austria-Hungary still had an uncertain future on a continent where political nationalism had come to stay.

Crisis in Bosnia. Just how the interplay of all these factors could add up to a genuine international crisis became apparent as the twentieth century opened. In 1903, a bloody coup against the pro-Austrian Obrenovic dynasty took place in Belgrade. Not content with murdering the king and queen, the conspirators hurled the bodies of their royal victims from the palace window. Serbia was now ruled by the house of Karageorgevic, which was far more friendly toward the Russians. Relations between the South Slavic kingdom and the Habsburg monarchy grew noticeably more tense. In 1906, Count Alois Lexa von Aehrenthal (1854-1912), a member of one of Bohemia's leading families, became the foreign minister of Austria-Hungary. Since the 1870s he had served in various diplomatic posts around Europe; from 1899 he was the Habsburg ambassador in St. Petersburg. Far more attuned to domestic politics than his immediate predecessors, he believed that Austria-Hungary had to behave more forcefully abroad to retain the support of the Germans and Hungarians at home. The Balkans were to be his proving ground.

The Habsburg defense establishment had urged for some time that its naval installations in Dalmatia be protected more heavily; in 1908 a nationalist uprising of the so-called Young Turks in Constantinople gave Vienna reason to be concerned about its Adriatic bases. The rebels in the Ottoman empire wanted their government to reverse its territorial decline; Bosnia-Herzegovina, though under Austrian military administration, was still technically subject to the sultan's suzerainty. Aehrenthal argued that Austria-Hungary should annex the two provinces outright, which it proceeded to do. It was a move bound to anger the Serbs at the very least, and Aehrenthal moved quickly to contain that problem. With protests taking place in the streets of Belgrade, the Habsburg government issued an ultimatum in 1909 demanding that the kingdom recognize the new arrangement in Bosnia. Powerless to block any strike from Vienna, the Serbs acquiesced. They were anything but happy however. They, along with the Croats in Bosnia-Herzegovina itself, had come to support the incorporation of the provinces into a greater Serbia. (*See Document No. 20.*) Even Croatian patriots in the Hungarian half of the monarchy were beginning to doubt that the Habsburgs were trustworthy protectors. Dalmatia and Bosnia, once part of their medieval kingdom, were now being administered from Vienna, not Zagreb. As far as they were concerned, Franz Joseph had replaced the sultan as the chief opponent of Slavic historical rights. In the kingdom of Serbia itself, organizations sprang up to keep national sentiments alive in the annexed territories. The government in Belgrade brought Bosnian students to the Serb capital for schooling and nationalist indoctrination. Especially important was the propaganda churned out by *Narodna Odbrana* (National Defense). A few Serb army officers founded *Crna Ruka* (Black Hand) which was dedicated to realizing a Greater Serbia through violence. None of this kept the Habsburg regime from continuing to frustrate Serbian territorial ambitions. During the general Balkan conflict in 1912, the Dual Monarchy supported the creation of an independent Albania to block Serbian expansion to the Adriatic coast.

Moreover, nationally minded Serbs and Croats were not the only people displeased by Austria-Hungary's new assertiveness. England became uneasy about the changing power relations in the eastern Mediterranean. And Russia, though just coming off of a humiliating defeat at the hands of Japan, was nevertheless freed from conflict in the Pacific theater. Its government too, was unhappy about the way the annexation had taken place. While foreign minister Alexander Izvolsky had informally agreed to the Austrian move, he and the tsar's government were much embarrassed by the peremptory way in which Vienna carried out the mission.

The whole affair added one more incident to the stockpile of *ressentiments* which the Russians were amassing against Vienna. None of these developments were of immediate consequence to the Habsburg empire and its agents. Indeed, from Aehrenthal's perspective, the annexation of Bosnia was just the sort of bold stroke that he thought would enhance the monarchy's reputation. But the reaction abroad to a foreign policy conceived in part to win respect at home showed that such an approach might not always end happily for the Habsburg empire in the world of power politics.

CHAPTER 9

A PERSISTENT ANACHRONISM

A European Fixture. The twentieth-century Austrian novelist Robert Musil (1880–1942) once remarked that Vienna's inhabitants were often at one another's throats over national issues. Yet, he hastened to add, they could bury their differences for long periods of time as well. Expanded economic and educational opportunities, official accommodation to genuine political reform, and widened channels for social mobility certainly did much to foster a public willingness to live and let live throughout the empire as a whole. To these might also be added the integrative effect of experiences such as service in the common army.

But, as we have seen, the institutional structure of the empire was far from secure. If it were to survive, the monarchy had to rely upon other conditions in its favor. One of these was simple fear of the unknown, not only among those who ran Europe's foreign ministries, but among Franz Joseph's subjects as well. The dynasty and the lands it ruled, in whatever constitutional guise, had been the central reality of their collective world for almost 400 years. What would happen to the various nationalities of central and east central Europe under its sway were that regime to collapse? The muscular intrusion of the new German empire into the ranks of the major powers did much to keep Austria-Hungary's peoples together, as strained as their relationship could sometimes be. The by-now reflexive concern about Russia's westward ambitions had the same effect. Intellectual inertia was a natural by-product of this kind of thinking. It was hard to picture a world without the Habsburgs, even for those who espoused a relentlessly egalitarian ideology such as Marxism. The empire's Social Democrats proposed many radical changes before World War I, but abolition of the monarchy was not among them.

Thus, following a tense start in 1848 and several crises after that, Franz Joseph still ruled his empire unchallenged. Indeed, like his equally long-lived contemporary in England, Queen Victoria, he had become something of an institution. Though age had only increased his natural reserve, he enjoyed both respect and, insofar as this can be a group sentiment, affection from the bulk of his subjects. He deliberately cultivated an aura of personal accessibility, holding audiences twice a week for up to a hundred people. Only age forced him to cut that number to fifty during the 1890s. Though these encounters were short, they did much to warm the public image of an otherwise stiffly formal man. He never broke with the elaborate ceremonial observed to the very end at the Habsburg court. Like many of his forebears, however, he kept to simple personal habits. His favorite meal, insofar as anyone could determine, was boiled beef and vegetables—*Tafelspitz*—a dish found on countless noontime tables throughout his lands, especially on Sundays. State banquets or even more intimate suppers for advisers and dignitaries could be ordeals for the truly hungry. The emperor put away food swiftly with the mechanical indifference of those for whom eating is a bodily duty. The Empress Elizabeth (1837–1898), a striking Bavarian princess whom he married in 1854, was determined to preserve her improbably slender waist and barely touched a thing, if she attended these functions at all. Since the plates for each course were cleared away as soon as the sovereign was done, many of his guests had half-finished dishes snatched from under their noses. They spent the rest of the evening longing for the moment when they could quit the imperial presence for some local inn or restaurant.

Franz Joseph preferred military ways to any others, and the furnishings in his private chambers were those of a spartan field commander. The conveniences of modern technology did not attract him. He was more comfortable in horse-drawn carriages than in automobiles; he never, apparently, gave serious thought to installing a bathroom for his private quarters at his suburban residence in Schönbrunn. Two water pitchers and bowls, a wash basin and a bucket which doubled as a chamber pot met his hygienic needs. But his public appearances, both in Vienna and throughout the empire, became occasions for outpourings of popular enthusiasm, particularly when he rode, utterly straight even in old age, on horseback. He had borne crushing losses in his family with dignified grace. His son and heir-apparent, Archduke Rudolf (1858–1889), committed suicide under scandalous circumstances with his alleged mistress. The empress, who had grown ever more estranged from her husband, was knifed to death by an Italian anarchist in 1898. Through it all he had fulfilled his duties and kept to his dawn-to-dusk work routine without major interruption. Such behavior may have been only one more side of the basically cold personality that some say he was. His subjects knew little of that; they measured him by what they imagined their own reactions to similar trials might be.

Dynasty and Empire. The day had long since passed when the dynasty had a functional proprietary relationship to the lands and peoples it governed. There were now clear legal distinctions between what belonged to the house of Habsburg and what belonged to the state. Public taxes supported the army, not the private credit and revenues of the ruling house as had once been the case. The financing for the court itself came from monies voted and raised by the parliaments in both halves of the monarchy rather from the resources of the imperial family.

Yet, in several important ways, some formal, some less so, the Habsburgs were not only central to the operation of their state but connected to it in very personal ways. No one expressed this more transparently than Franz Joseph himself. When assenting to legislation that came out of the parliament in Vienna, he spoke of "my peoples," and "my lands." A soldier swore his allegiance to the emperor and his commanders, not to his country or constitution. Officers pledged their loyalty to the emperor alone. The educational system reinforced such practices. At the turn of the twentieth century, a Vienna pedagogical college urged prospective elementary school faculty to teach their pupils with reverence for the emperor, the "father of the fatherland," and all the members of his house.

The Habsburg dynasty as a whole still occupied a position given to no other persons or groups of persons in the empire. Members of the imperial family, while legally part of the state, were not subject to it. The house, and the house alone, had the right to provide rulers for that state and to determine who, among them, would hold that position. The two parliaments actually authorized the funds for the court, but the dynasty, not the legislators themselves, made the policies that had to be financed. This included even private family arrangements such as the size of allowances and dowries given to various archdukes and archduchesses. Even when dead, the Habsburgs commanded unique treatment. The sanitary code of Vienna forbade churches and other religious establishments to bury private benefactors on their premises. Only the imperial dynasty could continue to be interred in the crypt of the Capuchins not too far from the *Hofburg* in the first district of the city.

Directly or indirectly, the presence of the ruling house made itself felt wherever one was in the monarchy. Should one be an academic, it was hard to forget that an imperial archduke was the patron of the Imperial Academy of Arts and Sciences in Vienna. Regardless of his pedes-

trian musical tastes, Franz Joseph appeared faithfully at gala perform-
ances of the opera. Theaters in Vienna both large and small had a "court
box" for spectators from the imperial family. How much use they made
of the facility was beside the point. Members of the dynasty distributed
among themselves appearances at some of the innumerable balls which
took place in the capital during the pre-Lenten season. Many of these
affairs were unmistakably plebeian. The Firemen's Ball and the Small
Businessmen's Ball, for example, were graced in one year by ceremonial
visits from two heirs-apparent, Archduke Franz Ferdinand (1863-1914)
and his nephew Archduke Charles (1887-1922).

Over the centuries the court had set the decorative and cultural tone
of its peoples. In early modern times, nobles from outlying parts of the
expanding empire had come to Vienna where they aped, in some instances even outdid, what they saw and heard in their sovereign's establishment. By the latter half of the nineteenth century, the most affluent among the middle classes could afford the habit of patronage. The
breadth and intensity of interest in the arts and sciences and the money
to support them drew talent from all over the monarchy to the city, making it a center for learning and the arts, as well as an administrative
capital.

Some of the greatest luminaries, not only of Austro-Hungarian, but
of European intellectual and cultural history, abandoned outposts of the
Habsburg realms to cultivate their gifts in Vienna. The Freuds, as
already mentioned, came from Moravia, the physicist Ernst Mach
(1838-1916), from Bohemia, as did the composer-conductor Gustav
Mahler (1860-1911). The parents of the playwright and novelist Arthur
Schnitzler (1862-1931) were from Hungary. The great pianist Arthur
Schnabel (1882-1951) was from Polish Galicia; his musical education
in Vienna was underwritten by a nobleman who asked in return that his
name remain unknown to the young musician. Though the emperor
himself had no serious aesthetic bent, some of his children did. One in
particular, Archduchess Valerie (1868-1924) was deeply committed to
supporting artistic and musical talents, particularly the organist and
symphonic composer Anton Bruckner (1824-1896), whose origins lay
in provincial Upper Austria.

In the latter half of the nineteenth and beginning of the twentieth
centuries, the style of the imperial city and its chief resident spread
throughout the monarchy as a whole. Budapest, Brno in Moravia, Za-

greb in Croatia, and to a lesser extent Prague, took on some of the architectural cast of Vienna. Travelers throughout the Habsburg lands, were they in an urban center or the countryside, found buildings on the properties of the dynasty or institutions under Habsburg patronage painted in the deep yellow (*Kaisergelb*) of the imperial house. Nor did the dynasty neglect to tell its humbler subjects that its members had very special rights in what was still *their* state. Every train station of the empire, large and small, had an antechamber reserved for all who belonged to the imperial-royal house. Most of these rooms were occupied about as frequently as the "court boxes" mentioned above. They served, nevertheless to remind local populations that remote as their community might be, it was linked to the dynasty that ruled from Vienna. The house did avail itself liberally of another privilege available to it in railroad waiting rooms, that of sending telegrams free of charge. Many of these missives had to do with matters of state, but a goodly amount of social trivia was dispatched in them as well.

The Emperor in Politics. The Habsburgs still dominated crucial operations of their governments. The head of the house, the emperor-king, no longer ruled as absolutely as did Maria Theresa or Joseph II. The Compromise of 1867 required that whatever orders he issued be countersigned by appropriate ministers to indicate that these measures were constitutional. Yet, there were still significant areas where Franz Joseph could act free of such intervention. Above all, he had supreme command of the army and final authority over its internal organization. He had the power to make war and conclude peace treaties. Even in matters where ministerial approval was needed, the emperor had privileges unmentioned in the constitution. The parliaments in Vienna and Budapest never knew the precise content of discussions between officials and their sovereign. Without such personal contact with the ruler, a minister had only indirect influence on policy and events. And in some ways, Franz Joseph still held to the idea that those who ran his government were household servants. After Schwarzenberg, he never had a supreme chancellor. The foreign minister of the Dual Monarchy developed informally into the first among equals, more than a clue to the emperor's understanding of the common good. Yet, in addition to his duties of state, that same foreign minister also functioned as chief officer for the imperial household's affairs.

A model of circumspection, Franz Joseph could nevertheless bring himself to interfere directly in domestic political matters when he believed that the integrity of his fractious state was at issue. He, too, was aware of the dangers which interethnic strife created for his dynasty's position and on occasion, intervened decisively to curb it. One of the powers the sovereign retained from the sixteenth century was the right to confirm the election of the Mayor of Vienna. Four times, from 1894 to 1897, Franz Joseph refused to allow Karl Lueger to take the office to which the city council had named him. The emperor believed that the anti-Semitism of the opportunistic politician would further envenom relations among the heterogeneous peoples in the capital. Only after yielding to Count Badeni's argument that Lueger's movement would help to contain the even more noxious appeal of the Social Democrats did the Habsburg ruler permit Lueger to assume the position.

An even more dramatic demonstration of the emperor's willingness to curb national particularism came in a crisis over army organization at the turn of the century. In 1903, the Hungarian parliament was asked to pass a bill authorizing an increase in the number of recruits for the common army. The governing party, the Liberals, were unable to steer the bill through the body. The substantial Hungarian Independence Party, led by Francis Kossuth (1841–1914), the son of the revolutionary leader of 1848, made its support conditional upon having soldiers from the Hungarian lands be assigned to Hungarian units. There they would get orders in Magyar from Hungarian officers and march under the Hungarian flag. Such demands were a direct attack on the common army, and the emperor would hear nothing of them.

The fortunes of politics fell Franz Joseph's way when, in 1905, the Liberals lost their parliamentary majority. The emperor named a new ministry of essentially nonpolitical figures and put the army bill before the legislators in Budapest once again. Almost all of them came from districts exquisitely gerrymandered to hold down the size of the electorate. They were therefore anxious to preserve both social and economic privilege for those who had it along with as much Hungarian autonomy as the Dual Compromise allowed. Franz Joseph coupled his renewed request for funding with a threat to introduce the secret ballot and universal suffrage. Both practices were anathema to the narrow clique that controlled political life in the kingdom beyond the Leitha. Magyars were less than half of the population, and expanding the franchise would unquestionably bring their preeminence to an end. The parliament voted as their king wished. Franz Joseph got his troops, and the franchise reforms were considerably modified.

National Unrest in Hungary. Age, however much it had deepened the respect of his subjects for him, was also visibly sapping the emperor's vitality. Among themselves and their intimates, ministers had come to discuss his demeanor and physical appearance in the same tone that they addressed matters of state. Indeed, these concerns were matters of state. The ethnic strife that erupted periodically, yet unpredictably in both halves of the monarchy, always reopened the question, at least in some minds, of whether Franz Joseph's state would survive him. The time was long since past when Palacky had called Austria's existence, meaning a collection of lands all more or less equally subject to the house of Austria, a historical necessity. An Austria-Hungary in which some nations were constitutionally more privileged than others was not what he had in mind. Furthermore, it was the Hungarian half of the empire which had given rise to many of the elements which were working to undermine Habsburg rule. The Romanians of Transylvania and the Croats deeply resented the Magyarizing policies coming out of the parliament in Budapest during the late nineteenth and early twentieth centuries. Should the venerable emperor's successor fail to cut a judicious path through this tangle of national *ressentiment*, there was good reason to think that the entire structure of the monarchy would break apart.

A curious mix of Hungarian liberalism and repression had led to the mounting discontent in Croatia. The South Slavic kingdom had not come off altogether badly in the *Nagodba*, its settlement with Budapest after the establishment of the Dual Monarchy. Its territories in the Balkans and along the Adriatic were somewhat enlarged, and its spokesmen could participate in the meetings of the delegations where joint Austro-Hungarian affairs were discussed. Croatians sent representatives to the parliament in Budapest for deliberations on common issues such as commercial policy. Cultural activities and local administration, including judicial institutions, were considered Croatian internal affairs and to be administered in the Croatian language. Though the region's people were basically poor, they were modestly assessed when the time came to pay the taxes which underwrote their joint expenditures with Hungary. A separate Nationalities Law for the entire kingdom of Hungary, enacted in 1868 as well, reinforced these provisions. While the language of the national government and the central administration in the capital was Hungarian, non-Magyar speakers could administer and adjudicate affairs from the county level down in their native tongue. Croatia had its own parliament, the *Sabor*, which, with its very restricted franchise, ensured the dominance of the more monied classes as was the case with its counterpart in Budapest. The Croatians of Hungary eagerly took advantage of all of the opportunity for autonomous development open to them. Zagreb became a significant intellectual center under the leadership of Bishop Joseph Strossmeyer (1815–1905), who hoped to see Croatia granted the same status that Hungary enjoyed within the Habsburg empire.

But the city became a center of more radical nationalist activism as well, in part due to Vienna's high-handed annexation of Bosnia-Herzegovina in 1908. Even more provocative were the policies emanating from Budapest. For all its concessions, the *Nagodba* had dashed Croatian hopes of becoming an autonomous state within the Dual Monarchy as a whole and forced them to accept a governor or *Ban* nominated by the Hungarian minister-president. As time went on, the Hungarian administration of the territory seemed to violate the spirit and letter of both the *Nagodba* and the Nationalities Law flagrantly and frequently. In sharp contrast to the more enlightened aspects of its initial relationship with Croatia after 1867, the government in Budapest was now intent on Magyarizing the Hungarian half of the monarchy. Its ultimate goal was a virtually indivisible Hungarian state. Officials throughout the kingdom were sternly advised to take Magyar names. Language was an especially sensitive issue. Efforts to make the study of Magyar obligatory and Magyar the actual language of instruction proceeded at first slowly because primary schools were largely run by local communes and churches. But from the 1870s on, all state-run schools beyond the elementary level taught in Magyar. Even for young pupils, the study of Magyar was made compulsory after 1879.

Two other measures ignited popular outrage in Croatia and elsewhere in Hungary at the end of the nineteenth and beginning of the twentieth centuries. One mandated that every place in the kingdom of Hungary to have a Magyar name. The policy gave local populations ample opportunity for demonstrations, especially at railroad stations where activists could always find a sign in Hungarian to destroy and keep their cause before the public. The promulgation in 1905 of a thoroughgoing set of language decrees set off a particularly nasty outbreak of dissent in Hungarian Croatia. So repressive were these measures that the Croats from the Austrian half of the monarchy hoped that the emperor would act to rescue the cultural integrity of their ethnic cohorts to the east. Franz Joseph chose to remain out of the fray, as under the terms of the Dual Compromise he was bound to do; his disappointed South Slavic subjects looked ever more favorably to the regime in Belgrade for support. Raising tensions even further, the Hungarians happily made what use they could of the hostility among Croatian Serbs toward the more particularistic forms of Croatian nationalism.

The Heir-Apparent. Could the monarchy rise above these mounting difficulties when Franz Joseph died, as he was certain to do? Reform of his state was the topic of countless discussions, but the emperor was absent from almost all of them. If change was to come, it would be after he had passed from the scene. An exceptionally energetic successor, his nephew Archduke Franz Ferdinand, was impatiently waiting to take his place; not everyone, however, especially in Hungary, took great comfort in this.

Franz Ferdinand was born to privilege; he nevertheless knew personal struggle at first hand. As a young man he had survived tuberculosis, the scourge of his age. Even greater testimony to the reserves of determination he could draw upon was his marriage. He had chosen as his wife Countess Sophie von Chotek (1868–1914), who was from a minor Bohemian noble family, and therefore below the ranks from which future emperors, indeed Habsburgs in general, married. The two were deeply in love however, and remained that way until the end of their lives. Franz Ferdinand respected the protocols of his dynasty and asked his uncle to allow the marriage to go forward. This Franz Joseph did, but on the condition that it be a morganatic union. The line of succession would therefore not pass to the couple's sons should they have any. Even under these limitations, the emperor disapproved of the whole affair thoroughly. He did not bother to conceal his feelings from his nephew, whom he disliked in any case. Franz Ferdinand, for his part, was no more fond of his uncle whose increasingly sclerotic regime both frustrated and angered him. The one thing that they did share was a concern for the future of the dynasty; their approaches to the issue were, however, very different.

The archduke had assumed important operational responsibilities in the empire, especially in the armed forces. His interest and unwavering commitment brought about the expansion of the small but accomplished Habsburg navy before the First World War. In 1913 he was made General Inspector of the Army in charge of all training maneuvers. Though modern technology intrigued him, his goal was traditional—increasing Habsburg military power to protect more effectively the dynasty and its thrones. But his plans did not stop here. He and a coterie of advisers who frequented his chancery at the Belvedere Palace, once the residence of Prince Eugene of Savoy, clearly intended to bring about structural changes in the monarchy once Franz Joseph passed from the scene. Unlike his discreet uncle who rarely if ever uttered any public thoughts about the peoples of his realms, the archduke was very open about his preferences and dislikes. Among the latter, the Hungarians were clearly in first place. He regarded their singular status as a threat to the integrity of the empire's multinational character and was especially concerned about the impact on the South Slavic peoples of policies that came from Budapest.

Though the archduke and his intimates were dedicated to the ideal of a unified Habsburg empire (*Gesammtstaat*) governed from Vienna, they somewhat reluctantly had concluded that this was politically impossible. Alternatively, they toyed with the idea of federalizing the monarchy, or creating a third entity to be on a par with Hungary. The latter scheme was called Trialism with the new unit to be cobbled together from the southern Slavic territories of both Austria and Hungary— namely Dalmatia, Bosnia-Herzegovina, Croatia, and Slovenia. By 1913 the archduke had concluded that this was the only way to undermine the Belgrade regime's drive for a "Greater Serbia." He realized that the effect of this ploy would be to keep Serbia small, but he had no ambitions to dismember it. The idea would offend Magyar nationalists, but Franz Ferdinand was prepared to ignore them. He planned to implement the project immediately upon succeeding his uncle, but before the Hungarian coronation.

However, for all of his confrontational approach to political problems and his keen interest in military matters, he was anxious to avoid war. At the very least, major armed conflicts would put off the thoroughgoing structural changes he believed had to be made for the monarchy and his house to endure. Worse yet, he feared that the empire, given its internal weaknesses, would simply fall apart. It was the threat of Russian mobilization that bothered him most, though, respecter of dynasties that he was, he bore the Romanovs themselves no ill-will. Indeed, he believed that should war break out between the two of them, both multinational states would go under. He argued against the annexation of Bosnia in 1908, and after some initial interest, opposed Habsburg intervention in two Balkan Wars in 1912 and 1913, where again he feared an Austrian presence might bring Russia into the conflict.

It was then in the person of this energetic, yet, for this very reason, threatening man, that much of the future of the Habsburg monarchy appeared to rest. Unlike his bland and aging uncle, he spoke of radical reform with confidence, inspiration for a few, but reason for fear among many. The Hungarians were certain to contest vigorously any reduction in their status. And not all of those likely to be angered by the archduke's plans were confined to the Habsburg monarchy. This was particularly true in the Balkans. The proponents of Greater Serbia, both within the kingdom of Serbia itself as well as within the Habsburg lands, clearly had much to lose should Trialism or even a quasi-federalized Habsburg state come into being. Just how inflammable these emotions had grown became gruesomely apparent on June 28, 1914. In Bosnia for a military inspection of the Habsburg forces there, Franz Ferdinand and his wife were assassinated in Sarajevo. The perpetrator was a Bosnian student of Serbian ancestry, Gavrilo Princip (1895–1918). Just how much the conspiracy, of which he was a part, was directly inspired by the government in Belgrade, if at all, has never been established. It was brutally plain, however, that the Habsburg empire and the intricate politics which had kept it alive had become the hated enemy of young Serbian nationalists and their followers.

CHAPTER 10

TO THE EDGE AND OVER

The Decision for War. The corpses of Franz Ferdinand and his wife were sent back to the Adriatic coast. From there they were transported by ship to Trieste, then to Vienna by train. In keeping with the morganatic status of their marriage, the couple could not be interred in the Crypt of the Capuchins with the archduke's more august ancestors. Rather they were given an exceedingly simple funeral in the cramped chapel of the *Hofburg*, then dispatched during a ferocious summer thunderstorm to Artstetten, their residence in Lower Austria, for private burial.

Though a mob in Vienna tried to attack the Serbian legation immediately after the funeral cortege passed through the streets of the capital, Franz Ferdinand was not deeply mourned in the Habsburg lands. While a familiar figure to many, he was hardly popular. His own uncle, the emperor, though genuinely shocked and horrified at the killings in Bosnia, had greater confidence in his new successor, his grand-nephew, Archduke Charles. Franz Joseph was very fond of the young man, something which could never have been said of his feelings toward the late heir-apparent. Charles was generally amiable, well-educated, devout and conscientious. His wife and distant cousin, Princess Zita of Bourbon-Parma (1892–1989), also befit his exalted status.

Privately relieved though Franz Joseph and his advisers might have been to have the strong-willed Franz Ferdinand off the scene, they agreed that the assassination called for a stern official response. Given the anti-Habsburg mood that had been noisily evident in Belgrade for several years, they suspected that the Serbian government lay in some way behind the killing in Sarajevo. Proving it, however, was very difficult, not to mention finding the guilty parties. Officials in Vienna saw the outlines of an organized plot, but no one had any knowledge of its details. The emperor therefore, received sharply conflicting advice from his ministers, whose views were based as much on opinion and political interests as fact. Only the sovereign could resolve the issue.

Field Marshall Joseph Conrad von Hötzendorf (1852–1925), the chief of the Dual Monarchy's general staff, argued vigorously for an incisive military strike. The assassination only confirmed his long-held belief that Serbia posed a mortal danger for the integrity of the monarchy. He welcomed the opportunity to move decisively against the troublesome kingdom and eradicate the problem once and for all. To do this, however, without precipitating a general war required a very swift attack, something that the more cautious among the emperor's ministers were reluctant to endorse. Count Stephen Tisza (1861–1918), the Hungarian minister-president, was among them. The volatile national rivalries in the Balkans had long concerned him; he wanted Hungary to be well-prepared for a war that might be crucial to its continued existence as a state. He also feared that Romania might support Russia should the tsar's government intervene on Serbia's side. This would free the regime in Bucharest to take up the cause of their ethnic cohorts in Hungarian Transylvania. It was in his interest to keep Vienna from acting recklessly, and he insisted that Belgrade's role in the assassination be clarified before doing anything serious. Positioned more or less between the two was Count Leopold von Berchtold (1863–1942), the joint foreign minister. He believed that it was wise for the Habsburgs to remain a significant presence in the Balkans. Military retaliation against Serbia was not out of the question, but he wanted to explore diplomatic remedies first.

This strategy the emperor more or less accepted, but the Hungarians continued to withhold their approval. A mission set off for Berlin to see just how far Germany would support Austrian-Hungarian armed intervention in Serbia. When William II and his government indicated that they would do so, Tisza's concerns about the Russian reaction abated somewhat. By July 14, Romania had also promised to meet its treaty obligations to the Dual Monarchy. But first the Serbs had to be given the opportunity to resolve the matter nonviolently. An ultimatum, which in essence was a compromise between Tisza's and Berchtold's views, was hammered out and sent to Belgrade in the middle of July. Franz Joseph had sanctioned it on the clear understanding that if war should come, the Habsburg empire would not take territory from Serbia or any other place. This policy was a concession to the Hungarians who had consistently opposed adding more Slavs to the Habsburg peoples. The text of the ultimatum, as well as the declaration of war that came a couple of weeks later, were never communicated to Austria-Hungary's German allies, some measure of the independence with which the empire could seemingly operate.

The tone and content of Habsburg demands and the diplomatic exchanges which followed upon them do little to persuade anyone that the government in Vienna wanted to end its Serbian problem peacefully. Indeed, the ultimatum virtually invited rejection by any state as sensitive to matters of sovereignty as was Serbia. At the very least, its provisions, if accepted, guaranteed that the government in Belgrade would not threaten the Dual Monarchy for a long time to come. Serbian officials would have to clamp down on any anti-Habsburg propaganda in their kingdom. The army was to rid itself of its anti-Habsburg elements. Most demeaning of all was the requirement that Austrian officials be sent to Serbia where they would participate in the investigation of the conspiracy which the Habsburg government was sure had existed. It was to this stipulation the Serbs refused to yield, seeing it as a intolerable breach of their territorial rights. (*See Document No. 21.*)

The Habsburg regime had therefore managed to talk itself into launching the military action that some in the government had promoted for some time, regardless of the international reaction. (*See Document No. 22.*) Having himself concluded that Serbia must be punished in a way that would remove it as a threat to the multinational Habsburg state, Franz Joseph signed the mobilization orders. His announcement to his peoples on 28 July (*See Document No. 23.*) that they were at war, illustrates clearly that for all the political changes that had gone on in his realms throughout the nineteenth century, personal and dynastic considerations were still uppermost in the emperor's mind. It was the "honor" of the monarchy, by which he meant its reputation and standing among states, which had to be vindicated. Serbia's offenses were against his family and himself, not against his subjects. It was his house, which had once furthered the independence of the small kingdom from Ottoman rule, only to receive hatred rather than gratitude in return.

Insuperable Weaknesses. Even the most ardent war hawks of the Habsburg regime wanted a short and territorially limited conflict. Those hopes evaporated the next day, July 29, when Russia announced a general mobilization, thereby living up to promises of aid to the Serbs made four days earlier. Like a broadening whirlpool which traps more and more debris in its swirls, the European alliance system fell into place. Within a few days, Austria-Hungary and Germany were at war with Great Britain, France, and Russia.

To the surprise of some, the various peoples of the Habsburg empire did not forsake their sovereign and his house at the earliest opportunity.

Pockets of dissent emerged here and there, but even the Czechs, whose loyalty seemed the shakiest, answered the call to arms. In Budapest, crowds cheered the men leaving the city for the front. Except for a few emigres, Romanian and Croatian leaders joined in professions of loyalty to the crown. Part of this support reflected no more than long-standing habit, but another part was inspired by the Russian mobilization. The latter reawakened fears among some of the nationalities, Germans and Hungarians especially, of being swept into the orbit of the giant Slavic state to the east. All this patriotic fervor was, however, quickly put to a demanding test. Habsburg military planning had been badly compromised on the eve of the war when an Austrian officer ensnared in a homosexual scandal betrayed strategic documents to the Russians. Tsarist forces had made good use of the intelligence, and initially scored impressive victories on the eastern front in Galicia. The Serbs put up effective resistance as well. Occupied with securing their western border against France, the Germans were not much help, so the Habsburg armies had no alternative but to fall back. The number and scale of these setbacks showed that Franz Joseph's forces were technically and logistically ill-prepared for a major conflict. The empire had never been among the most innovative competitors in the European armament race of the late nineteenth century. Moreover, within a year, national and ethnic divisiveness did indeed begin to weaken the Dual Monarchy's war effort. Italy saw an opportunity for using Habsburg vulnerability to fulfill irredentist yearnings among the Italians who remained in the empire. Though the kingdom was officially part of the Triple Alliance with Germany and Austria-Hungary, few expected Rome to meet its treaty obligations to the Central Powers.

Franz Joseph's government thought that the most it could hope was for Italy to remain neutral; Austria-Hungary opened negotiations to that end with the kingdom soon after the conflict began. The price for Italian cooperation was the port of Trieste and the Trentino in the south Tyrol. Despite the urging of his German ally, the emperor angrily refused to give up any fraction of his realms without having fired a shot in their defense. By 1915, he reluctantly agreed to hand over part of the Trentino, but by this time the Italians had raised their demands as well. To realize these, they joined with England and France, thus requiring the Habsburg forces to open a third front in the south. This was the very situation that everyone in Vienna had wanted to avoid. A second wave of patriotism surged through the Habsburg peoples, this time directed against Italian treachery. Indeed, the emperor-king's army and his Mediterranean navy fought quite well against their new enemy. But the entire enterprise further strained the already undersupplied Austrian-Hungarian forces.

From the outset, many Czech troops had fought less willingly and enthusiastically than their colleagues from elsewhere in the empire; in April of 1915, the first of their regiments to surrender as a whole did so to the Russians. Desertions multiplied, even when the military situation had brightened somewhat in the east. With the war stalled in the trenches on the western front, the Germans could redirect massive help to their beleaguered ally. Galicia was reconquered from the Russians, thus opening up a source of grain supply lost at the outset of hostilities. Serbia itself was defeated. However, the increased German presence in the east caused problems of its own. Not all the peoples of the empire reacted to it enthusiastically. Habsburg regiments had been directly incorporated into the German army in Galicia, and the German officer who took Belgrade, Field Marshal August von Mackensen, had commanded all of the troops of the Central Powers. This, despite the responsibility which the Habsburg government and its Serbian fixation carried for setting off the entire conflict. No subtle analytic gifts were needed to see that the Habsburg government was becoming ever more tied to its counterpart in Berlin. The notion that the empire existed to shield the smaller peoples of central and east central Europe from German or Russian hegemony seemed ever less credible.

The Attitude of Foreign Powers. At the beginning of the war, nationalist spokesmen had emigrated, to England and France particularly, where they mounted political and propaganda campaigns on behalf of the peoples they claimed to represent. Even before 1914, journalists and intellectuals in western Europe had written sympathetically about the travails of some ethnic groups in the Habsburg empire. One of the most prolific and committed among them was Robert W. Seton-Watson (1879–1951). Both as a professional scholar and well-connected publicist, he had studied Austria-Hungary and its peoples for many years. Though at first opposed to the dissolution of the Dual Monarchy into its component parts, he became convinced as the war went on that this was the best course of action. A Scot of strong Protestant convictions, who early in his career had toyed with the idea of writing a history of Hungarian Calvinism, he thought about ethnic relations in severely moral terms. Long repelled by Magyar domination of Slovaks and Croats, he viewed the German-Austro-Hungarian alliance as a threat to some of the most basic values of western civilization. (*See Document No. 24.*) He was convinced that the increased influence that Germany had over the Habsburg empire would eventually crush the individual nationalities ruled from Vienna. German behavior in Belgium, where some civilians had been brutalized by the occupying armies, showed that Hohenzollern rule did not respect Europe's less powerful peoples. Serbia was the cardinal proof of his argument.

It was also Seton-Watson who arranged a professorship in England for a leading Czech supporter of this position, Thomas Masaryk (1850–1937). Of Moravian and Slovak ancestry, Masaryk had hoped that the Habsburg empire would never have to test its viability in war. Once it came, however, he concluded that multinationalism, at least as officials in Vienna and Budapest understood it, had little bearing on genuine political freedom. To realize the latter, all of the small nations of central and east central Europe should be free. In Paris before going to England, he had formed a Czecho-Slovak national committee to promote the idea of an independent state made up of both regions. Aside from a closely related language, geographic proximity, and long experience with foreign rule, the two peoples had very little in common. The Czech kingdom of Bohemia had been a historic entity since medieval times. It was industrial and commercial, with a progressive and secular middle class. The Slovaks had never had their own state, having lived in the mountainous areas of northern and eastern Hungary for centuries in lands that were part of the Crown of St. Stephen. The population was overwhelmingly rural and intensely Catholic. Nevertheless, bringing both groups together would, as Masaryk saw it, liberate them from Vienna and Budapest respectively. They could then develop as nature, not man, had intended. It was toward this goal that he became a tireless worker. Similar thoughts were also stirring among the Croats and Galician Poles.

Evidence continued to mount that Germany would take little account of ethnic and historic niceties should the Central Powers win the war. A book published in 1915 entitled *Mitteleuropa* by a German clergyman and social activist, Friedrich Naumann, reinforced such opinions. Though a thoroughgoing progressive in social matters, Naumann urged an economic union of all central and east central Europe under the leadership of Berlin. His ideas found a receptive audience in the German government which began exploring the scheme with Habsburg representatives as the war was going on. The Germans were particularly interested in widening their influence in Poland, even in territory under Habsburg rule. They would press this with their ally, albeit unsuccessfully, until the end of the war.

Whatever independence from Germany the Habsburgs pretended they enjoyed had all but disappeared by 1918. Franz Joseph had finally died on November 21, 1916. As planned, Archduke Charles succeeded him, becoming Emperor Charles I (King Charles IV in Hungary) or "Charles the Last" as some have unkindly dubbed him. Though hardly a forceful personality, he believed that innovative leadership, even when it undercut established procedures, was the only policy which could rescue his monarchy. From the outset of the war he had been eager to keep the Habsburg empire from appearing overly attached to Germany. Nor was he irrevocably committed to seeing the conflict through to the end. He had not participated in the decisions that had launched the attack on Serbia. Therefore, he could conclude in good conscience that if the Dual Monarchy were to survive at all, he would have to withdraw it from the hostilities. The new Empress, Zita of Bourbon-Parma, whose opinions he took very seriously, shared these views.

From the end of 1916 to May of 1917, Charles and Zita conducted a set of private negotiations with the French president, Raymond Poincaré, to extricate Austria-Hungary from the war. In exchange for peace, Charles would support the return of Alsace-Lorraine, occupied by Germany since 1871 to France, and the restoration of Belgian independence. Though outwardly a betrayal of his alliance with the Germans, he had reassured himself that dynastic history justified this action. The full title of his dynasty since Maria Theresa's marriage to Francis of Lorraine in the eighteenth century was the house of Habsburg-Lorraine, and the Habsburgs themselves were the descendants of the medieval counts of Alsace. In April of 1918, prompted by a series of indiscretions on the part of the Habsburg foreign office, the French prime minister, George Clemenceau revealed what Charles and Zita had been up to. Pan-German elements in the Habsburg lands reacted furiously to their emperor's behavior toward his primary ally, the incarnation of their ethnic identity to the north.

The international attention given to this episode was a disaster for the Habsburg empire. The German regime, itself no stranger to covert initiatives, was nevertheless outraged over Charles's duplicity and wanted, at the very least, a show of contrition from him. The Entente and its allies had hoped to detach Austria-Hungary from Germany and had welcomed any openings that Vienna made along those lines. Indeed, it was just such a possibility that had kept them from calling for the break-up of the empire into its national components. This, the ultimate option, was a sure way to end Austria-Hungary's participation in the conflict, but one laced with uncertainty about the future territorial security of Europe as a whole. But Charles now had proven himself to be an untrustworthy negotiator. The Allies, who were also eager to end the bloodiest war Europe had ever seen, decided that the Habsburg empire had to go. The young emperor's abject trip to Spa, Kaiser William II's wartime residence, where he apologized humbly to his German counterpart for his unfaithfulness signaled plainly that Austria-Hungary had lost almost all the attributes of a sovereign state, at least internationally. (*See Document No. 25*.) On June 29, 1918, the French government recognized the Czecho-Slovak claims to independence and an emigre council to serve as a provisional government for the state to come.

The End Game. On the domestic front Charles fared little better. Even at the beginning of the war, members of the Habsburg government had disagreed over how to conduct it. Military dictatorship, in force as soon as hostilities got underway, was deeply resented by more liberal and reform-minded members of the regime, and opinions varied on how to handle the national issue as well. Just as he hoped to rescue his monarchy abroad with a peace, the emperor sought to preserve his position at home through conciliation. Here too, he blundered badly and often. Against the advice of the Austrian minister-president Heinrich Clam-Martinitz (1863–1932), he went ahead with his coronation as king of Hungary, in effect renewing the Dual Compromise which gave the Hungarians the leverage to stall any serious reforms of the monarchy. Several people at the ceremony noticed that the crown was too big for his slender head, a disturbing omen for those who looked for them. The *Reichsrat* in the Austrian half of the monarchy had been prorogued since March of 1914 by the minister-president at the time, Count Karl von Stürgkh (1859–1916). The prospect of so many Slavic representatives, at odds not only with the other ethnic groups of the monarchy but among themselves, convinced him that wartime Cis-Leithenia could conduct its business without parliamentary input. The empire had, therefore, been ruled by decree, allowed according to Article 14 of the 1867 constitution.

It was this view which led to Stürgkh's assassination in 1916 at the hands of a young Socialist, Friedrich Adler (1879–1960), who believed that domestic reform would never take place unless the count was permanently disposed of. (*See Document No. 26.*) Though the bulk of the Austrian population was not prone to such extremism, discontent with wartime government was mounting. Numerous clashes between civilians and military authorities had taken place. Officers in the empire were known to treat elements of the Habsburg populations, particularly of Czech or South Slavic origins, more as enemies than as fellow subjects. The collapse of the tsarist regime in Russia in February of 1917 and the entrance of the United States of America into the war suggested that Habsburg political interests would be better served by partial reintroduction of civilian rule.

For Charles, convoking the *Reichsrat* again seemed a way of renewing the trust of his peoples in their sovereign. Once more ignoring Clam-Martinitz's counsel, he called it back into session in May of 1917. Its deliberations followed Stürgkh's predicted scenario. Rancorous debates broke out once more, led by Czechs and Croats pressing for political reforms in their national interests. On May 30 a Slovene representative asked for an autonomous South Slavic state under Habsburg rule. But, as with so many similar requests, both past and present, this one was impossible to satisfy without offending some other group. It seemed clear that if the empire endured at all, it would be with a constitution that acknowledged national interests far more systematically and openly than had the Dual Compromise. (*See Document No. 27.*) Just as in 1848, the Habsburg monarchy was being challenged by nationalism and liberalism. But this time, it was not only at war within, but fighting for its life abroad.

Undaunted, Charles forged ahead with policies which he hoped would reknit his relationships and those of his house with his various peoples. On July 2, 1917, the name day of his oldest son and heir, Archduke Otto (1912–), the emperor ordered the release of political prisoners, many of whom had been sentenced for real or suspected nationalist agitation. The gesture may have had mollified some Czechs, among whom a number, including the prominent national leader, Dr. Karl Kramar, had been jailed for subversive activities. Their disaffection was therefore great. However, Germans throughout the empire were out-raged. Their sovereign appeared to be rewarding people who had given less than their total support to the war effort and the dynasty and there-fore sacrificed less. The economic and social situation in the Hungarian half of the monarchy deteriorated badly in 1917 as well. Inflation, food shortages, the disproportionately heavy casualties which troops from the kingdom suffered and the Bolshevik Revolution in Russia led to de-mands for peace. Military desertion increased markedly.

The need to deal with the empire's structural crisis plus a new bel-ligerent from abroad led to a last desperate attempt to solve the national question in the Habsburg monarchy. The United States had entered the war in 1917, persuaded that Germany had become a threat to what it defined as its national interests. Both the American president, Woodrow Wilson as well as influential figures in his State Department, believed that nationalism, or more precisely, frustrated nationalism was the root cause of the war. Wilson was not, at the outset of American participa-tion, wholly hostile to the Habsburg monarchy. As was the case with his European allies, however, the president changed his mind when he saw that neither Franz Joseph nor his nephew could break cleanly with Ger-many. A declaration of war on Austria-Hungary seemed the only way to end the conflict. The American press and members of Congress from districts with large Slavic constituencies reinforced the president's con-viction. Indeed, the agreement to form a Czecho-Slovakia was formally announced in the Declaration of Pittsburgh in 1918, Masaryk having come to the United States to guide it to its final form. Here he had met Wilson, who was deeply impressed by the Czech statesman and patriot whose wife was an American, born Charlotte Garrigue in Brooklyn.

On January 8, 1918, in an address to the United States Congress, Wilson outlined a peace program for the entire world. Much of it was shaped however, by his analysis of the hostilities in Europe. Known as the Fourteen Points, article ten dealt with Austria-Hungary. It did not call for the break-up of the monarchy, but rather for the peoples of the empire to have the opportunity for "autonomous development." Events which followed, particularly those which showed that it would be im-possible to detach the Habsburg empire from its German commitments, rendered the magnanimous fuzziness of that tenth point obsolete. How-ever, Charles had seized upon it at the time as a last possibility for pre-serving his position. The collapse of the German-Austro-Hungarian front in Bulgaria during September of 1918 spurred him to make every effort to fulfill what he believed was yet a live condition coming from Washington. On October 16, he issued a manifesto which turned the monarchy into a loose confederation. The only institution to hold it together was the sovereignty of the dynasty itself. The document instructed the various peoples of the Austrian half of the empire to begin forming national councils. These would do the preparatory work for the creation of autonomous polities within the new state.

However, the national leaders among the Habsburg peoples read this as an invitation to break their ties with the dynasty altogether. On the same day, Hungary declared the Compromise of 1867 to be at an end and began its own efforts to hold on to what it could of its historic territories. Five days later the Czechs declared their independence; on October 29 the Yugoslav National Council did the same thing for the South Slavs. An armistice between the rapidly disintegrating Austria-Hungary and the Allies was signed on November 3.

Charles formally renounced all his rights to participate any new government to be formed in Austria on November 11. The agreement was worded so as not to preclude the return of his house to political position in some future state, though the parliament of the new Republic of Austria passed a Habsburg Exclusion Act in 1919 that effectively canceled that possibility. Charles would make two attempts to regain a throne in his former lands before his death in 1922, but both of these took place in Hungary. For the time being, he left Vienna and his shattered empire the day after he formally removed himself from its political life. It was for the safety of his children, he said. The world that the Habsburgs had helped shape through four centuries had decided that the dynasty was no longer needed. Nevertheless, the head of the house continued to think, as his ancestors had always thought, in family terms.

PART II

DOCUMENTS

DOCUMENT NO. 1

FERDINAND I CREATES A MILITARY BORDER IN THE BALKANS AGAINST THE OTTOMAN EMPIRE*

In 1538, Ferdinand I established a standing defensive force in Upper Slavonia, today part of Croatia. Largely Serbs fleeing from earlier Ottoman offensives, these men and the fortifications they occupied were to keep the armies of the sultan, Suleiman the Magnificent, from advancing further into Christian Europe. The unusually generous privileges they were given shows how important a military role the South Slavic troops were being asked to play in the sixteenth-century Habsburg lands. It also illustrates the Habsburg identification with the supranational cause of European Christendom.

γ γ γ

We Ferdinand . . . make known and recognize that . . . our beloved Nicholas Jurisic, Baron in Güns (Hung: Köszeg) [and] our captain general has indicated to us that a significant number of both Serbian and Rascian [Rascia was an earlier name for the original Serbia—Editor] captains and military leaders (*Vojvodas*) have made known that they wish to honor us and remain true to us in perpetuity along with their dependents, subjects, and others living in the military districts (*Vojvodatibus*). For this reason we wish to see to rewarding these military leaders and captains of the Serbs and the Rascians, along with their families, subjects and their dependents, benevolently and with abundant generosity. Through the following words we bestow exceptional exemptions and freedoms from taxes for their pious feelings and intentions toward us and toward Christendom, in order that they apply themselves diligently to demonstrating these in action. Because they, these same Vojvodes and captains from Serbia and Rascia, along with those specifically mentioned persons, who are their subjects or dependents, take upon themselves to honor and and be unbreakably loyal toward us, through the words of the present document, we give, endow, concede, grant and promise the following to them, along with each family, each of whom lives in a single house and under one roof and on a piece of property.

*Frantisek Vanicek, *Specialgeschichte der Militärqrenze*, 4 vols. (Vienna: K.-k. Hof-und Staatsdruckerei, 1875) 1:26–28 n. 2. Trans. Paula Sutter Fichtner)

Each one, for twenty consecutive years, must, be able to and may live freely in our domains in a place assigned to them by the aforementioned captain general, cultivate the land, raise fruit, harvest grain, without any impediment or objection. Furthermore, we grant, raise, and pay in advance each captain and voyvode of these Serbs and Rascians, each of whom has 200 men under his command, a provision of 50 Rhenish gulden for each year that he serves us well and faithfully. Beyond this, whatever they themselves capture as booty from the unbelievers and the eternal enemies of the Christian faith, the Turks, must remain with the Rascians outside of the cities, markets, camps, and fortifications, captured captains and significant people whom we reserve for our own disposition. An additional condition is that during the time they are in the emperor's pay, whatever they take from the unbelievers, they must hand over a third of their gain or their booty to our paymaster. We are not indeed renouncing the privilege and the income of a third of this kind. On the contrary we wish that this works to the advantage and use of the Serbs and Rascians, as, for, example, ransoming captains who perhaps have fallen into the hands and power of the enemy and toward equipping and rewarding of those, who have distinguished themselves through a praiseworthy deed for Christendom against the eternal enemy.

DOCUMENT NO. 2

THE PRAGMATIC SANCTION, 1722–1723[*]

The Pragmatic Sanction was really a series of agreements arranged by Emperor Charles VI. Through them he hoped that the Habsburg lands as a whole would pass to a female successor should he die without legitimate male heirs as he indeed did. Charles was clearly thinking as a dynastic ruler who saw his territories as a kind of property of the ruling house rather than belonging to a state governed in the interests of its inhabitants at large. This selection, written in the florid constitutional language of the day, was part of the emperor's agreement with the Hungarian estates. It therefore also illustrates the so-called functional dualism with which the Habsburgs ruled their lands in early modern times.

γ   γ   γ

1. . . . Knowing well that kings and princes, like other men, are also subject to the fate of mortality, thus taking mature and studied account of how many great and reputable deeds have been consummated by his sacred majesty's forebears . . . and especially by his sacred reigning imperial and royal majesty to enhance the well-being of the state and the enduring benefit of his loyal subjects in war and peace, above all, through the opportunity of the most recent conflict against the Turks, his highness has not only kept intact but extended through the good fortunes of war, his hereditary kingdom of Hungary and its associated lands . . . as well as the security of the estates and every single inhabitant and also to the associated lands . . . in order that . . . in all the years to come the kingdom will be secured from foreign and domestic disturbances and dangers and will be blessed with continued peace and sincere unity of spirit against every external threat

2. and, besides this, in order to take care that all the inner uproar and evil of an interregnum be prevented, which can easily arise, as is well known to the estates of this kingdom from time immemorial. . . .

5. in the case that, God forbid, the male line of his sacred imperial and royal majesty becomes extinct, they [the Hungarian estates—Editor] confer upon the female line of the exalted house of Austria the he-

---

[*]*Die österreichische Verfassungsgesetze*, Edmund Bernatzik, ed. (Leipzig: Hirschfeld, 1906), pp. 14–16. Trans. Paula Sutter Fichtner.

reditary right of succession in the kingdom and crown of Hungary and its associated lands and kingdoms, which already, with the help of God, have been recaptured and in the future will again be won, thusly: first among the heirs of the currently reigning sacred imperial and royal majesty

6. failing these, to the heirs of the late Emperor Joseph

7. and, if there are none of these, to the heirs of the late Leopold, insofar as all these come from the lands of the emperors and kings of Hungary, and are legitimately born, of the Roman Catholic faith and archdukes or archduchesses of Austria in conformity with the primogeniture order established by his currently reigning sacred majesty for his other kingdoms and lands within and outside of Germany, which are to be held, ruled, and governed hereditarily, indivisibly, and inseparably with one another, along with the kingdom of Hungary and the divisions bound to it, according to the laws and orders mentioned above. . . .

10. [They] stipulate that the declared archdukes of Austria of both sexes through the female line of the illustrious house of Austria should be accepted and approved in the established manner as heirs and successors; and at the same time, that previously discussed freedoms and prerogatives of the estates of the kingdom of Hungary and the lands, realms and provinces associated with it . . . will be observed henceforth forever at the time of a coronation. . . .

DOCUMENT NO. 3

THE COMMON-SENSE EMPRESS[*]

The following letters of Maria Theresa, written during the last years of her life, are representative of her strongly pragmatic and personal, yet decisive style of rule. The first is to Joseph II and deals with affairs in the Austrian Netherlands where provincial estates were still very powerful and where government was unusually decentralized. The second is to her son, Archduke Ferdinand Karl Anton (1754–1806), who became governor of Lombardy in 1780.

γ γ γ

Schönbrunn 22 July 1780.

I am sending you this dispatch concerning the Netherlands; I have nothing to add to it, being altogether saddened and astonished. I am very happy to have anticipated your wishes concerning the departure of your sister, which I have arranged for a year from now, and we should have plenty of time for arranging the formalities and what you call pettifogging, because I don't think that there is anything to change in the basic constitution and way of governing this country; it is the only prosperous country and provides us so many resources. You know how these people are about their traditional, indeed ridiculous prejudices, if they are obedient and loyal and contribute more than our German lands, which are worn out and discontented! What more can one ask for? A governor will have to have complete authority, given the remoteness and separateness of this province, and on account of its powerful neighbors. . . .

15 December 1779

My dear son. This will get to you very near your departure . . . I am not going to dwell on anything and wish that with this bad weather and even worse roads, you begin your journey happily. I will not be easy in

[*]*Briefe der Kaiserin Maria Theresia an ihre Kinder und Freunde.* 4 vols. in 2, ed. Alfred Ritter von Arneth (Vienna: Braumüller, 1881)1:1; 2: 237–238. Trans. Paula Sutter Fichtner.

my mind until I know that you have arrived in Florence. Don't hurry the coach and horses ahead on the road, and as soon as you leave Milan, you will have to gird yourself with great patience and never act like a prince. You are nothing but a petty count, who demands nothing, but is receptive to all. Don't go running to the stables when the post horses are being changed, that way one only holds up what is being hurried along and you expose yourself to many nuisances and fabricated stories, and which, in this vulgar genre, are never favorable to us. My sole fear is that . . . you would like to arrange the entire trip and all the coaches yourself, that you would occupy yourself with this on the pretext of being well served. A stable boy, a courier could handle this detail and more properly, and I see no one on this list who could do this. It is however, a major issue, if you wish to be well served and attract the esteem of the land where you are traveling, not to act like a stable boy but like a cavalier. The same thing is true of tips; I myself do not have to do this. . . . Stinginess will not do at all there; the same for alms, because it is necessary to give them.

It would be very well if this trip could get you to be precise in giving times and arrangements, otherwise everything will be in confusion and you will be badly served. Be discreet with what you say in different lands and resting-places, or you will find yourself that everything will come back to haunt you. Keep in mind that trip to Parma where they were very discontented with the way you addressed them, informing yourself about them or acting as if you wanted to know everything, and disburdening yourself of your opinions and judgments; they did not like this. I pointed this out to you then; neither you nor anyone else has the right to undertake research in a strange land. One may, in the spirit of getting information, ask questions, but no decisions at all, no approval or disapproval, no making comparisons or pronouncements or confidences; speak less, observe and listen more; enter a little into the national spirit or that of the rulers. This trip being solely for your gratification and instruction, it is unnecessary to go beyond this in any way. From the moment you leave Milan, you will be in the great theater of the world, and all the world will have its eyes on you. However minor the activity, I want you to be seen advantageously, above all having your court and that of your family in Italy. This is more important for you than it was for your brothers and sisters who have been very successful. One will ask more of you, as a mature man. You must win the hearts of princes and ministers for the benefit of the service [to the monarchy] and your family. Much politeness, patience, listen much, but don't talk a lot, conform to the customs of the country, without appearing irritated by them; better to rest for a day or an evening in your lodgings rather than falling asleep at a public gathering or something else.

DOCUMENT NO. 4

LEOPOLD II MAKES A STRATEGIC RETREAT[*]

To restore order in Hungary and other Habsburg lands following the death of Joseph II in 1790, his brother, Emperor Leopold II had little choice but to accept some of the demands made upon him by the empire's rebellious provinces. Though not all of the Josephinian reforms were abolished, the new Habsburg ruler had to recognize once again many of the freedoms which the Hungarian estates had traditionally enjoyed.

γ   γ   γ

. . . .

ON THE INDEPENDENCE OF THE KINGDOM OF HUNGARY AND ITS DEPENDENCIES.

On the proposal of the estates and orders of the Kingdom, His Sovereign Majesty has been graciously pleased to recognize that, although the female succession of the august house of Austria, established by Laws 1 and 2 of 1723 in the Kingdom of Hungary and its dependencies, attaches to the same prince as in the other Kingdoms and hereditary States situated in Germany and outside of Germany, which must be possessed inseparably and indivisibly in accordance with the established order of succession, nevertheless, Hungary with its dependencies is a free kingdom, and independent in all that concerns the legal form of the government (with all its dicasteries), that is to say, that it is subject to no other kingdom or people, but that it has its own existence and constitution, and that it must be governed and administered by its hereditary King, legally crowned, and, consequently, by His Sovereign Majesty and his successors, the Kings of Hungary, in accordance with its own laws and customs and not on the model of other provinces, conformably to Laws 3 of 1715 and 8 and 11 of 1741. . . .

ON THE EXERCISE OF THE LEGISLATIVE AND EXECUTIVE POWER.

His Sovereign Majesty voluntarily and of his own accord recognizes that the power to make, abrogate and interpret the laws in this Kingdom

[*]Herbert F. Wright, ed., *The Constitutions of the States at War, 1914–1918* (Washington, D.C.: Government Printing Office, 1919), pp. 26–28.

of Hungary and its dependencies belongs, save for the provisions of Law 8 of 1741, to the lawfully crowned Prince and to the estates and orders of the Kingdom lawfully assembled in Diet, and he has been graciously pleased to declare that he would preserve intact this right of the States, and would transmit it inviolate to his august successors as he had received it from his illustrious ancestors, guaranteeing to the estates and orders of the Kingdom that the Kingdom and its dependencies shall never be governed by edicts or by what are known as patents, which can in no case be received by any of the tribunals of the Kingdom, the deliverance of patents being reserved only in the case where, on points in other respects conforming to the law, the publication can be effectively obtained only in this way. In consequence:

The organization of tribunals, established or to be established by the law, can not be modified by royal authority; the execution of lawful sentences can not be prevented by orders of the King, nor can he in person be permitted to prevent it; the lawful sentences of the tribunals shall not be altered or yielded to the revision of the King or any political administrative authority, but the judgments shall be rendered conformably to the laws at present existing or subsequently to be made, and to the recognized custom of the Kingdom, by judges chosen without religious distinction, and the executive power shall be exercised by His Royal Majesty only in the meaning of the laws.

ON SUBSIDIES AND CONTRIBUTION.

His Sovereign Majesty has also been graciously pleased to guarantee fully to the estates and orders of the Kingdom and the dependencies that no subsidies, under any name whatsoever, either in money, in kind or in recruits, shall be imposed by the royal will either upon the estates and orders or upon persons not of the nobility, nor shall they be solicited, under the pretext of a free gift or for any other reason, outside of the diet, save in so far as concerns the provision of Law 8 of 1715 confirmed by Law 22 of 1741. The amount of the contribution appropriated for the maintenance of the permanent army shall always be determined from one diet to the other in the comitia of the Kingdom; save for the other provisions of Law 8 of 1715 above cited, which are, presumably, confirmed. . . .

DOCUMENT NO. 5

A CONSERVATIVE VIEWS
POST-NAPOLEONIC EUROPE[*]

On 15 December, 1820, Prince Metternich, the Habsburg chancellor, sent an extended memorandum to Tsar Alexander I of Russia following a conference among Austria, Prussia and Russia held in Troppau. The three conservative powers had met to discuss the revolutionary movements then underway in Spain and Italy. In particular, they focussed on and eventually sanctioned Habsburg wishes to intervene in the Kingdom of the Two Sicilies where revolution had broken out against the Bourbon government. Metternich's Profession of Faith, as it has come to be known, is both a justification of the policies followed by Emperor Francis I and himself and a classic statement of the statist conservatism found among several European governments following the Napoleonic Wars.

γ   γ   γ

. . . The progress of the human intellect has been extremely swift over the course of the past three centuries. This advance, having been moved forward more rapidly than has wisdom, the sole counter-weight to passions and to error; a revolution prepared by the false systems, by the deadly mistakes into which many of the most illustrious sovereigns of the last half of the eighteenth century fell, broke out finally in one of the most enlightened countries, one of the most enervated by pleasures, in a land inhabited by a people whom one might think of as the most frivolous, in view of the ease with which it understands things and the difficulty it undergoes in judging things dispassionately.

Having cast a rapid glance at the primary causes of the current condition of society, one should show in greater detail the nature of the evil which threatens, in one blow, to disinherit it of the total of the very real benefits, fruits of a genuine civilization, and to disturb it in the midst of its pleasures. We find the evil completely defined in a single word:

[*]Clemens Wenzel Lothar Prince of Metternich-Winneberg. *Mémoires, Documents et Écrits Divers.* Edited by Prince Richard de Metternich with the assistance of M. A. de Klinkowstroem, 5 vols. (Paris: Plon, 1880–1882). 3: 430–431, 434, 436–437, 440, 443. Trans. Paula Sutter Fichtner.

presumption, the natural effect of so rapid an advance of the human spirit toward the perfection of so many things.

It is this which has led so many individuals astray, because the feeling has become so widespread.

Religion, morals, legislation, economics, politics, administration, all together have become communal goods, accessible to all. Knowledge seems to be innate: experience is of no value for the *presumptuous*; faith, in itself, means nothing to him, he substitutes for it a supposed individual conviction, and to arrive at this conviction, dispenses with all investigation and all study; because such ways appear to be beneath a mind which believes itself sufficiently powerful to encompass at a glance the totality of issues and data. *Laws* have no force for him because he has contributed nothing to making them, and it would be beneath a man of his quality to acknowledge boundaries laid out by savage and ignorant generations. *Power* lies in himself; why should he submit to something which is useful only for a man deprived of knowledge and understanding. That which, according to him, sufficed for the age of enfeeblement, will no longer be appropriate for an age of reason, of vigor, to the level of universal perfection which the German innovators designate with the idea, absurd in itself, of the *emancipation of peoples*! . . .

In thus sketching the character of the presumptuous man, we believed we have sketched that of the society today, composed of such elements, if one can apply the term society to an order of things which in principle tends only *to individualize* all the elements which make up a society and to make each man the master of his own belief, the arbiter of what laws he finds acceptable to govern himself with or through which he permits himself to be governed, he and his neighbors; in short, the sole judge of his faith, of his actions, and the principles according to which he understands how to regulate them.

Is it necessary to prove this last truth? We think we do it by pointing out that one of the most natural of human sentiments, that of *nationality*, has itself been erased from the liberal catechism, and that wherever the word is yet used, it serves only as a pretext for leaders of factions to put governments in fetters or as a lever in aid of disorder. The real purpose of these partisan ideologues is to fuse religion with politics, and, in the last analysis, it is nothing more than to create to the advantage of each individual an existence completely independent of all authority and no will other than his own, an idea which is ridiculous and contrary to the nature of man, and incompatible with the requirements of human society. . . .

The revolutionary germ . . . penetrated all countries and spread itself there more or less. It developed further under Bonaparte's military despotism. His conquests displaced a multitude of legitimate things, institutions and practices, breaking bonds sacred to all people, and those impervious to temporality, even more than certain benefits which the innovators have thrust upon us now and again. As a result of these disturbances, the revolutionary spirit could easily take on the guise of sincere patriotism in Germany, in Italy, and, later, in Spain. . . .

It is largely the middle classes of society which this moral gangrene has won over, and it is only among them that one finds the true partisan leaders.

The great mass of people are not vulnerable to its appeal and will not be. The work which this class—*the true people*—must devote itself to is too constant and too positive for them to abandon themselves to the uncertainty of abstractions and ambition. The people know what is good for them, that is, to be able to count on tomorrow, because it is only tomorrow which rewards them for the pains and the cares of the day before. The laws which assure rightful protection to the first of their goods, to the security of individuals and their families, and to their property, are basically simple. The people fear any movement which negates industriousness and brings endless new burdens in its wake. . . .

In Germany, as in Spain and in Italy, people want nothing more than peace and quiet.

In these . . . countries, the activist classes are the monied men, really cosmopolitans, assured of their profits at the expense of whatever order of things; state employees, lawyers, individuals who oversee public education. . . .

We are persuaded that society can no longer be saved without strong and vigorous resolve on the part of Governments which are still free to think and to act.

Likewise we think that this may yet be, if these governments face reality squarely, if they disabuse themselves of illusions, if they close ranks and settle themselves upon the path of correct principles, free of all ambiguity, boldly upheld and stated.

Conducting themselves in this way, the monarchs will, first of all, fulfill the duties imposed upon them by Him, who, by conferring power upon them, has charged them to attend to maintaining justice, the rights of everyone and especially, to avoid the byways of error and to proceed resolutely in the way of truth. Situated beyond the sphere of those passions which agitate society, it is in days of crisis that they are principally summoned to strip false appearance from reality, and to show themselves for what they are, fathers invested with all authority rightfully belonging to heads of families, to prove that in days of gloom, they know how to be just, wise, and, through this, even strong, and that they will not abandon the peoples, who it is their duty to govern, *to the games* of factions, to error, and to its consequences, which will inevitably bring with it the destruction of society. The moment where we are setting down our thoughts on these pages, is one of these moments of crisis; this crisis is serious; it will be decided according to whoever it is who takes it in hand or who does not.

There is a rule of conduct shared by individuals and states, set down by the experience of centuries as well as that of day-to-day living; this rule reads: "one should not think about reforms in the midst of upheaval; wisdom dictates that at such times one confine one's self to keeping things together. . . .

We are not certain . . . whether society can exist *with freedom of the press*, a scourge unknown to the world before the latter half of the seventeenth century, and kept in check until the end of the eighteenth, with few exceptions but England, in a part of Europe set off from the continent by the seas, as well as by its language and by its singular customs.

DOCUMENT NO. 6

LIFE IN THE METTERNICH SYSTEM[*]

While the political and social tranquility of the Metternich era was welcome to many, it was stifling to others. The police surveillance which the regime used extensively to discourage revolutionary activity extended beyond the capital to the provincial centers of the empire, Prague among them.

γ   γ   γ

. . . .

There are, in every department among the counsellors or assessors, at least two spies, who correspond regularly with the President of the supreme Police at Vienna, or with the Emperor himself. Two months before my arrival, the most distinguished Counsellor of the Government expressed his opinion, in the sittings of this tribunal, which is headed by the Chief of the kingdom, the Supreme Burggrave, respecting a question about duties on imported produce. He availed himself of this opportunity to give a comprehensive and clear statement of the system in all its bearings, saying, that the present system was not in accordance with the state of manufactures. He was speaking this at the same time that his preferment to the supreme financial department, as Aulic Counsellor, wanted only the signature of the Emperor, after having been recommended by the financial department, and approved by the State Council. What was the astonishment of this counsellor, when, eight days afterwards, the appointment of the youngest counsellor of the government arrived from Vienna, signed by the Emperor, who wrote with his own hand that a man who looked more at the spirit of the time, than at the expressed will of his monarch, could not be a fit subject for a counsellor of the court, and that his Majesty did not want reasoners, but faithful servants. There is no aulic counsellor of the Department of Justice, who would dare to ask his colleague of the financial branch respecting the measures of his department; it would be looked upon as a temptation, or as an interference with objects in which he has not, and should not take any concern, though it may be that, in a fortnight, he is appointed to the very committee or department, of the measures of which,

[*]From Charles Sealsfield [Karl Postl] *Austria As It Is Or Sketches Of Continental Courts By An Eye-Witness* (London: Hurst, Chance and Co., 1828), pp. 81–87.

134

to inform himself beforehand, would be considered as presumptuous and dangerous. When Count O'Donnel, Minister of Finances, died, the Emperor, then at Prague, looked round for a successor, and the then Supreme Burggrave, Count Wallis, was called before him. "Count," he was accosted, "I am going to reward you for your faithful services. O'Donnel is dead, I have designated you for his successor."—"Your Majesty," replied the Count, "will most graciously condescend to consider that I am entirely ignorant in this department, as I have never paid the least attention to it."—"That is what I want; never mind, you will learn it," resumed the Emperor; "every one to his business. You were a faithful Supreme Burggrave, you will be a no less faithful Finance Minister." The consequence was, as might be expected, a bankruptcy, which, in the financial history, will be recorded as disgraceful as the battle of Ulm, which was owing to nearly the same cause. These explanations will fully account for the painful ignorance, servility, and narrowness of conception of the Austrian officers, both civil and military. Out of a thousand secretaries, counsellors, and assessors, who have run through the whole course of studies, you will not find fifty who can give you an explanation of the financial state of the Empire. Out of a thousand Austrian captains, there will not be fifty who have the least idea of tactics, except those of the artillery and engineers. These gentlemen advance colonels, generals, field-marshals, lieutenants, not by dint of military prowess or knowledge, but according to the rule of seniority; while the others, plodding on in the same way, become counsellors of the court, of the state, and the managers of the household of the Emperor. Thus, while we see poor countries like Saxony and Prussia prospering, paying off their debts, and establishing a firm national credit; their armies, with a soldiery far inferior to the Austrian in discipline and military prowess, fighting their battles successfully: the Austrian Empire with its immense resources, is impoverished, every day more and more, through the ignorance of their financial men; and, owing to the same cause, their armies are beaten and captured like so many herds of cattle, through the supine idiotism of their commanders.

There are several omens which have induced his Imperial Majesty to direct his attention not only to his officers, whom he considers less as public servants than as his own, but to the inhabitants generally. In a country where the lower classes are servile and ignorant, the feeling of honour, of course, very precarious, it requires little pains for the agents of the police to induce servants to betray their masters. For every information the former carry to the police, they obtain one or two ducats. During my stay, a merchant gave a dinner to several of his friends. The conversation turned on the new loan. Every one gave his opinion, which was unfavourable to the measure. Next day he was called before the Chief of the Police, to account for the language used at his party. The merchant pleaded his right to discuss public pecuniary affairs: but he was answered, that it was no business of his, as he was not a banker; and that a repetition of such disrepectful language would be punished with imprisonment!

The merchant returned home and instantly dismissed his servants, being convinced of their having betrayed him. He is again summoned to answer the cause of the dismissal of his servants. Again he pleads his right to do as he pleases; and the Director and Chief of the Police, an Imperial Counsellor of the Government, holding the rank of a Colonel, and a Knight of an Order, has the impudence to assure him upon his honour, that he did not get his information from the servants! It was impossible to form an adequate idea of the ramifications of this product of a bad public conscience. Every footman in a public-house is a salaried spy: there are spies paid to visit the taverns and hotels, who take their dinners at the *table d'hôte*. Others will be seen in the Imperial library for the same purpose, or in the bookseller's shop, to inquire into the purchases made by the different persons. Of course, letters sent and received by the post, if the least suspicious, are opened; and so little pains are taken to conceal this violation of public faith, that the seal of the post-office is not seldom added to that of the writer. These odious measures are not executed with that *finesse* which characterises the French, nor with the military rudeness of the Prussian, but in that silly and despicable way of the Austrian, who, as he is the most awkward personage for this most infamous of all commissions, takes, notwithstanding, a sort of pride in being an Imperial instrument and a person of importance. One characteristic feature of this Government is particularly striking: its persecution turns less against foreigners than the people who communicate with them. They and their families are exposed to every sort of chicanery; and for this reason, it is almost impossible to associate, if we except noblemen, with the better classes, all of them dreading the crafty severity of their suspicious Government.

Without introduction into the circles of the nobility, it would be, indeed, impossible for a man of even the most moderate pretensions, to stay in this city for a week, every enjoyment being poisoned by the baneful influence of the secret police. The middle class of its inhabitants are a sober, well-informed, and respectable set, far above the sensuality of the Viennese; though the Government does not allow even those scanty means of public information which the latter possess. In Prague there is but one, and this the poorest newspaper imaginable, under the immediate control of the Supreme Burggrave. Another public paper in the Bohemian language had hardly made its appearance with the consent of the Government, when it was suppressed by an order from Vienna. . . .

DOCUMENT NO. 7

A CZECH INTELLECTUAL DEFINES HIS RELATIONSHIP TO THE HABSBURG EMPIRE*

Frantisek Palacky, both a historian and a leader of the Czech national movement, was invited by German nationalists to appear at the Frankfurt Assembly in 1848 as a delegate from the kingdom of Bohemia. His letter of refusal, dated 11 April, 1848, constituted a justification for the existence of the Habsburg empire in central and east central Europe which continued to figure in the thinking of its subjects through the First World War.

γ   γ   γ

This nation (Czech) is small, it is true, but from time immemorial it has existed independently with its own identity; for ages its rulers were part of the federation of German princes; however, the nation itself never counted itself as the German nation nor, throughout the centuries, did others see it that way. The entire connection of the Czech lands, first with the Holy Roman Empire, then with the German Confederation, was always purely dynastic, which the Czech nation, the Czech estates, hardly had anything to do with, without itself taking any interest in it. . . . And were anyone to declare it to be received truth that the Czech crown was a vassal to the German Empire (something Czech publicists have shied away from for ages), no Germans have any real basis to conclude that [they have] . . . any political and legal sovereignty in the Czech lands. The entire world knows that the German emperors, whose dignities have already been mentioned, had very little throughout the centuries to do with the Czech nation, that they had no legal, political, or executive competence within Bohemia nor over the Czechs; that none of them had the right to raise an army from the land, nor any *regalia*, that the Czech land, together with its crownlands did not count among any of the one-time ten German circles, that summons to the imperial court did not refer to them, etc. that therefore the entire connection between the Czech lands and the German Empire up to now must be thought about and considered, not as the bond of one nation to another, but as one sovereign to another.

*From Frantisek Palacky, *Politicke Myslenky*, (Prague: J. Otto, n.d.): 44–46. Trans. Paula Sutter Fichtner.

Certainly, if the Austrian state were not already in existence from long ago, it would have been in the interest of Europe, indeed of humanity itself, to begin work as soon as possible to create it. For what reason have we seen this state (Austria) that has been summoned by nature and history, be placed as the guardian of Europe before all sorts of Asiatic elements—for what reason do we see it in a critical moment powerless and almost without council before the face of the crush of the oncoming storm? Because in the lamentable blindness of long duration, it has not recognized the real legal and moral basis of its existence and has denied it: that is, the fundamental precept that all the nations unified under its scepter and all religious faiths together enjoy equal rights and nurturing. I am persuaded that even now it is still not too late for the Austrian empire to proclaim this basic principle of justice, this sacred anchor for a vessel in danger of capsizing, to state it clearly and sincerely and together, to put it into operation vigorously: but every moment counts, for God's sake, let us not delay yet another hour.

Should I train my sight beyond the Czech border, natural and historical reasons propel me to turn, not to Frankfurt, but to Vienna, there to seek out a center which is fitted and called to assuring and protecting the peace, liberty, and right of my nation.

Whoever orders, that Austria (and together with it the Czechs) attach itself nationally to the German empire, is asking of it to commit suicide, something which has neither moral nor political purpose.

DOCUMENT NO. 8

HUNGARY CALLS FOR INDEPENDENCE[*]

Led by Louis Kossuth, the Hungarian estates moved from demands for greater autonomy toward outright independence in the revolutionary years 1848–1849. The following declaration was issued in Debreczen, a traditional Calvinist center in the eastern part of the kingdom on April 14, 1849.

γ   γ   γ

"We, the legally constituted representatives of the Hungarian nation assembled in the Diet, do by these presents solemnly proclaim and maintain the inalienable natural rights of Hungary with all its dependencies, to occupy the position of an independent European State—that the House of Hapsburg Lorraine, as perjured in the sight of God and man, has forfeited its right to the Hungarian throne. At the same time, we feel ourselves bound in duty to make known the motives and reasons which have impelled us to this decision, that the civilized world may learn we have taken this step, not out of overweening confidence in our own wisdom, or out of revolutionary excitement, but that it is an act of the last necessity, adopted to preserve from destruction a nation persecuted to the limits of the most enduring patience.

"Three hundred years have passed since the Hungarian nation, by free election, placed the House of Austria upon its throne, in accordance with stipulations made on both sides, and ratified by treaty. These three hundred years have been a period of uninterrupted suffering for the country.

"The Creator has blessed this land with all the elements of wealth and happiness. Its area of 100,000 square miles presents, in varied profusion, innumerable sources of prosperity. Its population numbering nearly fifteen millions feels the glow of youthful strength within its veins, and has shewn temper and docility which guarantee its proving at once the mainspring of civilization in Eastern Europe, and the guardian of that civilization when attacked. Never was a more grateful task appointed to a reigning dynasty by the dispensation of Divine Providence, than that which devolved upon the House of Hapsburg Lorraine.

[*] E.O.S., *Hungary and Its Revolutions From the Earliest Period to the Nineteenth Century* (London: George Bell and Sons, 1896), pp. 431–43.

If nothing had been done to impede the development of the country, Hungary would now rank amongst the most prosperous of nations. It was only necessary to refrain from curtailing the moderate share of Constitutional liberty which the Hungarians united with rare fidelity to their Sovereigns, and cautiously maintained through the troubles of a thousand years, and the House of Hapsburg might long have counted this nation amongst the most faithful adherents to the throne.

"But this Dynasty, which cannot point to a single ruler who has based his power on the freedom of the people, adopted, from generation to generation a course towards this nation which meets the name of perjury. . . .

"Confiding in the justice of an eternal God, we in the face of the civilized world, in reliance upon the natural rights of the Hungarian nation and upon the power it has developed to maintain them, further impelled by that sense of duty which urges every nation to defend its own existence, do hereby declare and proclaim in the name of the nation, lawfully represented by us, as follows:—

"1st. Hungary with Transylvania, as by law united, with its dependencies, are hereby declared to constitute a free independent Sovereign state. The territorial unity of this State is declared to be inviolable, and its territory to be indivisible.

"2nd. The House of Hapsburg-Lorraine, having by treachery, perjury, and levying war against the Hungarian nation, as well as by its outrageous violation of all compacts, in breaking up the integral territory of the kingdom, in the separation of Transylvania, Croatia, Sclavonia, Fiume, and its districts from Hungary; further, by compassing the destruction of the independence of the country by arms, and by calling in the disciplined army of a foreign power for the purpose of annihilating its nationality, by violation both of the Pragmatic Sanction, and of treaties concluded between Austria and Hungary on which the alliance between the two countries depended,—is, as treacherous and perjured, for ever excluded from the throne of the United States of Hungary and Transylvania, and all their possessions and dependencies, and is hereby deprived of the style and title, as well as of the armorial bearings belonging to the Crown of Hungary, and declared to be banished for ever from the united countries, and their dependencies and possessions. They are therefore declared to be deposed, degraded, and banished for ever from the Hungarian territory.

"3rd. The Hungarian nation, in the exercise of its rights and sovereign will, being determined to assume the position of a free and independent State amongst the nations of Europe, declares it be its intention to establish and maintain friendly and neighbourly relations with those States with which it was formerly united under the same Sovereign, as well as to contract alliances with all other nations.

"4th. The form of government to be adopted in future will be fixed by the Diet of the nation. . . .

"And this resolution of ours we shall proclaim and make known to all the nations of the civilized world, with the conviction, that the Hungarian nation will be received by them amongst free and independent nations, with the same friendship and free acknowledgement of its rights, which the Hungarians proffer to other countries. . . .

DOCUMENT NO. 9

EDUCATING A MULTICULTURAL POPULATION IN THE NINETEENTH CENTURY[*]

One of the most difficult challenges that the Habsburg empire faced was that of accommodating the various confessional and linguistic demands of its population in the school system. Among the most ethnically and religiously diverse of the Habsburg lands was the Bukovina, now divided between southern Ukraine and Romania. Suczawa is now Suceava in Romania.

γ   γ   γ

I. Organization of Instruction

A. Summary of the Professors and of the Subjects Taught by Each

Dr Josef Marek, secular priest
    Provisional Director of the Secondary School, member of the Historical-Statistical Section of the Imperial-Royal Moravian Silesian Agricultural Society in Brünn, Honorary Curator of the General Welfare Institute allied with the Austrian Savings Bank in Vienna
    Subject taught: Latin (Class III)
    Hours per week: 6

August Klimpfinger, secular priest
    Subjects taught: Latin (Class II), Greek (Class III), German (Classes II, III)
    Hours per week: 19
    Master of Class II

Dr Blasius Knauer, secular priest
    Member of the Zoological-Botanical Society in Vienna
    Subjects taught: Mathematics (Classes I, II, III, IV), Natural History (Classes I, II, III), Physics (Class IV)
    Hours per week: 21
    Master of Class III

[*]*Programm des k.k. gr. u. unirten Gymnasiums in Suczawa für das Schuljahr 1862.* (Czernowitz: Eckhardt, 1862): 31–32, 40. Trans. Edward G. Fichtner.

Josef Rohrmoser, secular priest
  Subjects taught: Geography (Class I), German (Classes I, IV), History (Classes II, III, IV)
    Hours per week: 18
    Master of Class IV

Brother Otto Novotny, secular priest
    Subjects taught: Latin (Classes I, IV), Greek (Class IV)
    Hours per week: 18
    Master of Class I

Konstantin Andriewicz, secular priest of the Bukovina Diocese
    Subjects taught: Greek Uniate religion (Classes I, II, III, IV), Romanian (Classes I, II, III, IV)
    Hours per week: 20

Brother Martin Stieber, Vice-Canon and Pastor in Suczawa
    Regular Member of the Association for Knowledge and Culture of Bukovina
    Subjects taught: Roman, Greek, and Armenian Catholic religion (Classes I, II, III, IV)
    Hours per week: 8

B. Adjunct faculty

Anton Wallentin
    Organist of the Catholic parish church
    Subject taught: vocal music
    Hours per week: 2

Isaac Unterberg, private teacher
    Subject taught: Mosaic religion
    Hours per week: 2

VI. Summary Table
of the number of pupils at the
Imperial-Royal Greek Uniate Secondary School at Suczawa
in the school year 1862

| | Class | | | |
	I	II	III	IV
Number of pupils				
at the beginning of the school year				
public	48	56	22	21
private	2	-	-	-
total	50	56	22	21
at the end of the school year				
public	42	53	22	21
private	1	-	-	-
total	43	53	22	21
Of these, the following number				
had been promoted	-	47	20	15
were repeating a class	4	2	2	6
had transferred from other schools	39	6	5	21
had been exempted from tuition fees	14	25	8	14
paid tuition fees	29	28	14	7
held scholarships	-	4	2	2
Classification by religion				
Greek Uniate	25	21	17	15
Roman Catholic	11	27	4	3
Greek Catholic	-	-	-	1
Armenian Catholic	1	-	-	-
Armenian Oriental	1	2	1	-
Israelite	5	3	-	2
Classification by language				
German	12	18	3	2
Romanian	24	19	13	14
Polish	6	14	2	4
Ruthenian	1	2	4	1
Classification by pupil status				
withdrawn	7	3	1	-
not examined	-	-	3	-

	Class			
	I	II	III	IV
diplomas awarded				
First Class with Distinction	8	8	5	4
First Class	24	34	11	14
Second Class	6	8	2	–
permission to repeat examinaton	4	3	–	3

DOCUMENT NO. 10

HUNGARIAN NATIONALISM
SEEKS FOREIGN SUPPORT*

In exile for the rest of his life following his flight from Hungary, Louis Kossuth continued to advise the remnants of the revolutionary and constitutional movement in his native land and to look for support from the liberal states of Europe and North America. His appeals such as the one below delivered upon his arrival in Southampton, England on Oct. 23, 1851, were largely unproductive. Nevertheless, they show clearly the relationship between nineteenth century liberalism and nationalism.

γ   γ   γ

. . .

"It is indeed an honor to be welcomed by the people of England in this noble town. It is the highest gratification to me that it was the municipality of the first town I had the honor to meet, which receives me in such a generous manner. It is not on this day only, but from my early youth, that this glorious country had a mighty share in my destiny. I was used to look on England as on the Book of Life, which had to teach me and the nations of Europe how to live. Through three centuries the house of Austria has exhausted against Hungary the arts of open violence and secret intrigue, and it was our municipal institutions which still, among the most arduous circumstances, conserved to Hungary some spirit of public life and some part of constitutional liberty. It was at the time when this fatal sickness of political feeling to centralize every power and to tutor the people into this notion of political wisdom—when this fatal sickness, I say, spread over the continent, and made its way even to my own country, so that it became almost the fashion, and almost a mark of intelligence to bend towards the doctrine of centralization, that I, my humble self, with a few friends who stood by me, struggled against this storm—against those rushing waves coming over the spirit of Europe, because I regarded, and I ever shall regard, municipal public life as a public benefit, without which there is no prac-

---

*P. C. Headley, *The Life of Louis Kossuth* (Auburn, N.Y.: Derby and Miller, 1852), pp. 236–239.

tical freedom whatever, and for the loss of which I think all Ministerial responsibilities and Parliamentary privilege but a pitiful equivalent.

"In this land is seen the finest fruits of this conquest of liberty; the glory outside, the freedom within, unwithered by the blighting finger of centralization. When I first read the French constitution I foretold that great and glorious French nation should have to go through many storms, because it did not abandon its fatal principle of centralization; and because it is only in municipal institutions freedom can be developed. That is my conviction. Sir, I hope England will be forever 'great, glorious, and free;' but when I look to history, and see what is this land and the English race, the only single one which is free in both hemispheres of the world, and when I look for the key of this freedom, I readily confess I believe that it is not only those municipal institutions, which are not absorbed by the propensity to centralization, which so conserved that freedom though under different forms of government,— here in England, under a monarchical form, in America under a republican form,—that it was not those institutions only, but the spirit of the people embodied in those institutions, which made these two great offsprings of a mighty race great, glorious, and free. Therefore it is with the highest satisfaction I receive this address from your hands, and from the corporation of Southampton. As to my own humble self, conscious of no merit, and never aspiring to whatever reputation, but to that of a plain honest man, faithful to the duty of a true friend of freedom and of a patriot, I could not forbear to feel perplexed to see myself the object of such undeserved honors, were I not aware that this manifestation is intended rather openly to countenance that principle of freedom, of justice, of popular rights, for which my nation has valiantly struggled, and which you so happily enjoy.

"It is a glorious position the English race holds—almost the only one that is free—it is the only one, the freedom of which has neither to fear the changes of time nor the ambition of man, provided it keeps to its institutions, provided that the public spirit of the people continues to safeguard that which is best for the exigencies of the time, and that their manly resolution never fails to meet those exigencies in time. This watchfulness and resolution being the chief guaranty of your country's greatness and happiness, I take for the most consoling hope to oppressed humanity; for I have the most firm conviction that the freedom and greatness of England are in intimate connection with the destinies and liberty of Europe.

"It is not without reason that my native land, and all oppressed nations look up to you, as to the elder brother to whom the Almighty has not in vain imparted the spirit to guide the tide of human destiny. There is one thing that is a prominent feature in your race,—a result of no small importance in our struggles,—that the sentiments of this race are spreading over the world, and that it is not the least of the glories you call your own, that the people of England appear to be resolved to take the lead in the new direction of the public opinion of the world, out of which the highest blessings will flow. The generous sympathy of the people of England for my bleeding, struggling, down-trodden, but not broken, native land, is one, but not the only one manifestation, by which England shows she is ready to accept this glorious *rôle* of the elder brother of humanity.

"This country, though it has not to fear any direct attack on its own liberty, still knows that its welfare and prosperity, founded as they are on the continued development of your genius and industry, cannot be entirely independent of the condition of other nations. The people of England know that in neither social nor political respects can it be indifferent whether Europe be free or groaning under Russia and her satellites; the people of England are conscious of their glorious position—it knows that, while it conserves its freedom, it cannot grant the privilege to Russo-Austrian despots to dispose of the fate of Europe, but must have its weight in the balance of the destinies of Europe, or England would no more be an European Power. And it is this knowledge which is the source of hope and consolation to my oppressed country, as well as to all the fellow-nations of Europe, for by the principle on which your freedom continues, and on which your happiness is founded, and by your generous sentiments, we are assured that let the people of England once throw their weight into the balance of the fate of Europe, then they will never assist despotism, but freedom; not injustice, but right; not the ambition of a few families, but the moral welfare and dignity of humanity.

"Such were my expectations of the public spirit of Britannia, which you, by your generous address, have raised to the level of conviction by assuring me you have the belief and hope that those principles for which we have struggled have a future in my own native land. Seeing you to entertain this hope and belief is almost like a victory itself, because this manifestation cannot fail to influence in the most effectual manner the public spirit of my nation, and to double her perseverance and my own in her cause. And, besides the prophecy of freedom is almost realized, for when the people foretell it, you have the self-confident power to make good your own words.

"I hope the Almighty will grant, before I leave this country and cross the ocean, and go the young giant, the younger brother of your mighty race, and thank him for the generous protection bestowed on me, and entreat his brotherly hand for the future of Europe and of my own country, that I shall see established in full activity and spread over these glorious isles, some of those mighty associations by which you carry the triumph of every great reform and of every great principle in your constitution. I hope to see some of those associations lending its attention to the solidarity of the independence of Hungary, with the hope that the peace of Europe and the future of these glorious isles will take for its aim to give a practical direction to the sympathy of the people for my poor down-trodden country—that the people of England will look upon my unhappy land, and that they will reduce to a ruling principle that sentiment of the public spirit of Britannia which evidently shows itself to be ready to accept the solidarity of the destiny of mankind, and especially of the liberty of Europe itself. . . .

DOCUMENT NO. 11

SHARING POLITICAL RESPONSIBILITY IN AUSTRIA-HUNGARY AFTER 1867[*]

During 1867 and 1868 both the Austrian and Hungarian parts of the Habsburg monarchy adopted constitutions to conform to the new configuration of the monarchy. Both instruments stated the affairs which were considered common.

γ   γ   γ

ARTICLE 1. The following affairs are declared common to Austria and Hungary:

a. Foreign affairs, including diplomatic and commercial representation abroad, as well as measures relating to international treaties, reserving the right of the representative bodies of both parts of the Empire (Reichsrat and Hungarian Diet) to approve such treaties, in so far as such approval is required by the Constitution.

b. Military and naval affairs; excluding the voting of contingents and legislation concerning the manner of performing military service, the provisions relative to the local disposition and maintenance of the army, the civil relations of persons belonging to the army, and their rights and duties in matters not pertaining to the military service.

c. The finances, with reference to matters of common expense, especially the establishment of the budget and the examination of accounts.

ART. 2. Besides these, the following affairs shall not indeed be administered in common, but shall be regulated upon uniform principles to be agreed upon from time to time:

1. Commercial affairs, especially customs legislation.

2. Legislation concerning indirect taxes which stand in close relation to industrial production.

3. The establishment of a monetary system and monetary standards.

4. Regulations concerning railway lines which affect the interests of both parts of the empire.

5. The establishment of a system of defense.

ART 3. The expenses of affairs common to both Austria and Hungary

[*] Wright, *Constitutions*, pp. 4–9.

shall be borne by the two parts of the Empire in a proportion to be fixed from time to time by an agreement between the two legislative bodies (Reichsrat and Diet), approved by the Emperor. If an agreement can not be reached between the two representative bodies, the proportion shall be fixed by the Emperor, but for the term of one year only. The method of defraying its quota of the common expense shall belong exclusively to each of the parts of the Empire.

Nevertheless, joint loans may be made for affairs of common interest; in such a case all that relates to the negotiation of the loan, as well as the method of employing and repaying it, shall be determined in common.

The decision as to whether a joint loan shall be made is reserved for legislation by each of the two parts of the Empire.

ART. 4. The contribution towards the expense of the present public debt shall be determined by an agreement between the two parts of the Empire.

ART. 5. The administration of common affairs shall be conducted by a joint responsible ministry, which is forbidden to direct at the same time the administration of the joint affairs and those of either part of the Empire.

The regulation of the management, conduct, and internal organization of the joint army shall belong exclusively to the Emperor.

ART. 6. The legislative power belonging to the legislative bodies of each of the two parts of the Empire (Reichsrat and Hungarian Diet) shall be exercised by them, in so far as it relates to joint affairs, by means of delegations. . . .

ART. 11. The delegations shall be convened annually by the Emperor, who shall determine the place of their meeting.

ART. 12. The delegation from the Reichsrat shall elect a president and vice president from among its own members, and choose also its secretary and other officers.

ART. 13. The powers of the delegations shall extend to all matters concerning common affairs.

All other matters shall be beyond their power.

ART. 14. The projects of the government shall be submitted by the joint ministry to each of the delegations separately.

Each delegation shall also have the right to submit projects concerning affairs which are within its competence.

ART. 15. For the passage of a law concerning matters within the power of the delegations the agreement of both delegations shall be necessary, or in default of such agreement, a vote of the full assembly of the two delegations sitting together; in either case the approval of the Emperor shall be necessary.

. . .

ART. 30. Each delegation shall communicate to the other its decisions and, if the case requires it, the reasons therefor.

This communication shall take place in writing, in German on the part of the delegation of the Reichsrat, in the Hungarian language on the part of the delegation of the Diet; in each case there shall be annexed a certified translation into the language of the other delegation.

ART. 31. Each delegation shall have the right to propose that a question be decided by a vote in joint session, and this proposal can not be declined by the other delegation after the exchange of three written communications without result.

The two presidents shall agree upon the time and place of the joint meeting of the two delegations for the purpose of voting together.

ART. 32. In the joint sessions the presidents of the delegations shall preside alternately. It shall be determined by lot which of the two presidents shall preside in the first place.

In all subsequent sessions the presidency at the first joint meeting shall belong to the president of the delegation which has not had the presidency at the meeting immediately preceding.

ART. 33. In order to transact business in joint session the presence of not less than two thirds of the members of each delegation shall be necessary.

Decisions shall be reached by a majority vote.

If one delegation has more members present than the other, so many members shall abstain from voting as shall be necessary to establish an equality of the number of voters from each delegation.

It shall be determined by lot which members shall abstain from voting.

ART. 34. The joint sessions of the two delegations shall be public.

The minutes shall be kept in the two languages by the secretaries of the two delegations and attested by both.

ART. 35. Further details regarding the procedure of the delegation of the Reichsrat shall be regulated by an order of business to be adopted by the delegation itself.

. . .

DOCUMENT NO. 12

THE AUSTRIAN CONSTITUTION[*]

While the position of the emperor remained central to the operation of the constitution in the Austrian part of the Dual Monarchy, it contained many features that liberalized the political, social, and economic life of the peoples who lived there. The following excerpt incorporates some of the changes made to the original after 1867, including the laws governing elections.

γ   γ   γ

ARTICLE 1. For all natives of the various kingdoms and countries represented in the Reichsrat there exists a common right of Austrian citizenship. The law shall determine under what conditions Austrian citizenship is gained, exercised and lost.

ART. 2. All citizens are equal before the law.

ART. 3. Public offices shall be equally open to all citizens. The admission of foreigners to public office is dependent upon their acquisition of Austrian citizenship.

ART. 4. The freedom of passage of persons and property, within the territory of the State, shall be subject to no restrictions.

All citizens who live within a commune and pay therein a tax on real property, business, or income shall have the right to vote for members of the communal assembly (*Gemeindevertretung*) and shall be elgible to that body under the same conditions as natives of the commune.

Freedom of emigration is limited by the State only by the obligation to serve in the army.

Taxes on emigration shall be levied only as a measure of retaliation.

ART. 5. Property is inviolable. Forced expropriation shall take place only in the cases and according to the forms determined by law.

ART. 6. Every citizen may dwell temporarily or establish his residence in any part of the territory of the State, acquire real property of any kind and freely dispose of the same, and may also engage in any form of business, under legal conditions.

In the matter of mortmain the law may, for reasons of public policy, restrict the right of acquiring and of disposing of real property.

ART. 7. Every relation of vassalage or dependence is forever abol-

[*]Wright, *Constitutions*, pp. 11–19.

ished. Every burden or charge resting upon the title to real property is redeemable, and in future no land shall be burdened with an irredeemable charge.

Art. 8. Liberty of person is guaranteed. . . .

Every arrest ordered or prolonged in violation of law imposes an obligation upon the State to indemnify the injured party.

Art. 9. The domicile is inviolable. . . .

Art. 10. The secrecy of letters shall not be violated; the seizure of letters, except in case of a legal arrest or search, shall take place only in time of war or by virtue of a judicial order issued in conformity with the law.

Art. 11. The right of petition is free to everyone. Petitions under a collective name should emanate only from legally recognized corporations or associations.

Art. 12. Austrian citizens shall have the right to assemble together and to form associations. The exercise of these rights is regulated by special laws.

Art. 13. Everyone shall have the right, within legal limits, freely to express his thoughts orally, in writing, through the press, or by pictorial representation.

The press shall not be placed under censorship nor restrained by the system of licenses. Administrative prohibitions of the use of the mail are not applicable to matter printed within the country.

Art. 14. Full freedom of religion and of conscience is guaranteed to all. The enjoyment of civil and political rights is independent of religious belief; however, religious belief shall in no way interfere with the performance of civil duties.

No one shall be forced to perform any religious rite or to participate in any religious ceremony, except in so far as he is subject to another who has legal authority in this matter.

Art. 15. Every legally recognized church and religious society has the right publicly to exercise its religious worship; it regulates and administers its internal affairs independently, remains in possession and enjoyment of its establishments, institutions and property held for religious, educational and charitable purposes; but is subject, as other societies, to the general laws of the State.

Art. 16. Adherents of a religious confession not legally recognized are permitted to worship privately, in so far as their religious services are not illegal or contrary to public morals.

ART. 17. Science and its teaching shall be free. Every citizen whose capacity has been established in conformity with law shall have the right to establish institutions of instruction and education and to give instruction therein. Private instruction shall be subject to no such restriction. Religious instruction in the schools shall be left to the church or religious society to which the school is attached. The State shall have the right of superior direction and superintendence over the entire system of education and instruction.

ART. 18. Everyone shall be free to choose his occupation and to prepare himself for it in such place and in such manner as he may wish.

ART. 19. All the races of the State shall have equal rights, and each race shall have the inviolable right of maintaining and cultivating its nationality and language.

The State recognizes the equality of the various languages in the schools, public offices, and in public life.

In the countries populated by several races, the institutions of public instruction shall be so organized that each race may receive the necessary instruction in its own language, without being obliged to learn a second language.

ART. 20. A special law shall determine the right of the responsible governing power to suspend temporarily and in certain places the rights mentioned in Articles 8, 9, 10, 12 and 13.

LAW ALTERING THE LAW OF 26 FEBRUARY 1861
CONCERNING IMPERIAL REPRESENTATION. . . .

ART. 7. Every male person who has attained the age of 24 years, possesses Austrian citizenship, is not excluded from the right to vote by the provisions of the election law of the Reichsrat, and who at the time the election is ordered has resided for at least one year in the Austrian commune in which the right to vote is to be exercised, is qualified to vote for representatives.

Every male person who has been in the possession of Austrian citizenship for at least three years, has attained the age of 30 years, and is not excluded from the right to vote by the provisions of the election law of the Reichsrat, is eligible as a representative. . . .

ART. 14. If urgent circumstances should render necessary some measure constitutionally requiring the consent of the Reichsrat when that body is not in session, such measure may be taken by imperial ordinance, issued under the collective responsibility of the ministry, provided it makes no alteration of the fundamental law, imposes no lasting burden upon the public treasury, and alienates none of the domain of the State. Such ordinances shall have provisionally the force of law, if they are signed by all of the ministers, and shall be published with an express reference to this provision of the fundamental law.

The legal force of such an ordinance shall cease, if the government neglects to present it for the approval of the Reichsrat at its next succeeding session, and indeed first to the House of Representatives, within four weeks after its convention, or if one of the two houses refuses its approval thereto.

The ministry shall be collectively responsible for the withdrawal of such ordinances as soon as they have lost their provisional legal force.
. . .

ART. 19. The adjournment of the Reichsrat or the dissolution of the House of Representatives shall take place by decree of the Emperor. In case of dissolution a new election shall be held in conformity with Article 7.

ART. 20. Ministers and chiefs of the central administration are entitled to take part in all deliberations and to present their proposals personally or through representatives. Each house may require the presence of a minister. Ministers shall be heard whenever they desire. They shall have the right to vote only when they are members of one of the houses.

ART. 21. Each of the two houses of the Reichsrat may interpellate the ministers upon all the matters within the scope of their powers, may investigate the administrative acts of the Government, demand information from the ministers concerning petitions presented to the houses, may appoint commissions, to which the ministers shall give all necessary information, and may give expression to its views in the form of addresses or resolutions.

Law Concerning the Exercise of Administrative and Executive Power.

ARTICLE 1. The Emperor is sacred, inviolable, and irresponsible.

ART. 2. The Emperor shall exercise governmental power through responsible ministers and officers and agents subordinate to them.

ART. 3. The Emperor shall appoint and dismiss ministers and, upon the proposal of the respective ministers, appoint all officers in all branches of the public service, in so far as the law does not otherwise provide.

Art. 4. The Emperor shall confer titles, orders and other public distinctions.

Art. 5. The Emperor shall have supreme command of the armed force, shall declare war and conclude peace.

Art. 6. The Emperor shall conclude political treaties. The consent of the Reichsrat is necessary for the validity of any treaties of commerce or political treaties which impose obligations upon the Empire, upon any part thereof, or upon any of its citizens.

Art. 7. The right to coin money shall be exercised in the name of the Emperor.

Art. 8. Before assuming the government the Emperor shall take a solemn oath in the presence of both houses of the Reichsrat:

To maintain inviolable the fundamental laws of the kingdoms and countries represented in the Reichsrat, and to govern in conformity with them, and in conformity with the laws in general.

Art. 9. The ministers shall be responsible for the constitutionality and legality of governmental acts done within the sphere of their powers.

This responsibility, the organization of a court to try impeachments of ministers, and the procedure to be observed in such a court shall be regulated by a special law.

Art. 10. The publication of the laws shall take place in the name of the Emperor, with a note of their passage by the representative bodies in the constitutional manner and under the signature of a responsible minister.

. . .

DOCUMENT NO. 13

VOTING IN HUNGARY *

Written in the interests of a narrow electorate drawn chiefly from the Magyar nobility and upper middle classes, the Hungarian constitution was constructed to preserve not only traditional Hungarian freedoms but the political, social, and economic influence of these classes as well. The basis of their power was a restrictive election law.

γ   γ   γ

ON THE MODIFICATION AND AMENDMENT OF
LAW 5 OF 1848. . . .

CHAPTER I.—QUALIFICATIONS OF VOTERS.

ARTICLE 1. With the exception of females, the right to vote in the election of representatives may be exercised by all native or naturalized citizens who have attained the age of 20 years and who possess the qualifications mentioned in Articles 1 and 2 of Law 5 of 1848 and in Articles 3 and 4 of the Transylvanian Law 2 of 1848 and more particularly specified in the subsequent articles. . . .

ART. 3. In the royal free cities and in cities with an organized administration the right to vote shall belong to those who possess alone or jointly with their wives and minor children:

a. A house which, even if temporarily exempt from taxation, consists of at least three different parts, subject to the household tax; or

b. Land which is assessed on the basis of a net income of 16 florins.

ART. 4. In those sections of the country in which Law 5 of 1848 is effective, the right to vote shall belong to those who in the larger or smaller communes possess one fourth of an urbarial share or other land of an equal area either alone or jointly with their wives and minor children, it being immaterial in whose name this property is registered.

Lands upon which the tax imposed is equal to that of the most lightly taxed one-fourth urbarial share in the same commune shall be regarded as equal in size to one fourth of an urbarial share.

In case the urbarial system does not exist in a given commune, the

*Wright, *Constitutions*, pp. 34–37.

most lightly taxed one-fourth urbarial share of any neighboring commune resembling the given commune most nearly in land values shall be taken as the standard. . . .

Bottom land, gardens, vineyards, arable land and meadows shall be regarded as cultivated ground.

ART. 5. In those parts of the country in which the Transylvanian Law 2 of 1848 is in force, the right to vote may be exercised by those who in the larger or smaller communes:

a. Pay land taxes according to the present land-tax valuation on a net income of 84 florins, but if they own a house belonging in the first class of taxable property, on an income of 79 florins, 80 kreuzer, and if the house be rated in the second or a higher class, on an income of 72 florins, 80 kreuzer.

ART. 6. The right to vote shall belong also to those:

a. Who possess a house, either alone or jointly with their wives and minor children, in the manner provided by Article 4, upon which the house tax has been assessed on an annual income of not less than 105 florins.

b. Who pay the public-land tax mentioned under *a*, or a tax on capital or on both land and capital, upon a net annual income of not less than 105 florins.

c. Who as merchants or manufacturers are taxed upon an annual income of not less than 105 florins.

d. Who in the royal free cities or in cities with an organized administration are taxed as artisans upon an annual income of not less than 105 florins.

e. Who in the larger or smaller communes pay the income tax for not less than one employee.

ART. 7. The right to vote shall belong also to those who pay the income tax on an annual income of not less than 105 florins, which, according to Law 26 of 1868, is rated in the first class; or who pay this tax on an annual income of not less than 700 florins under the provisions of the second class; moreover, those State, municipal, and communal officers may vote who pay the income tax on an annual income of not less than 500 florins under the provisions of the second class.

Art. 8. In cases covered by Articles 6 and 7, it is required that electors, to be entered on the voting lists in accordance with the provisions there mentioned, must have already been taxed in the preceding year upon an income not less than that fixed above.

Art. 9. Without regard to income, the following may vote in the electoral districts in which they have their fixed residence: The members of the Hungarian Academy of Sciences, professors, members of academies of fine arts, physicians, lawyers, notaries public, engineers, surgeons, druggists, graduates of agricultural schools, foresters and mining engineers, clergymen, chaplains, communal notaries, teachers and licensed kindergarten teachers.

It is required, however, that pastors and chaplains in order to exercise the right to vote shall actively officiate as such in some officially established congregation.

Professors, school teachers, kindergarten teachers and communal notaries, on the other hand, shall have the right to vote only in case they have been legally appointed or elected to their position or have been confirmed therein.

Art. 10. Persons under paternal authority, under guardianship, or under employers' authority, even though they possess one of the qualifications mentioned in the preceding section, shall not have the right to vote.

The apprentices of merchants and artisans and those employed in public or private service as servants or domestics shall be regarded as being under employers' authority.

Overseers of estates are not regarded as under such authority. . . .

Art. 13. Every elector who has reached his twenty-fourth year shall be eligible as a representative, provided he is registered in the list of voters and is qualified in the Hungarian language, which in accordance with law is the legislative language. . . .

In case of the correction of the present valuation or of the adoption of a new valuation, the above-mentioned amounts of income shall be changed to agree with the change in ratio between the present assessments of apparent total net income from land in the Transylvanian districts and those of the altered valuation.

b. Or pay the public tax on a net annual income of not less than 105 florins, subject either to the land or house tax, or to the income tax of the first or third class.

In addition to those qualified in accordance with Law 12 of 1791, every commune which has at least 100 homesteads may also take part in the election of representatives through two informally chosen electors, smaller communes, however, having one elector.

DOCUMENT NO. 14

ECONOMIC RIVALRY IN THE DUAL MONARCHY[*]

Economic differences in the empire were even more problematic where national antagonisms reinforced them. The following article, heavily censored, appeared in a German-Liberal newspaper in Sarajevo. The "Kmet" mentioned in the body of the article was the Bosnian serf-peasant. Called by some historians the most exploited agricultural worker of the Habsburg empire, he held a hereditary lease from a landlord to whom he owed one-third of his earnings.

γ γ γ

What is incompatibility? Incompatibility is, when the president of a Croatian nationalist organization, the "Croatian National Union" becomes the director of the Hungarian Agrarian Bank for Bosnia.

Dr. Nicholas Mandic finds himself as a politician in an extremely delicate situation. In his innermost self a schism must have arisen with regard to the ideal and material conception of a political profession. It cannot be otherwise. How else could our beloved Croatian leader in Bosnia, filled with high-minded national principles, have changed what was up to now his political credo for the sake of a banking establishment. We do not want to impute a change of heart to the honorable and straightforward bearing of Dr. Mandic. However, remembering his many fine speeches, both public and in private circles, his friends have been taken aback by his entry into the Hungarian bank. Throughout Sarajevo in general yesterday, his new position as the director and legal consultant of the Agrarian Bank was the subject of the widest variety of comments. It would be a mistake and inappropriate to pass judgment on Dr. Mandic, without a thorough and objective evaluation of the motives which led him to this sensational step.

In order to do this, we must understand two notions clearly. First of all, what are the purposes of the "Croatian National Union?" Secondly, what goals is the Hungarian Agrarian Bank trying to realize in Bosnia and Herzegovina?

Before the annexation, the "Croatian National Union" was the lone

[*]*Sarajevoer Tagblatt*, vol. 2, no. 17 (22 January 1909): 1–3. Trans. Paula Sutter Fichtner.

cultural and economic organization of the Croats in Bosnia and Herzegovina to defend and maintain the sacred national patrimony received
from their forefathers. Following the annexation, the committees of the
"Croatian National Union" declared themselves to be the political representatives of the local autochthonous population as well. Dr. Mandic
has often said that the aim of Croatian politics is the union of Bosnia
and Herzegovina with the Croatian mother kingdom. For this reason,
the Croatians in Bosnia long to bring about amalgamation with the
Habsburg monarchy. Trialism under the Habsburg scepter is the political ideal of every genuine Croat.

The concept of "Trialism," the creation of a new basis of the
Habsburg Empire, is naturally unacceptable to representatives of the
Hungarian state idea. Hungary does not recognize the kingdom of
Croatia as an independent political entity which is tied to it only
through a personal union. Legally there is much disagreement about
this. However that may be—we want to discuss this only on an academic
basis—one can understand Hungarian efforts to obstruct the future realization of Trialism through exploitation of its current political hegemony in the lands of the Holy Crown of St. Stephen. To this end the Hungarian regime has now for a long time used tactics to guard against the
separation of Croatia from the concept of the Hungarian state.

The annexation changed the whole picture in one fell swoop. And
when Wekerle [Austro-Hungarian finance minister—Editor] before this
had claimed Bosnia for the Holy Crown of St. Stephen, he was in no
way thinking of incorporating this province into the mother kingdom
of Croatia, but rather a single vision passed before his eyes, out of which
with time, one could create what might be called a "Bosnian Fiume."
Hungary is now a lively competitor in the Bosnian market. She will at
first conquer Bosnia and Herzegovina economically. Once that is actually under economic control, then the extension of the Hungarian state
to Bosnia is legally feasible. Austria is naturally thinking about the Bosnian hinterland because of Dalmatia. Accordingly, following the annexation of Bosnia we are in the area of a peaceful, but nevertheless in-
tense contest between Austria and Hungary.

The founding of the Hungarian Agrarian Bank is a massively conceived
and ingeniously thought-out advance of future Hungarian economic policy
in the Balkans.

Hungarian capital is the weapon in Bosnia and Herzegovina through
which the decisive victory for the future of these lands over notions of

Trialism, very congenial to Austria, with Croatia as the third part of the confederation, is supposed to be battled out. Orthodox-Serbian peasants vastly outnumber Catholic-Croatian ones. The Hungarian Agrarian Bank has not come here in order to redeem the debts of the Croatian peasant. As a matter of fact, the Bank of the Province already has a program to do this and has already done so for several thousand peasants. Economic need did not bring about the establishment of the new Hungarian Agrarian Bank. And although, as one hears from many quarters, the interest rates of the Bank of the Province are too burdensome, nevertheless the upcoming diet surely could have reduced these significantly by resolution of the agrarian issue through constitutional procedures.

What will and what could happen? The Hungarian Agrarian Bank will make loans for redemptions. The Kmet will become a heavily burdened, indebted free peasant; will he not be able to meet his bank obligations, his property will be put up for sale. The Hungarian bank could then buy him out, establish a colony according to its own specifications and pocket the difference between the amount of the loan and the sale price of the collateral land. We have yet, by the way, to publish a series of details on this subject.

Therefore *Croatian National Union*, the champion of the Croatian national idea for the reunification of Bosnia and Herzegovina with the Croatian-Slavonian-Dalmatian mother kingdom has every reason to regard the big, new Hungarian undertaking as a further obstacle to the realization of Greater Croatia and Trialism.

If, in view of the large financial institutions already in place, an agrarian bank had been needed, the *Croatian National Union* should have allowed the capital to come out of Agram (Serbo-Croat: Zagreb) or from Austria which is favorably inclined toward Trialism.

The *Croatian National Union* must use all the leverage it has to keep the Serb element from becoming economically stronger at the expense of the Croatians, for they too pay taxes. . . .

The *Croatian National Union* has every reason to counter the disproportionate strengthening of Hungarian economic influence in Bosnia, since, through economic dependency, the people will also become political dependents of the Hungarians—the most resolute opponents of the Croatian national ideal.

Until recently, Dr. Nicholas Mandic, the president of the Croatian National Union, also represented this point of view.

Therefore, the general surprise when people learned of the entry of Dr. Nicholas Mandic into the Board of Directors of the Hungarian National Bank. This was kept secret from even his most intimate political friends, and they, as well as the *Croatian National Union*, were confronted with a *fait accompli*.

Certainly no form of logic would recognize this as a necessary consequence of Dr. Nicholas Mandic's political convictions.

Combining national leadership—through his presidential dignity in the *Croatian National Union*—with that of bank retainer and attorney, the combining of ideal views of the world in one person is, in this case, an impossible thing.

As president of the "Croatian National Union" Dr. Nicholas Mandic has no place in the Hungarian Agrarian Bank.

Therefore, we cordially advise Dr. Nicholas Mandic to look at both positions from a national perspective and to choose between the Hungarian board of directors and leadership of the Croatian party. There is no other way out for Dr. Mandic; we would prefer him as a free, independent Croatian patriot to an accomplice of Hungarian imperialism. That is the counsel which a truly good and straightforward political friend can give him.

DOCUMENT NO. 15

NATIONALISM AND ECONOMIC DEVELOPMENT IN AUSTRIA-HUNGARY*

The Compromise of 1867 had relatively little to say about economic relations between the two parts of the Habsburg monarchy. The empire as a whole had been a customs union since 1851 and remained so to the end, though there were deep differences between the Austrian and Hungarian halves about customs policies in foreign trade. There was considerable room for disagreement in matters of internal economic policy as well. Hungary began to industrialize later than many of the Austrian parts of the monarchy and was therefore eager to protect fledgling industries—and the taxes they paid to the treasury in Budapest—from Austrian competition.

γ   γ   γ

. . . There is a specific precondition for every customs union: complete freedom of movement for people and commodities, without distinction as to whatever part of the entire customs area they want to go to or come from. In Berlin, there is no difference between products which are made in Chemnitz or Elberfeld, and the freight costs on the Hamburg exchange are the same for all German products, whether they come from Breslau or Frankfurt. The same laws, the same language and customs facilitate the internal movement of the population to those areas where their work will serve the common interest. If this freedom of movement of people and products did not exist in America and Germany, then Pittsburgh and Cleveland, Dortmund and Breslau would still be small towns today, and each individual state in the American union and in the German empire would have its own small and expensively operating industry. In those two customs areas, then, there would be no higher levels of production, and at no lower cost, than in our country; consequently, they would not be better off than we are. Without that freedom of movement, there would be a race between the various parts of the respective countries, to the disadvantage of the whole, and the area which has more imports, but fewer exports, would be left holding the bag.

Austria finds itself in this very position vis-a-vis Hungary: Austria

---

*Karl Wittgenstein, "Ungarisches Getreide und Österreichische Sensen," *Neues Wiener Tagblatt*, 28 February 1902, pp. 13–14. Trans. Edward G. Fichtner.

has been left holding the bag, because people and commodities can quite easily come over from Hungary, but cannot go unhindered to Hungary. The question, where and how a product can be produced most economically, is beside the point. For Hungary, there is only one question: on this side or that side of the Leitha. For many Austrian products, the high Russian tariffs are less of an obstacle than the Hungarian prohibition system, which allows the import of Austrian products into Hungary only when they cannot be obtained in their own country. To be sure, imports from Hungary over the last two years, according to the statistics, have attained the level of 1810 million Crowns, and our exports to Hungary the level of 1810 million Crowns. Whoever would conclude from these figures, however, that imports and exports are in equilibrium, would be mistaken. Ninety percent of our exports to Hungary are industrial articles which we produce out of raw materials and semifinished goods. Only a part of the value of those articles which we ship to Hungary are the product of our work and our effort. The remainder is paid by Austrian industry in cash to foreign countries. Wool, cotton, silk, and jute fibers, fresh fruits and vegetables, spices, clothing, soap and cleaning products, instruments and timepieces, as far as their value as exports from Austria, have not even half the value which is stated in the official statistics. On the other hand, what comes to us from Hungary is the product of Hungarian workers exclusively.

If our Ministry of Trade wanted to make clear in the lists of imported and exported items what proportion of Austrian exports to Hungary in fact benefit us, it would emerge that the balance of trade with Hungary is in deficit by several hundred million Crowns annually. Such a comparison would demonstrate statistically the bloodletting which the customs union with Hungary imposes upon us. It is not the fault of the Hungarians: the stupidity lies in the system. Hungary is only making full use of its rights, and it would be ridiculous to suggest that they should concern themselves with the interests of the Austrian peasant or Austrian industry. Hungary is doing what it is supposed to do: looking out for itself.

A few months ago, the following telegram was to be read in the papers: "Today, in the city of Raab, the first Hungarian factory for cotton, wool, and fashion textiles was opened in the present of the Minister of Trade. On this occasion, the Minister of Trade made a speech which contained a clear appeal to the Austrian industrialists to open factories in Hungary. "We will create an industry at all costs . . . The way which we have taken is, to be sure, a very difficult one. Yet we will follow that way tirelessly, and not be frightened in the face of any difficulty." The Hungarian minister says what all Hungary thinks. It will take only domestic products. In order to be able to sell beyond the Leitha, a series of Austrian manufacturers has had to open branches there. It is the opposite of what we have seen in Germany and America: sharing of industries. As a result, small factory plants which are expensive to operate, and this condition becomes more acute in the same degree as the Hungarian minister succeeds in transforming his words into deeds.

A few days ago, the Austrian Minister-President stated: "We want the harmony to continue which results from the fact that the two states complement one another economically." We want to—but Hungary does not. The government in Budapest invites the Austrian manufacturers to emigrate to Hungary with capital and experience. Even that is not so easy. They and their workers must be inclined to learn Hungarian in the shortest possible time, and to become Hungarians in their flesh and bone. Since this inclination exists only in the rarest cases, the children of our country emigrate to Germany and America, whose culture and language is closer to them. . . . When Viennese musicians and singers perform in Budapest, it is the cause of public annoyance; in Munich or Dresden, they are welcomed.

DOCUMENT NO. 16

ECONOMIC COMPETITION AND
ETHNIC RANCOR AMONG WORKERS[*]

The German National Workers' Party of Bohemia was one of the more radical of national movements within the Habsburg monarchy, fueled as it was by both social and national resentments which crossed political boundaries. The organization professed to speak in the name of German labor wherever it was found. Both Jews and Slavs were frequent targets of its polemic in its party newspaper.

γ　　　　γ　　　　γ

It is hard for a German worker in Gablonz (Gablonz on the Neiße River-Jablonec nad Nisou, a city in northern Bohemia which was a textile and glass manufacturing center in the nineteenth century) to find a job there, because Czechs get preferential treatment in every respect, because the Czech works more cheaply, in contrast to the German who is accustomed to a better standard of living. Whoever has the occasion and can observe the roads that lead into Gablonz, will come to different opinions; he will see how, in the morning, loads of Czech workers come with whatever they need for the day. One will notice this especially well in Schiller Street at the Giersig establishment which employs mostly Czechs. Mr. Giersig will use this excuse—I get no Germans. Just pay better wages, then they'll come. If one reads the Gablonz papers, one finds classified ads for beltmakers' assistants, painters, female help and so forth. Could not the master say, I take only German help, or is he ashamed to use the adjective German. It is preferable for the businessman when a Czech comes, because he works for 10 to 20 Heller (100 Heller = 1 crown) a day cheaper. Proprietors do not want to see that, through such practices, the industry is less productive. Should a Czech have received any kind of vocational training, he gives some thought thereafter to settling in Gablonz or the surrounding area and competing with Germans in manufacturing.

γ　　　　γ　　　　γ

The election campaign for control of the city hall in Budweis has

[*] (From the "*Arbeiter=Stimme*" no. 1 (12 Jan. 1907): 5 and no. 13 (31 Dec. 1906):4. Trans. Paula Sutter Fichtner)

brought along with it a bitter economic conflict. The economic boycott against German merchants and manufacturers announced by Czech leaders even during the communal elections is being carried on by all means. The entire Czech part of southern Bohemia is being mobilized for its implementation. "Yours from your own" (Czech: Svuj k svemu) agitation has been organized at a massive gathering of Czech women and girls. In addition to the Czech-national Socialist leaders Stribrny and Frinta from Prague, a woman, a professor, and a Roman Catholic clergyman also spoke.

Wives of government bureaucrats and faculty of the state middle schools are particularly involved in the movement. To understand what this means, one should know that in the government offices in Budweis, indeed in the administrative district, there are around 285 Germans as opposed to 1,260 Czechs in the court offices, the district financial administration, the postal and telegraph offices, the railroad management and the heating compartments of the imperial-royal railroads. Most of these men have families and little by little are being advanced in the government offices in Budweis by higher authorities. The families of the Czech bureaucrats now number more than four thousand people.

Hand in hand with this agitation against the Germans comes that of the clergy, for whom the example of the bishop of Budweis, Dr. Rziha, who ostentatiously allowed a Czech leader to cast his vote, has been very encouraging. As the *Bohemia* reported, the following communication was read from pulpits in the parishes around Budweis. . . . : "This afternoon a meeting will take place at Mr. N. N.'s inn, in which the inhabitants of the region will be instructed where they should shop when they arrive in Budweis." Beyond this, the agitation on the part of the Czech clergy goes on through the establishment of many clubs; just recently a new periodical from the Czech clergy, *The People's Voice* (Czech: *Hlas lidu*), has appeared, which the clergy works to distribute in the same way. Czech priests are in the front lines of battle everywhere.

Understandably the Germans are now carrying the fight to the economic arena and the events of the last election have, for the first time, really made them understand why. The German unfortunately often learns only in the struggle for existence to think and act on national principles. However, as long as such conditions prevail and the Czechs give full rein to their hatred of Germans, there can and should not be any commonality in any area between Czech and German, even in sports.

DOCUMENT NO. 17

LANGUAGE RIGHTS AS POLITICAL RIGHTS[*]

The right to conduct one's life in the language one spoke at home was perhaps the most widely spread source of dissatisfaction with Habsburg rule throughout the empire. It was especially difficult to discuss it in public forums, such as the Bohemian parliament in which the following exchange took place. Representatives Größl and Schreiner were Wenzel Größl (1856–1910) and Gustav Schreiner (d. 1922), founding members of the German Agrarian Party in the kingdom. Representative Pacak is Bedrich Pacak (1846–1914) a member of the Czech Party. A "beseda" is a Czech word for a group meeting on an informal basis to exchange ideas. The comments in parentheses are interruptions, or refer to interruptions, made by those listening to the speakers.

γ   γ   γ

Representative Dr. Schreiner: The Czech minorities in the German cities are composed (God help us) for the most part of Czech officials. (That's the way it is! Objections! Noise!) They accuse the government of discriminating against them in every way, but I can assure you that our justified wishes to see the filling of offices with German officials remain disregarded. (Agreement.) The Czech officials in the German areas do not mix in, they first set up a "beseda," and the rest follows all by itself; then various artisans are attracted; the Germans are so clumsy as to support them, and overnight the minority is there.

Representative Größl: That is a pretty picture.

Representative Peschka: We often get officials who do not know German.

Representative Kirchhoff: And the clergymen.

Peschka: We have a clerk in the district administration who doesn't know German.

Representative Pacak: That is not true.

Peschka: Excuse me, Dr Pacak, it is true, and the same thing was true of a surveyor.

Schreiner: In addition to the officials there is the clergy. Anyone who

[*] *Prager Tagblatt*, no. 5 (5 Jan. 1902), p. 3. Trans. Edward G. Fichtner.

171

has followed the developments in Southern Bohemia in the last decades with any attention. . . .

Representative Horica: Since Riha has been bishop, isn't it?

Schreiner: I don't want to comment on Bishop Riha.

Kirchhof(f): They have now gotten their comeuppance from the Pope.

Schreiner: Anyone who, then, has followed the situation in the Bohemian Forest and in Southern Bohemia knows that under the influence of Bishop Zirsik it has gone so far that by far the most parishes, even in German communities, have been staffed with Czechs. (Lasting noise.) These factors have been the cause of the fact that such artificially created Czech minorities have been formed. To be sure, recently it has become somewhat better. Those people have recognized that the German population also has a claim to German clergymen. (Bravo! Bravo! That's right!) As long as the Czech bishops spread their agitation activity across Southern Bohemia and over Eastern Bohemia, no one heard a word of outrage from them. (Heckling.) Today, however, when capable persons from the priesthood have assumed the responsibility of meeting their responsibilities to the people, and seeing to it that a German priesthood is being trained, today Representative Herold makes that a cause of reproach with such force, as if it were some kind of crime, for Heaven's sake! . . .

Horica: Representative Herold was talking about something quite different.

Schreiner: It is nothing other than a sacred right of the Germans, that they also have German priests. (Applause and objections.)

Representative Mastalka: In our undivided kingdom. (Laughter among the Germans.)

Größl to Mastalka: You are going to become the King of Bohemia. Just put on the crown.

Horica to Größl: You are becoming the Elector. [German princely title that vanished with the dissolution of the Holy Roman Empire.—Editor]

DOCUMENT NO. 18

ECONOMIC PROBLEMS AS POLITICAL FAILURE[*]

Karl Wittgenstein saw the national problems of the Habsburg monarchy from the perspective of one who was not caught up in the daily cut and thrust of these controversies. He had, however, no higher opinion of government in the Dual Monarchy than many others among Franz Joseph's subjects.

γ γ γ

. . . Certain assertions, you see, when they are repeated again and again, harden into a kind of dogma to which the entire world gives assent without applying any critical analysis.

If one were successful, the official refrain goes, in reconciling the quarreling nationalities, if one could make the Imperial Council "effective," then—

The Governor of Bohemia has recently expressed the very thought in the following way: "What intellectual achievements, what prosperity would be granted to this land, if only peace among its various nationalities would enter into its realms!"

Really?

Let us assume that the miracle took place. German Bohemians and Czechs and all the other nationalities outdid themselves in reciprocal protestations of friendship: what then?

Nothing! For it is not true that our backwardness is due to the discord among the nationalities. We are poorer than the Germans and the French because, on average, we are less industrious and not as well educated, and because we are not so fortunate as to have a government which clearly grasps where to apply the leverage to lift us out of this stagnating atmosphere. . . .

We really do not work hard enough. The long series of holidays, unknown in solidly Catholic France, and the laws limiting the hours of labor, which we alone have introduced, are only a symptom. Far more than calloused hands, what is lacking are the minds, the persistence, the thrift, and enterprise in those whom, by virtue of their education, one

[*]*Prager Tagblatt*, 26 Jan 1902, pp. 1–2. Trans. Edward G. Fichtner.

173

should be able to call upon to get everyone into motion who is willing and able to work. We possess too few of those enterprising individuals who have taken the lead in the culturally advanced countries.

Instead of dispelling indolence, the pressure of poverty and deprivation vents itself in complaining, and instead of action, it fosters envy and malice. Only to a certain extent are the nationalities quarreling about ideas; it is poverty which provides the intensity, the impetus, and the hatred, and the government is incapable of showing the people how to deal with this.

The "kingdoms and lands represented in the Imperial Council" see only one way of getting out of these dreary circumstances: they seek to capture for their sons salaried positions in the towns, in rural areas, in government service, and in the church; meanwhile, the government attacks the effect, not the cause. It is more correct to say that it is poverty which fuels national antagonism, than the other way around.

Thus it happens that in the near future a decision will be made concerning our relationship with Hungary, a question which the entire population views with complete indifference and ignorance. Although the agricultural sector has to put up with the tariff-free importation of Hungarian agricultural products—and here is the source of its problems—although industry has the greatest interest in a flourishing agricultural sector because well-off farmers would be their best customers, and although it is precisely the workers in industry who suffer most under the lack of work, it is nevertheless easier to get 999 out of 1000 voters interested in some question involving Africa than in the question of severing the customs union with Hungary.

If, therefore, the miracle took place which the governor and so many others are hoping for, it would change nothing, because the servant is like the master, i.e., the voters are like those they elect. Nothing is to be hoped for from these representatives; it would be easier for a camel to go through the needle's eye.

Actually, it is only under the leadership of a strong hand that parliaments are capable of accomplishing anything. Even the optimists could see how little is to be expected of the Imperial Council, even from an "effective" one, from the debates in November and December of the previous year. The Imperial Council was effective exactly twice. In the first instance, Tirolese, Pan-Germans, and Czechs, nobility, peasants, and intelligentsia were, for a change, unanimous in trying to help the threatened agricultural sector. . . . After a series of long sessions, untroubled by the nationalities controversy, what was passed, almost unanimously, were the prohibition of futures contracts and the establishment of professional societies.

To understand the helplessness and naivete of the "effective" Imperial Council, one has to read Paragraph 2 of the law passed, along with the speech of the spokesman for the bill. Paragraph 2 defines the purpose of the societies as: "the improvement of the moral and material conditions of the peasants through the preservation of a spirit of common interest, mutual instruction and support, preserving and raising the sense of social awareness, etc.," and the spokesman began in the following way: "Finally we have arrived at the moment which our peasants have been waiting for years and years, and which, I hope, future generations will regard as a milestone in the history of Austrian agriculture."

As if the peasant can be helped by the cultivation of a spirit of common interest! What a difference between them and the German peasants! These want high prices for cattle and agricultural products, and ours content themselves with the elevation of a sense of social station. At the same time that the German peasants reject a law raising tariffs once again, our representatives—unanimously and enthusiastically—call a law which provides for mutual instruction and support a milestone in the history of Austrian agriculture.

This is the way the Imperial Council functions when it is left to its own devices, specifically in a matter for which it could have, by virtue of its composition, the greatest understanding.

If theoreticians like those politicians who are concerned with the needs of society, or industrialists who do not understand the importance of the domestic markets and cling tenaciously to uncertain opportunities for export, if the workers' leaders who do not see the connection between tariffs and wages, all clamor against grain tariffs, that is quite natural, indeed, the same thing happens in the French and German parliaments. It is unnatural and incomprehensible, however, that not [one] single representative of agriculture has risen to demand what the peasants of France and Germany already have or are to get, and that the policies of the French and German governments have no influence whatsoever on our government.

As long as no government appears which has the courage and conviction to move forward on the basis of the experience of more advanced countries, those who devote so much effort to the problem of national reconciliation will have to arm themselves with patience. They are working in vain on the pendulum of the clock, when the problem is that the clock has not been wound up.

DOCUMENT NO. 19

PARLIAMENTARY DEBATE IN IMPERIAL VIENNA[*]

Personal attacks and ethnic slurs were normal features of deliberations in the imperial House of Representatives, the lower chamber of the Reichsrat. *The following exchange took place on Feb. 14, 1902. At issue were the election campaign tactics of Karl Lueger and his Christian Social movement in Vienna, particularly their relationship to the Jewish community of the city. Engelbert Pernerstorfer (1850–1918) had moved through several political circles, but was now a Social Democrat; Franz Schuhmeier (1864–1913) was his party colleague. Vincent Malik (1854–?) belonged to the All-German party; Constantine Noske was a Liberal and a gentile who publicly opposed anti-Semitism. The reference to him as "Noskeles" is a Yiddishism and intended to be derogatory. Lueger was defended by Albert Gessman (1852–1920), a co-founder of the Christian Social party, Joseph Strobach (1852–1905), an important local organizer for the movement in Vienna.*

γ   γ   γ

Representative Pernerstorfer (speaker in favor of the motion) observed that persons mentioned in the interpellation as well as political parties, particularly the Social Democratic Party, had been insulted. Dr. Lueger had opened his big mouth yesterday and stated that he would document everything he said in the interpolation word for word. Dr. Lueger, however, never keeps a publicly made promise. His principle is always: better cowardly than stupid. Today, however, he was both cowardly *and* stupid. (Stormy applause among the Social Democrats, the German Progressive Party, and the People's Party.) He was cowardly; for his duty as a man of honor should have compelled him to speak first here today.

Representative Noske: Any decent man would have done that.

Representative Strobach: Noskeles, quiet!

Representative Dr. Lueger: The maker of the motion has the right to speak first.

Noske: You have to offer evidence if you make assertions. Pernerstorfer: Whoever has raised such accusations also has to offer proof.

Lueger: That has been done. . . .

[*]*Prager Tagblatt*, No. 45 (Feb. 15, 1902), pp. 11–12 Trans. Edward G. Fichtner.

Pernerstorfer: . . . Dr. Lueger is a typical political chameleon, a man without character. (Stormy cries of outrage among the Christian Socialists, turmoil, approval and applause among the Social Democrats and German Progressives.)

Representative Gessmann: Who are you, anyway, you, a member of the German National party, in the pay of the Jews? You have the effrontery to say such a thing, you who have swum around in all the political camps?

Lueger: Strange that he speaks of character.

Pernerstorfer: I can afford to let anyone speak of my political past. . . .

Representative Strobach: The genuine Jewish liberal!

Pernerstorfer: Dr. Lueger played a certain role in the Vienna Democratic Party. He was at that time a close friend of many Jews, and not exactly of the nicest ones. At the time when Dr. Lueger was friendly toward the Jews, he had the strange weakness of associating with quite disreputable Jews.

Schneider: Now you see Pernerstorfer with disreputable Jews. (Laughter among the Christian Socialists)

Pernerstorfer: When Representative Lueger had reached the necessary age, he made the effort to become a member of a representative body. It is a known fact that Representative Dr. Lueger at that time cultivated the electorate in a very endearing way. At that time, he was known in all of Vienna as the "carriage door opener". (Lively laughter)

Strobach: That is an old Jewish joke. . . .

Pernerstorfer: In the year 1885, he became a member of Parliament, and then it seemed to him that anti-Semitism would be a good way to advance his fortune. . . . There he would have gone far. He would not have become Mayor of Vienna. (Lively laughter)

Gessman: If you had completed your studies and gotten a decent position, you would not have joined the Social Democrats.

DOCUMENT NO. 20

SERBS AND BOSNIANS*

The annexation of Bosnia-Herzegovina in 1908 brought Habsburg government to a particularly concentrated assortment of peoples and religions—Moslems, Jews, Orthodox and Roman Catholic Christians. To those who supported the regime, the ambitions of Serbia were the chief threat to peace in the territory. The following selections are from the German-language Sarajevoer Tagblatt, *which announced itself as a defender of "Austro-Hungarian interests in the Balkans." It was owned and edited by a woman, Hermenegild Wagner, a liberal with feminist leanings, yet strong pro-Habsburg sympathies. The article, "What Is the Moslem National Organization?" was written by an anonymous "Austro-Hungarian Moslem."*

γ　　　　　γ　　　　　γ

The distributer of sweepings from the Serbian press bureau, *Musavat* [a Serbian periodical—Editor] brings two articles in its most recent issue, which this time, contrary to our normal custom, we will not ignore. In the first of these, with the heading "Over us—without us" *Musavat* complains that our provincial government supposedly ordered the district superintendents to send two respected citizens from each confession in their area to the inquiry concerning development of a draft constitution for our fatherland; through this, "national organizations" (?) were circumvented. How far the above contentions correspond to the truth, we do not know. Assuming however, that they are completely true, they are fully in order. Rather than whisper this in *Musavat*'s ear, we are going to proclaim, frequently and loudly, how we regard and think about so-called "national organization" and its representatives.

We all know, including the "national (?) organization" itself, that the people who represent it are without any education, that they do not have a dozen supporters among the Islamic population of these lands for the childish Great Serbian politics. We know, that the "national (?) organization" does not have one man in their ranks who has academic training. The Great Serbian propagator *Musavat* must realize, that all the better and more cultivated elements are like a strong phalanx in another camp. The "national (?) organization" knows itself what vile ways and means

*Sarajevoer Tagblatt, vol. 2, no. 13 (17 January 1909):1–2 Trans. Paula S. Fichtner.

have created such silliness. The emissaries go from house to house . . . with a white sheet of paper and under the pretext that it is no less a matter than that of driving the "Swabians" [people of German extraction—Editor] out of Bosnia and reincorporating it into Turkey, that our Islamic religion is in danger, and so forth; they have wangled impressions of official rubber stamps (for those carrying out these tasks are as illiterate as those in power). This has all taken place under the eyes of the authorities. These are well aware of their machinations, and the "national (?) organization" is so shameless as to ask the government to be recognized as a completely valid entity to be drawn into working out the national constitution, which means that intellectual Moslems can simply take their leave.

As far as the recognition of the Islamic religion in Austria-Hungary is concerned, the ignorant editors and owners of *Musavat* have to learn that history is not so simple. To avoid theoretical discussions, I shall offer a practical example, since otherwise the *Musavat* would not understand it. Islam allows polygamy. It is punishable according to Austrian and Hungarian law. The articles dealing with marriage, rights in marriage, etc. must be changed in the code of civil law. These changes must be accepted in the Austrian and Hungarian parliaments and so on and there is still a lot of preparation to be done for the recognition of our religion. *Musavat* has screamed a great deal about the constitution, and until yesterday, we were laboring under the delusion, that it understood something about history. It occurs to us now, that *Musavat*, as is the custom with ignorant people, does most readily what it knows the least about. Here we cannot let the opportunity slip to chide our government justly. We Moslem intellectuals demand, that in every situation, where the general welfare of our fatherland and its peoples is under discussion, we have a place appropriate to our numbers and education open for us. We demand the strictest measures against the falsification of public opinion on the part of the "executive committee" and its press, since the authorities know the way in which they have come to power. Their press is naturally childish and laughable in the eyes of reasonable men; but they are still in a position to mislead a gullible people.

DOCUMENT NO. 21

THE HABSBURG GRIEVANCES*

The Austrian Ultimatum of 23 July 1914 summarized the Habsburg government's perceptions of its relationships with Serbia from the Bosnian Crisis of 1909 until the assassination of Archduke Franz Ferdinand. Milan Ciganovic (Ciganovitch), a minor functionary on the Bosnian railway, was suspected of being an informant on the activities of the Black Hand Society, also called Union or Death, for the Serbian Prime Minister, Nikola Pasic (1846–1926).

γ   γ   γ

The Austro-Hungarian Government felt compelled to address the following note to the Servian Government on the 23rd July, through the medium of the Austro-Hungarian Minister at Belgrade:—

"On the 31st March, 1909, the Servian Minister in Vienna, on the instructions of the Servian Government, made the following declaration to the Imperial and Royal Government:—

" 'Servia recognises that the *fait accompli* regarding Bosnia has not affected her rights, and consequently she will conform to the decisions that the Powers may take in conformity with article 25 of the Treaty of Berlin. In deference to the advice of the Great Powers, Servia undertakes to renounce from now onwards the attitude of protest and opposition which she has adopted with regard to the annexation since last autumn. She undertakes, moreover, to modify the direction of her policy with regard to Austria-Hungary and to live in future on good neighbourly terms with the latter.'

"The history of recent years, and in particular the painful events of the 28th June last, have shown the existence of a subversive movement with the object of detaching a part of the territories of Austria-Hungary from the Monarchy. The movement, which had its birth under the eye of the Servian Government, has gone so far as to make itself manifest on both sides of the Servian frontier in the shape of acts of terrorism and a series of outrages and murders.

*Edmund von Mach, ed. *Official Diplomatic Documents Relating to the Outbreak of the European War* (New York: Macmillan, 1916, pp. 40–49).

"Far from carrying out the formal undertakings contained in the declaration of the 31st March, 1909, the Royal Servian Government has done nothing to repress these movements. It has permitted the criminal machinations of various societies and associations directed against the Monarchy, and has tolerated unrestrained language on the part of the press, the glorification of the perpetrators of outrages, and the participation of officers and functionaries in subversive agitation. It has permitted an unwholesome propaganda in public instruction; in short, it has permitted all manifestations of a nature to incite the Servian population to hatred of the Monarchy and contempt of its institutions.

"This culpable tolerance of the Royal Servian Government had not ceased at the moment when the events of the 28th June last proved its fatal consequences to the whole world.

"It results from the depositions and confessions of the criminal perpetrators of the outrage of the 28th June that the Serajevo assassinations were planned in Belgrade; that the arms and explosives with which the murderers were provided had been given to them by Servian officers and functionaries belonging to the 'Narodna Odbrana'; and finally, that the passage into Bosnia of the criminals and their arms was organised and effected by the chiefs of the Servian frontier service.

"The above-mentioned results of the magisterial investigation do not permit the Austro-Hungarian Government to pursue any longer the attitude of expectant forbearance which they have maintained for years in face of the machinations hatched in Belgrade, and thence propagated in the territories of the Monarchy. The results, on the contrary, impose on them the duty of putting an end to the intrigues which form a perpetual menace to the tranquillity of the Monarchy.

"To achieve this end the Imperial and Royal Government see themselves compelled to demand from the Royal Servian Government a formal assurance that they condemn this dangerous propaganda against the Monarchy; in other words, the whole series of tendencies, the ultimate aim of which is to detach from the Monarchy territories belonging to it, and that they undertake to suppress by every means this criminal and terrorist propaganda.

"In order to give a formal character to this undertaking the Royal Servian Government shall publish on the front page of their 'Official Journal' of the 13/26 July the following declaration:—

" 'The Royal Government of Servia condemn the propaganda directed against Austria-Hungary—*i.e.*, the general tendency of which the final aim is to detach from the Austro-Hungarian Monarchy territories belonging to it, and they sincerely deplore the fatal consequences of these criminal proceedings.

" 'The Royal Government regret that Servian officers and functionaries participated in the above-mentioned propaganda and thus compromised the good neighbourly relations to which the Royal Government were solemnly pledged by their declaration of the 31st March, 1909.

" 'The Royal Government, who disapprove and repudiate all idea of interfering or attempting to interfere with the destinies of the inhabitants of any part whatsoever of Austria-Hungary, consider it their duty formally to warn officers and functionaries, and the whole population of the kingdom, that henceforward they will proceed with the utmost rigour against persons who may be guilty of such machinations, which they will use all their efforts to anticipate and suppress.'

"This declaration shall simultaneously be communicated to the Royal army as an order of the day by His Majesty the King and shall be published in the 'Official Bulletin' of the Army.

"The Royal Servian Government further undertake:

"1. To suppress any publication which incites to hatred and contempt of the Austro-Hungarian Monarchy and the general tendency of which is directed against its territorial integrity;

"2. To dissolve immediately the society styled 'Narodna Odbrana,' to confiscate all its means of propaganda, and to proceed in the same manner against other societies and their branches in Servia which engage in propaganda against the Austro-Hungarian Monarchy. The Royal Government shall take the necessary measures to prevent the societies dissolved from continuing their activity under another name and form;

"3. To eliminate without delay from public instruction in Servia, both as regards the teaching body and also as regards the methods of instruction, everything that serves, or might serve, to foment the propaganda against Austria-Hungary;

"4. To remove from the military service, and from the administration in general, all officers and functionaries guilty of propaganda against the Austro-Hungarian Monarchy whose names and deeds the Austro-Hungarian Government reserve to themselves the right of communicating to the Royal Government;

"5. To accept the collaboration in Servia of representatives of the Austro-Hungarian Government for the suppression of the subversive movement directed against the territorial integrity of the Monarchy;

"6. To take judicial proceedings against accessories to the plot of the 8th June who are on Servian territory; delegates of the Austro-Hungarian Government will take part in the investigation relating thereto;

"7. To proceed without delay to the arrest of Major Voija Tankositch and of the individual named Milan Ciganovitch, a Servian State employé, who have been compromised by the results of the magisterial enquiry at Serajevo. . . .

"9. To furnish the Imperial and Royal Government with explanations regarding the unjustifiable utterances of high Servian officials, both in Servia and abroad, who, notwithstanding their official position, have not hesitated since the crime of the 28th June to express themselves in interviews in terms of hostility to the Austro-Hungarian Government; and, finally,

"10. To notify the Imperial and Royal Government without delay of the execution of the measures comprised under the preceding heads.

"The Austro-Hungarian Government expect the reply of the Royal Government at the latest by 6 o'clock on Saturday evening, the 25th July.

"A memorandum dealing with the results of the magisterial enquiry at Serajevo with regard to the officials mentioned under heads (7) and (8) is attached to this note."

I have the honour to request your Excellency to bring the contents of this note to the knowledge of the Government to which you are accredited, accompanying your communication with the following observations:—

On the 31st March, 1909, the Royal Servian Government addressed to Austria-Hungary the declaration of which the text is reproduced above.

On the very day after this declaration Servia embarked on a policy of instilling revolutionary ideas into the Serb subjects of the Austro-Hungarian Monarchy and so preparing for the separation of the Austro-Hungarian territory on the Servian frontier.

Servia became the centre of a criminal agitation.

No time was lost in the formation of societies and groups, whose object, either avowed or secret, was the creation of disorders on Austro-Hungarian territory. These societies and groups count among their members generals and diplomatists, Government officials and judges—in short, men at the top of official and unofficial society in the kingdom.

Servian journalism is almost entirely at the service of this propaganda, which is directed against Austria-Hungary, and not a day passes without the organs of the Servian press stirring up their readers to hatred or contempt for the neighbouring Monarchy, or to outrages directed more or less openly against its security and integrity.

A large number of agents are employed in carrying on by every means the agitation against Austria-Hungary and corrupting the youth in the frontier provinces.

Since the recent Balkan crisis there has been a recrudescence of the spirit of conspiracy inherent in Servian politicians, which has left such sanguinary imprints on the history of the kingdom; individuals belonging formerly to bands employed in Macedonia have come to place themselves at the disposal of the terrorist propaganda against Austria-Hungary.

In the presence of these doings, to which Austria-Hungary has been exposed for years, the Servian Government have not thought it incumbent on them to take the slightest step. The Servian Government have thus failed in the duty imposed on them by the solemn declaration of the 31st March, 1909, and acted in opposition to the will of Europe and the undertaking given to Austria-Hungary.

The patience of the Imperial and Royal Government in the face of the provocative attitude of Servia was inspired by the territorial disinterestedness of the Austro-Hungarian Monarchy and the hope that the Servian Government would end in spite of everything by appreciating Austria-Hungary's friendship at its true value. By observing a benevolent attitude towards the political interests of Servia, the Imperial and Royal Government hoped that the kingdom would finally decide to follow an analogous line of conduct on its own side. In particular, Austria-Hungary expected a development of this kind in the political ideas of Servia, when, after the events of 1912, the Imperial and Royal Government, by its disinterested and ungrudging attitude, made such a considerable aggrandisement of Servia possible.

The benevolence which Austria-Hungary showed towards the neighbouring State had no restraining effect on the proceedings of the kingdom, which continued to tolerate on its territory a propaganda of which the fatal consequences were demonstrated to the whole world on the 28th June last, when the Heir Presumptive to the Monarchy and his illustrious consort fell victims to a plot hatched at Belgrade.

In the presence of this state of things the Imperial and Royal Government have felt compelled to take new and urgent steps at Belgrade with a view to inducing the Servian Government to stop the incendiary movement that is threatening the security and integrity of the Austro-Hungarian Monarchy.

The Imperial and Royal Government are convinced that in taking this step they will find themselves in full agreement with the sentiments of all civilised nations, who cannot permit regicide to become a weapon that can be employed with impunity in political strife, and the peace of Europe to be continually disturbed by movements emanating from Belgrade. . . .

DOCUMENT NO. 22

THE DECISION FOR WAR[*]

In his instructions to Frederick Szapary (1869–1935), the Austro-Hungarian ambassador to Russia, Count Leopold von Berchtold, the empire's joint foreign minister, makes clear the thinking which prompted the Habsburg mobilization that began that day.

γ　　　　　γ　　　　　γ

Vienna, July 25, 1914.

In resolving to proceed firmly against Servia, we are fully aware that a conflict with Russia may result from the existing Servian differences. Yet, in determining our attitude toward Servia, we could not allow ourselves to be influenced by this possibility, because fundamental considerations of our home policy have forced us to put an end to a situation which enables Servia, under Russia's promise of immunity, to threaten this empire constantly and to do so unpunished and unpunishable.

In case Russia should consider that the moment for an accounting with the Central European Powers has come, and therefore *a priori* be resolved to make war, the following instructions would appear to be useless.

Nevertheless, it is still conceivable that Russia might reconsider her attitude and not permit herself to be carried away by the warlkie element, in case Servia should refuse to comply with our demands and we should be compelled, in consequence, to resort to force.

The following is designed for the latter emergency and it is left to your discretion to make proper use of it at the right time and in a suitable manner in your conference with M. Sazonow and the prime minister.

I presume that under the present circumstances you are in close touch with your German colleague, who has surely been instructed by his Government not to allow the Russian Government any room for doubt that Austria-Hungary would not stand alone in the event of a conflict with Russia.

I have no doubt that it will not be an easy task to bring Sazonow to

[*]*Austro-Hungarian Red Book*, pp. 64–66.

a true appreciation of our action at Belgrade, which has been forced upon us.

But there is one point which cannot fail to impress the Russian Foreign Minister, namely, an emphatic statement by you to the effect that Austria–Hungary, in conformity with her established principle of disinterestedness, is guided by no selfish motive in the present crisis, although the situation has culminated in warlike action.

The Monarchy is sated with territory and has no desire for Servian lands. If war with Servia be forced upon us, it will be for us not a war of conquest, but of self-defence and self-preservation.

The contents of the circular note, which in itself is sufficiently comprehensive, may be placed in a still more convincing light by a study of the dossier referring to the Servian propaganda against the Dual Monarchy and the relation between this propaganda and the crime of June the 28th.

You will therefore, call the Russian Foreign Minister's special attention to this dossier and point out to him that there is no precedent of a Great Power tolerating so long and with such unexampled forbearance the seditious agitations of a small neighbor.

We had no wish to adopt a policy adverse to the free development of the Christian Balkan States, and therefore we have permitted Servia to almost double her territory since the annexation crisis of 1908, although we knew how little Servian promises are worth.

Since then the subversive movement fostered against the Monarchy in Servia has become so excessive, that Austria–Hungary's vital interests and even her dynasty are seriously menaced by Servia's underground activities.

We must presume that conservative and dynastic Russia will not only understand our energetic action against such a menace to public order, but will even regard it as imperative.

On reaching this point in your conversation with M. Sazonow it will be necessary to state, in addition to your explanation of our motives and intentions, that, although we have no ambitions for territorial expansion and do not intend to infringe upon the integrity of Servia, as you already have pointed out, still we are determined to go to any length to ensure the acceptance of our demands.

The course of the last 40 years, as well as the historical fact that our gracious Sovereign has acquired the glorious name of "Guardian of the Peace," attest that we have always held peace to be the most sacred blessing of the people, and that, in so far as it depended on us, we have endeavored to maintain it.

We would all the more regret a disturbance of the peace of Europe, because of our conviction that the evolution of the Balkan states toward national and political independence could only improve our relations with Russia, eliminating all possibilities of a clash of interests with that empire, and because in framing our own policy we always have been disposed to respect the important political interests of Russia.

To tolerate the Servian machinations any longer, however, would undermine our national existence and our standing as a Great Power, and would, therefore, imperil the European balance of power—an equilibrium the maintenance of which, we are convinced, the peaceloving statesmen of Russia regard as essential to their own interests. Our action against Servia, whatever form it may take, is altogether conservative and has no object except the necessary maintenance of our position in Europe.

DOCUMENT NO. 23

AN EMPEROR NOTIFIES HIS PEOPLES*

Franz Joseph was at his summer residence in Bad Ischl on July 28, 1914, when he issued his declaration to his subjects that they were at war with Serbia. The document, which met with an enthusiastic response throughout his lands, was carefully phrased to make clear that the Dual Monarchy's quarrel was with Serbia alone.

γ   γ   γ

To my peoples!

It was My most deeply felt wish to dedicate the years which through God's grace remain to Me to the works of peace, and to protect My peoples from the grave sacrifices and burdens of war.

In the councils of Providence, it was decided otherwise.

The intrigues of a hate-filled opponent force Me after many years to reach for the sword—to maintain the honor of My monarchy, to protect its reputation and position, to secure its possessions.

Years ago, the Kingdom of Serbia, suddenly and ungratefully forgetting that it had been supported and encouraged by My ancestors and Myself from the earliest beginnings of its national sovereignty up to the most recent past, entered upon the path of open enmity to Austria-Hungary.

When, after three decades of effort in the cause of peace in Bosnia and Herzegovina, I extended my rule to these lands, this order of Mine called forth outbreaks of unrestrained passion and of the bitterest hatred in the Kingdom of Serbia, whose rights were affected in no way whatsoever. My government at that time availed itself of the accepted right of the stronger, and with the greatest forbearance and generosity demanded from Serbia only that it reduce its armies to peacetime levels, and that it promise to follow the path of peace and friendship in the future.

Two years ago, when Serbia was engaged in the struggle with the

*Streffleurs Militärische Zeitschrift. 2 (no. 8, 1914), pp. 1135–1137. Trans. Edward G. Fichtner.

Turkish empire, My government, prompted by the same spirit of moderation, limited its conditions to those most important for preserving the life of this monarchy. It was due to this policy that Serbia was able to realize its military aims in the first place.

The hope that the Serbian kingdom would respect My government's patience and love of peace and keep its word has not been borne out.

The hatred against Me and My house rages higher and higher, the attempt to tear loose inalienable territories of Austria-Hungary becomes more and more apparent.

Criminal activity is advancing across the border, which seeks solely to undermine the foundations of the political order in the south-east of the monarchy, to unsettle the loyalty of the people, to whom in paternal love I devote My full attention, to the ruling house and to the fatherland, to mislead young people and to incite them to criminal acts of madness and high treason. A series of attempted murders, a deliberately prepared and executed conspiracy, the success of which has struck Me and My loyal peoples to the heart, can be recognized, even at a distance, as the bloody evidence of those secret machinations which Serbia has guided and set into motion.

This intolerable activity must be stopped, the constant challenges of Serbia must be ended, if the honor and dignity of My monarchy are to be preserved intact, and its political, economic, and military development shielded from constant aggression.

In vain has My government again undertaken one last attempt to reach this goal peacefully, to persuade Serbia by means of a stern warning to reverse its course.

Serbia has rejected the just and appropriate demands of My government, and has declined to meet those obligations, the observance of which constitutes the natural and necessary foundation of peace in the life of peoples and states.

For this reason, then, I must proceed to impose by force of arms the indispensable guarantees which will assure internal calm to My states and continuing peace with their neighbors.

In this grave hour, I am fully aware of the whole range of implications of My decision, and of My responsibility before the Almighty.

I have examined and considered everything.

With a clear conscience, I enter upon the course to which duty directs Me.

I rely on My peoples, who in every peril have always gathered around My throne in unity and loyalty, and who were always ready to make the greatest sacrifices for the honor, greatness, and power of the fatherland.

I rely on Austria-Hungary's brave defense forces, who are filled with dedicated enthusiasm.

And I trust in the Almighty, that He will grant victory to My arms.

Franz Joseph

DOCUMENT NO. 24

THE LIBERAL WEST TAKES STOCK OF AUSTRIA-HUNGARY[*]

A remarkable linguist, Robert Seton-Watson knew the Habsburg monarchy and many of its leading figures both from extensive travels in the area and formal academic study at universities in Oxford, Berlin, Paris and Vienna. He had hoped that Archduke Franz Ferdinand would reform the nationality arrangements of the empire on a more equitable basis. With these prospects dashed by the Sarajevo assassination of 1914, he supported the break-up of Austria-Hungary. He was especially helpful to Thomas Masaryk, gaining the latter French, British, and Russian leaders' support for an independent Czechoslovakia. His and Masaryk's principles were put before the public in The New Europe, *a journal which Seton-Watson established, financed, and for which he did much of the editorial work.*

Albert Sorel (1842–1906) was an influential French historian of diplomacy.

γ   γ   γ

. . . .

One fact has already become abundantly clear since those words were uttered—that whereas the victory of the Central Powers means an absolute German hegemony over enemies and allies alike, the victory of the Entente will be the joint work of an ever-expanding group of Powers. While Germany, if she wins, will justly regard herself as having saved Austria-Hungary from destruction, not one of her rivals, in the event of the triumph of the Entente, will be able to claim a monopoly of the credit. Each will have contributed to the common cause, but in each case that contribution will have been an indispensable part of the total effort. Here at least it is possible to find some consolation. The victory of William II would be a victory for the spirit which inspired Louis XIV or the first Napoleon, a reversion to the vanishing era of insolent conquest and plunder. The victory of the Allies will be a victory for Europe and the European system. What might have been a mere war for French or British or Russian Imperialism, has thus become a conflict

[*]Robert W. Seton Watson, *What Is at Stake in the War*. Papers for War Time. No. 35 (London: Humphrey Milford/Oxford University Press, 1915), pp. 6–13.

in which all good 'Europeans', to say nothing of Americans, are ranged against a single renegade foe.

The creed of the Allies is a creed of diversity, that of the Germans is a creed of uniformity. The openly avowed aim of their political and academic thinkers is the imposition of a single form of 'culture'—the German—upon a world which has blindly failed to appreciate its merits. Hence their victory would mean the subjection of Europe to a new doctrine of Infallibility as demoralizing for its inventor as it would be intolerable for its victims. The victory of the Allies, on the other hand, will be the joint work of widely different ideals and traditions, and will vindicate the right of every people to preserve and develop its own national individuality. As a writer in the *Nation* has well said, the allied nations oppose to Germany's senseless worship of the 'Will-to-Power' an invincible faith in the 'Right-to-Live' of small and great nations alike.

Let us turn from theory to practice, and consider briefly what the victory of the Allies involves in the language of hard political facts. We are fighting three enemies of widely differing character, quality, and strength—Germany, Austria-Hungary, and Turkey. In any consideration of our policy towards them, it is advisable to treat them in the inverse order to their importance, for reasons which will soon become obvious. In peace-time all save the extremists favoured palliatives. To-day only the most drastic measures will meet the case. Hence the victory of the Allies means the dismemberment of Turkey and Austria-Hungary— first because only thus can we hope to isolate and bring Germany to her knees, and secondly because only on their ruins can we erect the new Europe of our dreams. . . .

With its twelve principal races and ten chief languages, with its seven religions and twenty-three legislative bodies, [Austria-Hungary] provides at every turn pitfalls for the unwary or superficial student: and the bare idea of its collapse has filled with terror every advocate of the *status quo*. Small wonder that Palacky's famous phrase, 'If there were no Austria, it would be necessary to create one', should have been re-echoed as a parrot cry for the last sixty years. A true instinct made even the most ignorant feel that the continued existence of the Habsburg Monarchy was essential if a European cataclysm was to be avoided. And yet M. Sorel, was unquestionably right when he declared that 'on the day when the Eastern Question appears to have been solved, Europe will inevitably be confronted by the Austrian Question'. The troubles which precipitated the great struggle were due to the inter-action of Balkan and Austrian racial problems—the jetsam of the receding Turkish tide. During the long reign of Francis Joseph, Austria-Hungary has made marked progress in many directions—politically as well as materially; but the attitude of her governing classes has always been a fatal drag upon the wheel. Her statesmen, far from realizing that so conglomerate a state could not rest upon a negative basis, openly proclaimed and acted upon a policy of 'jogging along' (the famous 'Fortwursteln' of Count Taaffe), of half measures alike in internal and in external affairs. The House of Habsburg, with all its faults and shortcomings, has earned the gratitude of Europe as the champion, for three centuries, of Christendom against the Turks. But with the disappearance of all danger from that quarter a fresh policy was needed, in order to weld into a single whole the medley of peoples whom the dynasty had gradually gathered round it. The necessity for a strong lead in this direction became more and more urgent with every decade, as national feeling gathered force; and yet Francis Joseph has consistently refrained from giving such a lead. At last, when the approaching dissolution of the Dual Monarchy was already the theme alike of superficial observers outside and acute thinkers within, there appeared in the person of the late Archduke Francis Ferdinand a man who seemed to possess the energy, knowledge, and gifts of leadership without which so herculean a task as the regeneration and reconstruction of the state would have been foredoomed to failure. His shortcomings were obvious, but his honesty of purpose and his belief in the mission of his house could not be gainsaid. It is the fashion to regard his uncle as the victim of some elemental Oedipean tragedy: but surely the fate of the nephew is infinitely more tragic. At the moment when he awaited with growing impatience the supreme moment of opportunity, confident that he would rally round him in his effort all the best brains of the Monarchy—at that moment he was struck down by the hand of an assassin, and his place was filled by a thoughtless and inexperienced youth better versed in light opera than in even the simplest problems of the political world.

His death removed the one man capable of restoring order to an internal situation which—for lack of any positive action—was rapidly becoming desperate. It removed, too, the chief restraining influence in the councils of the Monarchy and left the war parties supreme in Central Europe. The reactionaries of Berlin and the reactionaries of Budapest joined hands over the inanimate body of Austria. German and Magyar are inspired by a common resolve to maintain their domination over the Slav, to prevent the rising democracies of Western Slavdom from coming to their own. To-day we see Germany mercilessly draining the resources of Austria-Hungary in a quarrel which is altogether hateful to a majority among the latter's population; we see the exploitation of close upon thirty million people by their traditional enemies. If the menace of German military hegemony is to be removed from Europe, the first and most obvious task of the Allies must be the emancipation of the Slav and Latin races of Austria-Hungary, the vindication of their right to a free national development.

Before the war much was heard of the alleged attempt to 'ring round' Germany by a superior combination of hostile Powers. The events of the last nine months have effectually exploded the theory of the Entente's menace. Germany has not only proved herself a match for her three great rivals, despite the seccession of one member of her own group, but has even succeeded in galvanizing her remaining ally into fresh life. But this is the last spasmodic effort of a system which belongs to the age of feudalism rather than to modern times. The great war is a hideous proof that the policy of racial dominance and forcible assimilation is morally bankrupt, but through its long-drawn-out horrors we believe that more than one dream of national unity and liberation will be realized, and that those racial minorities whose separate existence reasons of geography and economics render impossible, will attain guarantees of full linguistic and cultural liberty.

The moment is still far distant when we can attempt to define the new frontiers of Europe; but in view of the complicated issues involved it is already necessary to weigh very carefully the various alternatives. The dissolution of Austria-Hungary—an event which is only conceivable if Germany should be completely defeated—would involve a complete re-grouping of Central and South-eastern Europe. The chief features of the new situation would be (1) the union of Polish Galicia with the new Poland; (2) of Ruthene Galicia with the Russian Ukraine; (3) of the Trentino, Trieste and Western Istria with the Kingdom of Italy; (4) the creation of an independent Bohemia—including not merely the Czechs, but their Slovak kinsmen in Northern Hungary; (5) of a Greater Roumania, including the Roumanian populations of Hungary and the Bukovina; (6) of a new Southern Slav state, composed of the present Kingdoms of Serbia and Montenegro, the ancient but dormant

Triune Kingdom of Croatia-Slavonia-Dalmatia, Bosnia-Herzegovina, Eastern Istria and perhaps the Slovene districts of Austria, and finally (7) of an independent Hungary, a national state shorn of the races whom she has so long and so grossly misgoverned, and herself set free for a new era of democratic development. In some cases it may prove difficult to reconcile the rival claims of ethnography and strategic necessity, but by accepting nationality as the guiding principle of any settlement, and insisting that no race shall be handed over to an alien rule without being previously consulted, a great step will have been made towards placing Europe upon a new and surer foundation.

But even with the establishment of free and vigorous national states upon the ruins of the old order, there must inevitably remain the difficult problem of racial minorities, whose interests are of secondary but none the less of vital importance. And just as every effort must be made to ensure the survival of the smaller nations, as the surest bulwarks of true culture and tolerance, as the guardians of racial individuality and diversity of type, so also they in their turn must be induced to offer the fullest political and intellectual liberty to all racial minorities within their boundaries. A guarantee of linguistic rights in schools, churches, local bodies and cultural institutions must be a *sine quâ non* in the settlement of every problem. Thus the Germans of Bohemia and Southern Hungary must enjoy the same privileges as the Magyars in the new Roumania, the Slovenes in Italy, and the tiny group of Italians in the new Jugoslavia. Those who see their monopoly threatened by such an arrangement will describe it as Utopian, but it is certainly attainable on a basis of careful study and good intentions. . . .

DOCUMENT NO. 25

CUTTING LOOSE[*]

Thomas Masaryk had made his reputation before 1914 both as an academic and as a political leader. Though never part of any of the major parties that emerged in the Bohemian lands, he combined both national and democratic convictions in ways that inspired the confidence of both his countrymen and, after 1914, the allied powers. Following the First World War, he became president of the new Czechoslovakia.

γ   γ   γ

. . . .

Since the accession of the new Emperor of Austria-Hungary a part of the British Press has expressed hopes of a separate peace with Austria. These hopes have no real foundation, but they are characteristic. The last few weeks have witnessed a rising tide of these expectations, although Austria has given a good enough answer by following Germany and breaking with the United States. . . .

Recent history shows clearly that Pangermanism in Austria is not the policy of "a few fanatics," but that of the whole German people and of the dynasty. Austrian Pangermanism dictated the policy against Serbia and the Slavs in general; the annexation of Bosnia-Herzegovina was accomplished under the direct protection of Germany and the Kaiser's "shining armour"; the same burgomaster of Vienna, whose audience with the new Emperor is now reported, spoke to William in the name of the population of Vienna and of the Germans in Austria, accepting Bismarck's policy of making Austria the German vanguard in the Balkans. It was this very policy that provoked the war; Austria-Hungary attacked Serbia knowing quite well that her action meant war against Russia and the Entente. But this very provocation of the world conflagration—with England neutral—was the aim of Vienna and Berlin. In Austria-Hungary and in Germany the merest child in politics was aware of the fact that "this war is in all its Mid-Europe and Eastern Europe aspects a war of Germanism against Slavdom, in which a victory . . . would be a German triumph"; that was the reason given by William and the Chancellor for waging this war. . . . The author of the

[*]Thomas Masaryk, "Austria Infelix," *The New Europe*, 3 (no. 29, 1917), pp. 76–82.

renowned pamphlet "Berlin-Bagdad" is an Austrian-German; and all German parties in Austria, even the Catholic *Christlich-Soziale*, have accepted the Pangerman programme which assigns to the Germans and Magyars the immediate leadership of the Balkans.

This war is the war of the Germans *and* Magyars; the Poles and Ruthenians in Galicia were divided, but all other nations of Austria-Hungary have been on principle against the war. The Czechs, with the Slovaks, the Southern Slavs, the Italians, and Roumanians were against the war. Bohemian regiments have surrendered to Russia to facilitate the victory of the Allies; and others have been punished by "decimation"; thousands of civilians in the Bohemian countries have been sentenced to death, and all the leading Bohemian deputies have been imprisoned or exiled and sentenced to death; and the same bloody persecution is known to have been carried out in the Southern Slav and Italian countries, even as in the Roumanian districts. These are *known facts*, whose political significance can escape none but the wilfully blind.

It is well known that the Austrian Parliament has not been summoned since March, 1914, that war was decided and declared without its consent; only the chauvinistic and oligarchical Hungarian Parliament accepted and ratified the Emperor's autocratic declaration of war. The majority of the Austro-Hungarian nations were—and are—against the war; the German and Magyar minority forced the whole Empire to serve as the obedient slave of Pangermanism.

The late Emperor Francis Joseph accepted the Pangerman policy. To strengthen the German minority in the Reichsrat he promised autonomy to Galicia, and the Germans were to be further rewarded by the disintegration of Bohemia into administrative departments, and by the proclamation of German as the language of the State; the Magyars were to retain their dominion in Hungary, even if the Southern Slavs were united in a trialistic body. The fate of Croatia—nominally self-governing under the Compromise of 1868—is a clear indication of what would be the meaning of this Southern Slav formation under Magyar and German rule. Meanwhile a new Poland was created as a tool of Berlin and Vienna against Russia; and, since Poland is Catholic, an Austrian or Bavarian prince on the throne would play in the East the *rôle* of Ferdinand and Constantine in the South.

Francis Joseph died. The new Emperor continued the old policy, but as he has used some new methods, he is believed by ingenuous politicians to be changing the entire Austrian policy and tradition. He appointed as his ministers two Bohemian aristocrats, who are Bohemian only in name, both of them staunch Conservatives and Clericals, not national Bohemians at all. Yet there can be no doubt about it that the new Emperor was setting out to win the lost confidence of the Bohemians. The Bohemian question is life and death to Austria. Without Bohemia there is no Austrian Empire; so Counts Martinic and Czernin toil and travail to reconcile Bohemia to the Habsburgs. But the Bohemian nation has expressed its feelings and convictions since the outbreak of the war clearly enough to show the futility of the Martinic-Czernin negotiations as long as the political leaders of the Czechs remained in exile or in prison. Meanwhile the new Emperor pursues the old Emperor's path of unredeemable promises. Francis Joseph gave pledges to the Germans against the Bohemians; the new Emperor gives promises to both. Galicia's autonomy and the proclamation of German as the State language are postponed, and Bohemia is tempted with a promise of autonomy, but what kind of autonomy we are not told. Peculiar news from Vienna suggests that the Emperor and his two ministers have succeeded in framing a compromise between the Bohemians and the Germans; but what compromise can it be if the Bohemians are deprived of their political leaders? Who negotiated on behalf of the Bohemian nation?

The Emperor, it is said, wishes to summon the Parliament; and we read that the Emperor himself points to the Russian Revolution as proof of the necessity of such a step. The Bohemian situation was dangerous enough in itself; but now comes the new Russian peril. A free and democratic Russia is the gravest possible threat to Austrian and German absolutism; the Slavs of Austria-Hungary, like the Italians and Roumanians, never loved Russian absolutism; but they could not successfully fight Austrian absolutism so long as the greatest Slav country itself was absolutist. Tsarism was for the Slavs the heel of Achilles; free Russia is the end of Austrian absolutism, and that means the death of Habsburg Austria. The Emperor Charles sees this and tries, therefore, by convoking Parliament, to give his *régime* a new democratic air. But no one is deceived. A Parliament sitting under the military pressure of Vienna has no democratic significance; more than half the political representatives of the Czechs and Jugoslavs are in prison or exile, and a Reichsrat without them is merely a packed jury. The whole is only a bluff for Neutrals and the Allies, or, perhaps, more truly, for that part of the political public in Europe that is willing to accept words for realities.

The Germans and the Magyars now begin to realise the results of their Pangerman policy in raising vast racial obstacles, and hence their attempt to save Austria. They will even be ready to sacrifice some territory to save essential Austria.

. . .

The Austrian peace-offers consist of abandoning the Poles to Poland, the Trentino to Italy, and perhaps a part of Bukovina to Roumania; Vienna is even merciful to Serbia, which "can be restored"—on condition of a change in the Serbian dynasty—says Count Czernin. But these sacrifices, which are the price Austria is willing to pay for peace, are no sacrifices at all. Supposing Polish Galicia is ceded to Poland, what constitution will Poland have, and what dynasty? Austria and Germany will not establish a Republic, and in that they will be met by the powerful Polish aristocracy; that goes without saying; and a Poland with an Austrian or even a Bavarian king is nothing more than an autonomous province of Austria and Germany; the more so, if the Poles in Germany are to remain where they are. . . .

We know, of course, that the Austrophils and Magyarophils among the Allies talk of Anti-Prussianism in Austria; and they tell us "Austria is awakening and turning against Germany." Emperor Charles, no doubt, sorely feels his dependence upon Germany, but Francis Joseph felt it even more, for he waged a war against Prussia; yet he became the executor of Bismarck's policy. The Emperor Charles cannot and will not change the Germans of his empire, and he will not change the Magyars. For the moment he cannot even liberate his army from the Prussian grip, since it now consists of regiments in which Prussian and Austrian troops are closely interlocked. The Allies must not forget that Germany has *saved* Austria so far, inasmuch as Germany's army succeeded in forcing the Russians to retreat from Galicia. This is known not only to the Germans of Germany, but also to those of Austria-Hungary; and this knowledge is a great moral force for the near and for the more remote future. Let us see things clearly, and let us speak as politicians. What would the Allies say if Italy made a separate peace with our common enemy? Why are those people, who desire a separate peace with Austria, so nervous if the possibility of Russia making a separate peace is suggested? If Austria made a separate peace, that would mean an Austrian betrayal of Germany; Austria provoked the war; Germany used the occasion for her political aims, and, incidentally, saved Austria by forcing the Russians to retreat. How, then, would the German nation accept

Austria's treachery? For treachery it is, since twice two make nothing but four, whether in Germany, Austria, Britain, France, Russia or Italy!

To work for Austria's salvation is to work against Italy, against Roumania, against Serbia and the Southern Slavs, against Bohemia and against Russia. The Allies proclaimed solemnly that they were fighting for the principles of democracy and nationality, for the re-construction of Europe, for the restoration and liberation of Belgium, Serbia, Poland, the Czecho-Slovaks, Southern Slavs, Roumanians, Italians; and if this is still their aim, it is irreconcilable with any attempt to save the Habsburg dynasty. Either the Habsburgs, or free democratic Europe; that is the question. Any compromise betwen these two is bound to be an unstable condition. Austrophilism in Entente circles can only be explained by the excessive Westernism of those who cherish it and take no account of the essential features of the Habsburg Dynasty and the turpitude of its most distinguished servants. THE NEW EUROPE has already proved how in this country the Magyarophils have operated by forgery; and the Austrian side is little better; it is essentially anti-democratic and distasteful to the British mind. In fine, any kind of Austria-Hungary, ruled by the Habsburgs, is the German vanguard for an advance into Asia and Africa. On these terms, Austrophilism, if conscious, is political perversity; if unconscious, political *naïveté*.

DOCUMENT NO. 26

DEMOCRATIC OPPOSITION
BECOMES RADICAL[*]

Friedrich Adler, the son of the Social Democratic leader Victor Adler, had been working in Switzerland until the outbreak of World War I. His democratic convictions led him to assassinate the Austrian minister-president, Count Karl von Stürgkh, in 1916. His statement before the court at his trial appeared in print under the title J'accuse, a reference to the open letter to the president of the French Republic published in 1898 by the French novelist Emile Zola. This was an impassioned indictment of those who supported the conviction for treason of Alfred Dreyfus, a Jewish major in the French army.

The Neue Freie Presse *referred to in the text was Vienna's leading daily with close connections to the Habsburg government. The* Arbeiter-Zeitung *was the Social Democratic newspaper. Ernest von Koerber (1850–1919) replaced Stürgkh as Franz Joseph's minister-president, Dr. Julius Sylvester (1854–1944), a jurist representing Salzburg, became president of the lower chamber of the* Reichsrat *in 1914. "Bernatz" refers to Dr. Edmund Bernatzik (1854–1919) a distinguished constitutional scholar who taught at the University of Vienna.*

γ   γ   γ

. . .

Now I will tell you what it was that particularly worked upon me: During the investigation I spoke openly and at some length. Here I may confine my remarks to things that are already proven, occurrences that may be read in the papers, that have become notorious. I will speak only of *political oppression*.

I could not rid myself of the feeling of degradation that preyed upon me.

Are we dogs that we allow ourselves to be beaten? Have we no honor, that we should bear it?

You cannot conceive what it means to live under Austrian censorship. A propaganda newspaper, the "Volk," which I edited at that time, was

[*]Friedrich Adler, *J'accuse. An Address in Court.* (New York: the Socialist Publication Society, 1917?), pp. 28–33.

the only German paper in Austria that was wholly suppressed. And I was satisfied that it should be so—for so, at least, it could not be misused by the censorship for its own purposes. But I continued to edit the "Kampf," our scientific organ, under the greatest difficulties, with untold sacrifices. I was constantly placed in the most trying situations.

So, for instance, one of my articles was withheld by the censor for weeks. Then it was returned—one line had been stricken out. Other articles were held back for months—there was method in their madness. . . .

In the "Neue Freie Presse" a poem was published that passed the censorship without objections. It contained only a few lines and was the translation of an American song of a mother who protests because her sons are to be drafted into the army, to kill the sons of other mothers. The song calls to the sons to throw aside their weapons. One of my comrades, Lang of Freiwaldau, discovered the poem, it appealed to him and he was seized with the unfortunate impulse to make 15 or 20 copies of it, which he distributed among a number of comrades. He was haled before court and condemned to death. Later his sentence was commuted to five years in prison. He is now languishing in Möllersdorf, and his health is rapidly failing. . . .

The military reserve courts have meted out over 900 years in jail, have passed and executed 26 death sentences. Among the former there is the shameful sentence of five years in jail meted out to a woman for a letter written to her husband. . . .

Russia and China have their Parliament, we are the only truly degraded nation. We have no popular representation. We are not consulted, when money is needed, nor do our rulers trouble to account for the money they have spent.

During this whole absolutist regime it was Stürgkh who played the leading role. He was always violently opposed to election reform, and was its bitterest enemy in the election reform commission. The whole opposition to the extension of a popular franchise grouped about him. This man later became Prime Minister, and from the beginning, he tried to prove the soundness of his opposition, by showing that Parliament was impossible, by proving, ad absurdum, its ineffectuality. Stürgkh saw, with joy, how Parliament became more and more incapable; and purposely he finally brought about its adjournment.

It was clear to me, even then, that Stürgkh had far-reaching plans. That he proposed to set aside Parliament completely was evident. Even though it had navigated successfully through the difficulties of the taxation debate, Stürgkh nevertheless succeeded in bringing about its downfall.

When war came, and with it, the most critical period in the history of the Austrian nations, Parliament was not called. Absolutism reigned. And this undiluted absolutism, to which we were subjected, was quite a different thing from the absolutism of peace times. It was an open coup d'etat. The whole fate of the country rested upon one man.

What did our government do during the war?

Stürgkh conferred with the "Deutschradikale," with Wolf and his followers as to ways and means of forcing new constitutional amendments upon the nation. This party stood ready to support any and every measure. I was assured by its deputies that the industrial future of Austria lay in the hands of Stürgkh alone. Without even consulting his colleagues he undertook to regulate the whole Hungarian question, and drew up a commercial treaty to be effective for two decades, with Tisza alone, and enforced its measures under Paragraph 14. War starvation was to be kept up for decades to come. By the terms of this treaty, duties on foodstuffs were to be levied, i.e., prices were to be screwed up still higher. Austria, even after the war was over, was to be held upon the very brink of starvation.

During the summer the demand for a parliament became more and more audible. Even feudal lords began to talk constitutionality. Attempts were made to force a calling of Parliament. But Stürgkh was at work, systematically, ruthlessly, coldly calculating to prevent it.

A caucus of social-democratic deputies adopted a resolution, in the first half of September, 1916, demanding the convocation of Parliament as an absolute necessity. Stürgkh ordered that the public not only be kept in ignorance of this resolution, but receive no news of the session of such a caucus. At this meeting Pernerstorfer told Stürgkh had personally done his utmost to prevent the calling of Parliament, how he had succeeded in keeping from the Emperor all news of what was going on. Stürgkh practically isolated the Emperor from the outer world. At one time President Sylvester demanded an audience. And this, too, Stürgkh managed to circumvent—so completely had he cut off the emperor from the population.

Stürgkh was generally recognized by all proletarians as the personal bulwark of opposition against constitutional government. But at that time numerous elements in Austria still hoped that it would be possible to re-establish constitutional government in Austria. It was at the time when the feudal lords held their conference; when Sylvester called his conference for the middle of October.

This brings me to the concrete situation that immediately preceded my deed.

At that moment everything plainly indicated that, for some time to come, constitutionality in Austria was dead. In September the reins had been slightly slackened. But the middle of October brought a new period of rigorous censorship, and nothing was permitted to appear in the Arbeiter-Zeitung.

On the day before I committed my deed there came the announcement that to speak of the re-establishment of a constitutional government was against the law. In his movement for the calling of Parliament, Sylvester had called a meeting of the party leaders to the House of Deputies. Hereupon Stürgkh declared that, so far as he was concerned, there was no such institution as a conference of party leaders, that he refused to discuss it, and that he would not attend its sessions. For me this was decisive. The third, and final decisive movement, also a part of this movement for Parliament, was the following:

A number of professors of the Juridical Faculty of the University of Vienna called a meeting in the hall of the Musical Society to discuss "The Parliament.". . . . The police forbade a public gathering altogether, and announced that the meeting could be held only according to the provisions of Paragraph E, as an assemblage of invited guests.

On the 20th of October . . . I received a message over the telephone, that the meeting had been prohibited in any form. This was to me of the greatest importance, not as a concrete case, but as a precedent for the future.

Thus matters stood on the 21st of October. Then came the four revolver shots. Two days later a conference was held at Sylvester's home, emphatically demanding the calling of the Reichsrat. Eight days later the Koerber administration was already in sight, and all Austria was openly declaring that conditions had become unbearable, that things must be changed. Everywhere it was taken as a matter of course that a complete upheaval must come.

From more than one point of view, the 21st of October has been a crisis. If my deed had not occurred, we should still be living under the rule of Stürgkh. I felt that we should choke if something was not done. Things had become unbearable. If no one cried out, I would have to cry out. . . .

DOCUMENT NO. 27

THE NATIONAL QUESTION SEEN ANEW[*]

The reopening of the Austrian Parliament by Emperor Charles in 1917 gave many of the national groups within the Habsburg empire the opportunity to demand far greater roles for themselves in the political and legal life of the state. Even if it were to continue to exist, the monarchy would be conducted on a very different basis. Nor, as the Social Democratic leaders Karl Renner and Karl Seitz saw it, could reform wait for the end of the war.

γ   γ   γ

Should you rummage through our laws, gentlemen, you won't find "nations" in them. We don't have nations in Austria, there are no nations, there is, only in one paragraph, so-called races. The definition of a race is also unclear, as is who has or has not the status of a race. But that is the only suggestion, otherwise there are no nations. Our old constitution is nation-blind, there are only *citizens with different languages*; there are, therefore, only German-speaking Austrians, Czech-speaking, Polish-speaking, Ukrainian-speaking Austrians, thus, it [the constitution— Editor] literally cannot see the forest for the trees, it does not see the Czech nation as a whole, likewise the Polish, probably because it sees too many Czechs and Poles, it in no way sees the totality of a nation and can never bring it into the picture. On the contrary, our constitution makes an effort to serve our national totality in single portions, in fragments. The entire nation consists of citizens capable of speaking individual tongues. For this reason, there appears to be only a language issue, not a national issue. Now, however, this condition, which takes no account of the national as a whole, is, at this time, unsustainable, where *the nations as a totality are drawing up* and declaring, they also want a *legal existence*, they want *to be something whole*. That is the final and decisive basis of all demands, which are here called political demands and which essentially are no longer the political demands which once always were. There is a very basic difference between what is now and was once said.

[*]Karl Seitz and Karl Renner, *Krieg und Absolutismus. Friede und Recht. Zwei Parlamentsreden.16. 17. Juni 1917* (Vienna: Volksbuchhandlung, 1917): 42–45. Trans. Paula Sutter Fichtner.

What I have presented may appear somewhat paradoxical to many gentlemen; I would like, however, to explain it very briefly through historical analogy. Our history has never seen the sort of nations, which today function historically. It is absolutely wrong when some nations look back into God knows how many centuries earlier. What represented the kingdom of Bohemia were the estates, what stood for Hungary in the old kingdom of Hungary were the Hungarian estates. And if you read something of the protocols of the assembly in 1791 of the Hungarian estates, you will find that these lords in the estates there felt themselves to be Hungary, made major and far-reaching demands as Hungary. When you read, however, who these Hungarians were, you will find names such as Liechtenstein, Kinsky, Auersperg along side of Apponyi and so on, along with Croatian grandees and all speak neither Hungarian, nor German, nor Croatian with one another, but *Latin*.

Those were meetings of the estates and the estates were the estates of the land, that means the estates of the entire kingdom of Bohemia were a land, a community. And so, in 1723 and in the following years, Austria was altogether logically constructed on the principle of having the estates of the archduchies of Austria and the kingdoms of Bohemia and Hungary coming together and concluding a Pragmatic Sanction in which they said: we, the estates of these kingdoms and provinces, declare, that we wish to create a permanent community under the glorious rule of the House of Habsburg. They were saying, thus, we, the estates of these lands, wish to form a mutual defence community, and, although each persists in its own legal structure, we nevertheless wish, as it says in the Pragmatic Sanction, to form a unity, undivided and indivisible.

Those who came before us knew very well what they were doing; each one was securing the autonomy of his land and together they created a totality that was an undivided and inseparable unity. And it also follows logically, that as representatives of the community, observing the customs of those times, a time that was monarchical through and through, they even installed and confirmed the monarch.

However, what, gentlemen, is the situation today? *Today the territorial groupings no longer* are decisive, today we no longer say: we Bohemians, we Moravians, we Silesians and so forth; let us sit down together, each one think about his own rights and we shall form a community. For where, here, do the Styrians and the Salzburgers and the Vorarlbergers and the inhabitants of the free city of Cattaro come forward separately? Or where then, do the Bohemians, Moravians, and Silesians, insofar as they are Czechs, come forward separately? This is what appears: the German nation, the Czech nation, the Polish nation, and so on, each one as a total nation, a clear and important sign, *that the nation has taken the place of the province* and that today is the time, to grant a constitution, which establishes the nations as the underpinnings and the bearers, as the pillars of this empire. (Vigorous applause).

That is the most elementary and simple fact in the world, and should there be an Austrian constitution, reason should have it, if Austria should even have a constitution, I could not imagine it otherwise than as the American constitutions, which there begin with the words, we, the people of Virginia, wishing to establish laws and to be governed by justice, have taken upon themselves, etc. Ours should read the same way: We, the Germans from Austria, the Czechs, the Poles, Ruthenians, and so on wishing, to found a community of states, reserving to ourselves our national rights, agree that the following are our common affairs and the following are our particular affairs.

SELECT BIBLIOGRAPHY

The following list has been constructed to help an English-speaking reader. Non-English sources consulted by the author do therefore not appear here. Most of the titles suggested contain more exhaustive bibliographies which include works in other languages.

Banac, Ivo. *The National Question in Yugoslavia, Origins, History and Politics.* (Ithaca, N.Y.: Cornell University Press, 1984).

Barany, George. *Stephen Szechenyi and the Awakening of Hungarian Nationalism, 1791–1841.* (Princeton, N.J.: Princeton University Press, 1968).

Beales, Derek. *Joseph II.* 2 vols. (Cambridge: Cambridge University Press, 1987-).

Beller, Steven. *Vienna and the Jews, 1867–1938. A Cultural History.* (Cambridge, New York: Cambridge University Press, 1989).

Bled, Jean Paul. *Franz Joseph.* trans. Teresa Bridgeman. (Oxford: Blackwell, 1993).

Body, Paul. *Joseph Eotvos and the Modernization of Hungary, 1840–1870: A Study of Ideas of Individuality and Social Pluralism in Modern Politics.* Transactions of the American Philosophical Society, new ser. vol. 62, Pt. 2. (Philadelphia: The American Philosophical Society, 1972).

Bottomore, Tom B. and Patrick Goode. *Austro-Marxism.* (Oxford: Oxford University Press, 1978).

Boyer, John W. *Political Radicalism in Late Imperial Vienna: Origins of the Christian Social Movement, 1848–1897.* (Chicago: University of Chicago Press, 1981).

———. *Culture and Political Crisis in Vienna: Christian Socialism in Power, 1897–1918.* (Chicago: University of Chicago Press, 1995).

Bridge, F. R. *The Habsburg Monarchy Among the Great Powers, 1815–1918.* (Oxford: Berg Publishers, 1991).

Brock, Peter. *The Slovak National Awakening: an Essay in the Intellectual History of East Central Europe.* (Toronto: University of Toronto Press, 1976).

Cohen, Gary B. *The Politics of Ethnic Survival: Germans in Prague, 1861–1914.* (Princeton, N.J.: Princeton University Press, 1981).

Davies, Norman. *God's Playground. A History of Poland.* 2 vols. (New York: Columbia University Press, 1982)

Deak, Istvan. *The Lawful Revolution: Louis Kossuth and the Hungarians, 1848–1849.* (New York: Columbia University Press, 1979).

——. *Beyond Nationalism. A Social and Political History of the Habsburg Officer Corps 1848–1918*. (New York/Oxford: Oxford University Press, 1990).

Evans, R. J. W. *The Making of the Habsburg Monarchy, 1550–1700*. (Oxford: Oxford University Press, Clarendon Press, 1979).

——. *Rudolph II and His World. A Study in Intellectual History 1576–1612*. (Oxford: Clarendon Press, 1973).

—— and Hartmut Pogge von Strandman, eds. *The Coming of the First World War*. (Oxford: Clarendon, 1988).

Fichtner, Paula Sutter. *Ferdinand I of Austria: The Politics of Dynasticism in the Age of the Reformation*. (Boulder, Colo. and New York: East European Monographs and Columbia University Press, 1982).

Garver, Bruce M. *The Young Czech Party 1874–1900 and the Emergence of a Multi-Party System*. (New Haven, Conn: Yale University Press, 1978).

Geehr, Richard S. *Karl Lueger: Mayor of Fin de Siècle Vienna*. (Detroit: Wayne State University Press, 1990).

Gerschenkron, Alexander. *An Economic Spurt that Failed*. (Princeton, N.J.: Princeton University Press, 1977).

Good, David. *The Economic Rise of the Habsburg Empire, 1750–1914*. (Berkeley, Cal.: University of California Press, 1984).

Hanson, Alice M. *Musical Life in Biedermeier Vienna*. (Cambridge: Cambridge University Press, 1985).

Ingrao, Charles. *The Habsburg Monarchy. 1618–1815*. (Cambridge: Cambridge University Press, 1994).

Janik, Allan and Stephen Toulmin. *Wittgenstein's Vienna*. (New York: Simon and Schuster, 1973).

Jelavich, Barbara. *History of the Balkans*. 2 vols. (Cambridge: Cambridge University Press, 1983).

——. *Modern Austria. Empire and Republic 1815–1986*. (Cambridge/New York: Cambridge University Press, 1987).

—— and Charles Jelavich. *The Establishment of the Balkan National States*. (Seattle, Washington: University of Washington Press, 1977).

Jenks, William A. *Austria under the Iron Ring, 1879–1893*. (Charlottesville, Va.: University of Virginia Press, 1965).

——. *Francis Joseph and the Italians, 1849–1859*. (Charlottesville, Va.: University of Virginia Press, 1978).

Johnston, William M. *The Austrian Mind: an Intellectual and Social History*. (Berkeley, Cal.: University of California Press, 1972).

Kann, Robert A. *The Multi-National Empire*. 2 vols. (New York: Columbia University Press, 1950; rpr. Octagon, 1964).

——. *A History of the Habsburg Empire 1526–1918*. (Berkeley, Cal.: University of California Press, 1974).

——, Bela K. Kiraly, and Paula Sutter Fichtner, eds. *The Habsburg Empire in*

World War I. Essays on the Intellectual Military, Political and Economic Aspects of the Habsburg War Effort. (Boulder, Colo. and New York: East European Quarterly and Columbia University Press, 1977).

—— and Zdenek David. *The Peoples of the Eastern Habsburg Lands, 1526–1918.* (Seattle, Washington: University of Washington Press, 1984).

Kiraly, Bela K. *Hungary in the Late Eighteenth Century. The Decline of Enlightened Despotism.* (New York and London: Columbia University Press, 1969).

——. *Ferenc Deak.* (New York: Twayne, 1975).

Knapp, Vincent J. *Austrian Social Democracy, 1889–1914.* (Washington, D.C.: University Presses of America, 1980).

Komlos, John. *The Habsburg Monarchy as a Customs Union: Economic Development in Austria-Hungary in the Nineteenth Century.* (Princeton, N.J.: Princeton University Press, 1983).

Kraehe, Enno. *Metternich's German Policy.* 2 vols. (Princeton, N.J.: Princeton University Press, 1963–1983).

Levy, Miriam J. *Governance and Grievance: Habsburg Policy and Italian Tyrol in the Eighteenth Century.* (West Lafayette, Ind.: Purdue University Press, 1988).

Luft, David S. *Robert Musil and the Crisis of European Culture, 1880–1942.* (Berkeley, Cal.: University of California Press, 1980).

Lukacs, John. *Budapest 1900. A Historical Portrait of a City and Its Culture.* (New York: Wiedenfeld and Nicolson, 1988).

Magocsi, Paul Robert. *The Shaping of a National Identity: Subcarpathian Rus', 1848–1948.* (Cambridge, Mass.: Harvard University Press, 1978).

Malcolm, Noel. *Bosnia: A Short History.* (London: Macmillan, 1994).

May, Arthur. *The Passing of the Habsburg Monarchy, 1914–1918.* 2 vols. (Philadelphia: University of Pennsylvania Press, 1966).

McGrath, William. *Dionysian Art and Politics in Austria.* (New Haven, Conn.: Yale University Press, 1974).

——. *Freud's Discovery of Psychoanalysis. The Politics of Hysteria.* (Ithaca, N.Y. and London: Cornell University Press, 1986).

Morton, Frederic. *A Nervous Splendor: Vienna, 1888–1889.* (Boston: Little Brown and Co., 1979).

Orton, Lawrence D. *The Prague Slav Congress of 1848.* (Boulder, Colo.: East European Monographs, 1978).

Palmer, Alan. *Metternich.* (London: Weidenfeld and Nicolson, 1972).

——. *Twilight of the Habsburgs: The Life and Times of Emperor Francis Joseph.* (London: Weidenfeld and Nicolson, 1995).

Pech, Stanley A. *The Czech Revolution of 1848.* (Chapel Hill, N. C., 1969).

Rath, R. John. *The Viennese Revolution of 1848.* (Austin, Texas: University of Texas Press, 1957).

Robertson, Ritchie and Edward Timms, eds. *The Habsburg Legacy. National*

Identity in Historical Perspective. Austrian Studies, vol. 5 (Edinburgh: Edinburgh Press, 1994).

Roider, Karl. *Austria's Eastern Question, 1700–1790*. (Princeton, N.J.: Princeton University Press, 1982).

Rothenberg, Gunther. *The Army of Francis Joseph*. (West Lafayette Ind.: Purdue University Press, 1976).

Rozenblit, Marsha. *The Jews of Vienna, 1867–1914: Assimilation and Identity*. (Albany: State University of New York Press, 1983).

Rudolph, Richard L. *Banking and Industrialization in Austria-Hungary: the Role of Banks in the Industrialization of the Czech Crownlands, 1873–1914*. (Cambridge: Cambridge University Press, 1976.

Schorske, Carl E. *Fin-de-siècle Vienna: Politics and Culture*. (New York: Alfred Knopf, 1980).

Shedel, James. *Art and Society: The New Art Movement in Vienna. 1897–1914*. (Palo Alto, Calif: Sposs, 1981).

Sked, Alan. *The Decline and Fall of the Habsburg Empire 1815–1918*. (London and New York: Longman, 1989).

Spielman, John P. *Leopold I of Austria*. (London: Thames and Hudson, 1977).

Sugar, Peter F. and Peter Hanak, eds. *A History of Hungary*. (Bloomington, Ind.: Indiana University Press, 1990).

Waissenberger, Robert, ed. *Vienna, 1890–1920*. (New York: Rizzoli, 1984).

Wandruszka, Adam. *The House of Habsburg*. (Garden City, New York: Doubleday and Co. Anchor, 1965).

Wandycz, Piotr S. *The Lands of Partitioned Poland, 1795–1918*. (Seattle/London: University of Washington Press, 1974).

Wangerman, Ernst. *The Austrian Achievement, 1700–1800*. (New York: Harcourt, Brace, Jovanovich, 1973).

Wegs, J. Robert. *Growing Up Working Class. Continuity and Change Among Viennese Youth, 1890–1938*. (University Park, Pa. and London: Pennsylvania State University Press, 1989).

Whiteside, Andrew G. *Austrian National Socialism Before 1918*. (The Hague: Nijhoff, 1962).

———. *The Socialism of Fools. Georg Ritter von Schönerer and Austrian Pan-Germanism*. (Berkeley, Cal.: University of California Press, 1975).

Williamson, Samuel R., Jr. *Austria-Hungary and the Origins of World War I*. (Houndsmills, Basingstoke, Hampshire, London: Macmillan, 1991).

Wright, William E. *Serf, Seigneur and Sovereign: Agrarian Reform in Eighteenth-Century Bohemia*. (Minneapolis: University of Minnesota Press, 1966).

Zacek, Joseph Frederick. *Palacky: the Historian as Scholar and Nationalist*. (The Hague: Mouton, 1970).

Zeman, Z. A. B. *The Break-Up of the Habsburg Empire, 1914–1918*. (London: Oxford University Press, 1961).

INDEX

Adler, Friedrich, 115, 203–7
Adler, Viktor, 81*ff*, 89–90, 203
Adrianople, treaty of, 47
Aehrenthal, Count Alois Lexa von, 94, 95
agriculture. *See under* economics
Albrecht-Carrié, René, 92
Alsaçe-Lorraine, 113
Andrassy, Count Julius, 86*ff*
Anna, of Bohemia and Hungary, 5, 6
Anti-Semitism. *See* Jews
army: administration, 5, 58, 96, 101, 151; conditions in, 50–51; financing, 129; inadequacy of, in Italy, 52; morale, 9
Ausgleich. See Compromise of 1867
Austria: alliances, 28, 30; constitutional rights of citizens, 154–56; electoral process, 156, 204; executive power, 157–58; trade with Hungary, 167, 174. *See also* Imperial Council (*Reichsrat*)
Austria-Hungary: constitution of, 151–60; creation of, 57–58; dismemberment of, 117, 196–97; economic conditions in, 62–72, 166–68; electoral process in, 59, 73, 77, 83, 204; foreign affairs, control over, 151; foreign policy, 58; politics in, 73–84, 100–6; Seton-Watson's view of, 193–97

Bach, Alexander, 45, 49, 52*ff*
Badeni language ordinances, 67, 77. *See also* languages of the realm
Badeni, Count Casimir, 77, 101
Balkans, 86–88, 92–95, 108*ff*
banks. *See* economics

Batthyany, Count Louis, 45
Bavaria, 7, 56
Beethoven, Ludwig van, 35
Belgium. *See* Netherlands
Benso di Cavour, Count Camillo, 51
Berchtold, Count Leopold von, 108, 187–89
Bernatzik, Dr. Edmund, 203
Biedermeier, 35, 38
Bismarck, Otto von: and Bosnia-Herzegovina dispute, 87; as strategist, 55–56; role of Habsburg Empire in overall strategy, 88–92, 198
Blum, Robert, 44
Bohemia: and Pragmatic Sanction, 209; becomes hereditary monarchy, 15–19; Czech-German conflict in, 67, 75–78, 90; earliest Habsburg ties with, 5, 6, 7; inclusion in Cis-Leithenia, 57; independent state, 196; iron processing in, 39, 64; resentment against taxation, 33; radical activity in, 38, 75; textile manufacture in, 32, 33, 39, 64. *See also* Czecho-Slovakia; languages of the realm, Czech
Bosnia-Herzegovina: ambitions of Serbia as threat, 179–80; crisis in, 94–95; history of, 86–87; Islamic population, 179–180; rivalry of Hungary and Croatia for, 163; Seton-Watson's view of, 197; Trialism, 105
bourgeoisie. See middle classes
Bratislava. *See* Pressburg
Bruckner, Anton, 99
Budapest, 64–65; Jews in, 71

215

Marie Antoinette, 25

marital diplomacy, 4–6, 27

Marxism, 79, 80–84; hostility to Christian Socialists, 84

Mary, Archduchess, 5

Mary of Burgundy, 5

Masaryk, Thomas, 112, 116, 193, 198–202

Matthias Corvinus, king of Hungary, 4

Maximilian I, 5–6

Maximilian II, 9, 15–16, 17

Metternich, Prince Clemens von: administrative proposals, 31; and economic growth, 33, 49, 55, 63; curbing nationalism, 28–30, 37, 38; during reign of Emperor Ferdinand I, 38; insurgents against, 42–43; memorandum to Tsar Alexander I, 130–33; Profession of Faith, 130–33; use of repressive methods, 34, 35; view of society, 130–33

middle classes, 32, 39, 65, 80. *See also* economics

Milan Obrenovic, 87, 93

mineral resources, 32, 39, 64, 66

Mitteleuropa. See Naumann, Friedrich

Modena, 12

Mohacs, battle of, 7

monetary system. *See under* economics

Montenegro, 86–87, 92, 196

Moravia, 8, 19, 90

multinational state, beginning of, 10–13

music, 35, 67

Musil, Robert, 96

Nagodba of 1868, 73, 102

Naples, 37

Napoleon I, Emperor, 27–28, 29*ff*

Napoleon III, Emperor, 51, 56, 85

Napoleonic era, 38–39

Narodna Odbrana, 95, 183

Nathan the Wise, 34

nationalism: as cause of World War I, 116; confronting Marxism, 81; Czech, 75–78; demands for, in 1917, 208–10; discouraged by Metternich, 28–30; during reign of Franz Joseph, 45–46, 62; fomented by Romantics, 36–37; German, 46–47, 55*ff,* 90; in Austria-Hungary, 73; liberalism and, 147–50; Metternich and, 28–30, 131–32; military suppression of, 37; proposed subdivisions of Austria-Hungary, 196–97

Nationalities Law of 1868, 102–3

Naumann, Friedrich, 112–13

navy, 105, 151

neo-absolutism, 45–46

Nestroy, Johann, 35–36

Netherlands: impact of Joseph II's reforms on, 24; loss of area to become Belgium, 29; restoration of Belgian independence, 113; Spanish, 12; Maria Theresa's opinion of, 125

New Europe, The, 193

New Year's Eve Patent of 1851, 46, 50

Nicholas I, Tsar, 45, 86

nobles, fear of constitutional liberalism, 31

Noske, Constantine, 177–78

Novi Pazar, Sanjak of, 92

Obrenovic, Milos, 47

October Diploma, 53–54

O'Donnel, Count, 135

Old Czechs, 75, 76

origins of the Habsburgs, 3–5

Otakar II, king of Bohemia, 3